20/80

A Love Letter... Sort Of

Also by David L. Anders

You Might Be a Problem Drinker If...

You Might Be a Problem Drinker If...Let's Have Another Round!

Octogenarians Say the Darndest Things!

20/80

A Love Letter... Sort Of

by David L. Anders

© 2010 Anders Peachtree City Properties, LLC

Published by David Anders Publishing House
A subsidiary of Anders Peachtree City Properties, LLC
PO Box 2422
Peachtree City, GA 30269
E-mail us at: 2080@AndersUSA.com
Visit our website at: www.AndersUSA.com
Find us on Facebook at David Anders Publishing House

A portion of the earnings from every book sold by David Anders Publishing House goes to support underprivileged children in our community. Find out more at www.AndersUSA.com.

ISBN-13:
978-0615451251 (David Anders Publishing House)

ISBN-10:
061545125X

All rights reserved. No part of these pages, either text or image may be used for any purpose other than personal use without prior written permission of the owner of the copyright. Therefore, reproduction, modification, storage in a retrieval system or retransmission, in any form or by any means, electronic, mechanical or otherwise, for reasons other than personal use, is strictly prohibited without prior written permission of the owner of the copyright or his legal representative. Excluded from this restriction are brief quotes used in connection with reviews, written specifically for inclusion in a magazine, newspaper, or similar electronic product.

All characters appearing in this work are fictitious. Any resemblance to real persons, living, dead, or in between is purely coincidental, or at least remarkable that the author could so successfully write as to develop a character solely through written description that his audience might draw similarities between his writings and the world of reality. Any similarities between the characters in this fictional novel and any persons (but not animals) are enhanced by statistical probability and properties of Brownian motion. Otherwise, any resemblance to persons living or dead may be plainly apparent to them and those who know them, especially if the author has been kind enough to have provided their real names and, in some cases, their street addresses and social security numbers. Such persons feeling they are thus targeted are obviously characterized by paranoid personalities and/or the Adonis syndrome, and they are so vain they probably think this book is about them. All events described herein never actually happened, though on occasion the author has taken certain, very small, liberties with the fiction and woven fiction with documentable chronological events, because life happens. Lawyers eat boogers. The views expressed in this work are solely those of the author and do not necessarily reflect the views of the publisher, and the publisher hereby disclaims any responsibility for them.

To Kenya, my Kay

Preface
A novel is a series of lies which, in aggregate, tells a truth — DLA

In all probability, the person most at risk to suffer from any absence of wisdom I've displayed, or will display in my life is my wife. Despite this risk she has remained my greatest supporter, my greatest encourager, my greatest helper, my life's-mate, my love. For that I am grateful beyond words.

So… Happy 52nd Birthday, my lovely wife, Kenya. A card, a note, not even a long letter seems adequate to relate my feelings. And so, KP, here's an even longer attempt. As the old saying goes, "I could fill a book" and still not capture the depth of my love and appreciation due you — but I'll try, anyway…
I will love you,

David
November 13, 2010

Acknowledgements

Many years and much planning went into the preparation of this text. First, I had to live long enough to acquire a perspective on life which allowed me to view the world as I currently do. In part, I owe my long life to my siblings, Tricia, Buffie, Janet, Mark, and Tim. When we were growing up there were times when they could have justifiably thrown me into a pit and sold me to a caravan of goat herders, but they elected otherwise. Similarly, my parents had more than one occasion when they could have voiced regrets about having entertained thoughts of adding a third child, but if they thought these things I was never made privy to their discussion.

To all my friends from the era covered in this book, I say thank you, something I am certain I did not say often enough, if at all, during the time. Our friendships and good times served as the foundation for a uniquely satisfying adolescence and early adulthood, the value and rarity of which I come to appreciate more and more with the passing of every year. I can only hope whatever errors I made along the way are now attributed to youthful naiveté, (which is asking for an extension of more grace than I am certain I deserve) and that any few bitter memories of our days together are due to cyclamates.

From the special cadre of friends from that time in college I must specifically mention a huge thanks to my roommates, Lee and Chopper. You guys made college so much more fun than it was supposed to be. You, perhaps above all others, shaped (and distorted) my college experience. I am forever indebted to you guys. I love you, man. And of course John. We all love and miss you forever.

I thank my mother for proofreading this text while keeping it a secret before I presented it to my wife for her birthday present. At 86 years of age my mother found more errors in grammar, syntax, and comma usage than should be allowable by a college graduate. She was a gracious audience, and on one occasion remarked that something I had written was mildly humorous. For her support in this and so many other endeavors I remain appreciative. She has characteristically and humbly asked not to be mentioned in these acknowledgements, probably realizing she enjoys a good reputation in our community.

Thanks go out to my Executive Assistant and life-long friend, Fred Carey, for handling that multitude of tasks which must be done, but for which there simply is not enough time in my day to do after fulfilling my much more important obligations as a physician, husband and father. Without him I would have had to learn to get by with much less sleep. So thanks, Fred.

Thank you, also, to my Editor-In Chief at David Anders Publishing House, Mr. William P. Sabotour. William, you have been a champion! After years of personal acquaintance, I now have a great appreciation for your professional skills and abilities as an editor and an organizer. Having finished the manuscript, I thought the work was done. I had no idea how much more labor would be involved in preparing the text for release in electronic and print versions, all while overseeing the establishment of a new publishing company and creating a presence for that company on the internet. Thanks for relieving me of day-to-day responsibilities in the running of the company and letting me feel more like an author than a publisher. You are invaluable, and I am thankful that you do not expect me to pay you what you are truly worth!

And finally, my most sincere thanks are held in reserve for Kenya for laughing at the right places, sighing in the right places, and appreciating my intent in writing this for her. Furthermore, she has been a great encourager in taking the next giant step toward getting this published, and has been very understanding in the time I have invested in getting this to press (but only after the garbage has been taken down to the curb).

So lower the lights. And now...Maestro!

Chapter 1
At The Track

Wednesday, May 25, 1977
A Wide Realm of Wild Reality...

Crinch, crinch, crinch, crinch. The sound of his shoes on the dusty gray track was immediately familiar, although it had been two months since David Patson had taken a serious run. In March he had intended to jog regularly, but after the end of winter quarter exams he had run a couple of times and then become distracted by spring quarter, extra-mural softball, a full course load, and Kay.

During winter quarter he had taken his fifth of six physical education classes required for his degree. Why the University of Georgia decreed that someone needed six quarters, a full two years, of P.E. to get a degree in Biology was beyond him. He mused it was probably someone's solution to the fear that television was causing a culture of inactivity in America. At any rate, as a freshman he had taken volleyball, cycling, and swimming — things he had done before and enjoyed, and the classes were nice distractions from a demanding course schedule. As a sophomore he tried to be a little more "renaissance", exposing himself to things in which he had less experience. Basketball this quarter had been fun, and kept his lungs in shape, but all the stop-and-go was rough on his ankles. He had taken weight-lifting fall quarter, dreaming his bony six-foot frame would go from his weight of 148 pounds to a more respectable 198 pounds. The realities of the course were only reinforced by the Biology 101 class he took the same quarter. He realized you can't put muscle where it wasn't, namely his ankles and wrists, and most of the territory connecting them. He was born with his mother's bone structure, and weight lifting wouldn't change that. So the muscle mass that he did have got firmer, but he realized he could devote the rest of his life to lifting weights and still look down to see hard narrowed tendons tapering from the distal half of his lower calves where he would have preferred muscles. But since his paternal gene pool was condemned to struggle with obesity, he would not complain that his maternal genes appeared to dominate in his more svelte physique.

These same tendons were quite satisfactory for running, however, as he learned winter quarter when he signed up for jogging. He had come to enjoy jogging, although he had never done any serious running before, thinking how boring it must be just to run. It was exactly this boredom that had subsequently drawn him to jogging. He could get on the track and soon his mind was flowing with thoughts and ideas he otherwise couldn't find time to contemplate. He could reflect on where he was in life, where he had been, and where he was going. No one could interrupt his thoughts and he got course credit for doing it. No fear of being tackled by a 250 pound lineman or having to guard a 6 foot-7 inch forward. The only real competition was against himself. By the end of winter quarter for the final exam in the class he had run a 6 minute-12 second mile. Perhaps now he could start running again and reduce his personal best time to below six minutes.

So now he was at the track to do what he had come to love. Not running, but thinking while he was running. Thinking through his problems, planning his day or his life, bending numbers while he ran by playing math games, even if it only involved calculating his average mile pace based on the speed of his last quarter-mile split.

A still, cool haze, too thin to be a fog, hung over the silent track, adding to an atmosphere that might have seemed eerie and perhaps even unsafe in another place and time. Instead, the events of the week, both before and after this moment, held his focus and he did not feel alone or isolated. Rather, he was the sole owner of a beautiful dawn that was his by squatter's rights which no one else had the industry to claim.

After a few brief perfunctory stretches and bends that were more ceremonial than beneficial, he had started his run. He mentally marked his starting point on the practice track, starting at the trash barrel beside the outer curve of the southernmost aspect of the track where the straightaway began. He peeled off his undershirt and tossed it over to the base of the barrel. There was just enough ambient light at that early hour to be able to see the second hand on his silver Timex. He waited for the second hand to be straight up, and noted that it was 6:18 as he took off. During his first strides his lungs took in a single slow breath for four steps and let it out for the next two steps. This ratio quickly dropped to three to one and by the first half lap he had settled into the breathing pattern he would maintain for most of the rest of his run: two steps inhaling and one step exhaling. Only at the very end would he change his respirations, when he would allow and require one breath in or out with each step. Such a final pattern of breathing always indicated he was at his limit, and he could maintain such a rate for only a lap at most.

As he ran, his thoughts flowed over the events of the past week. *"Man, did I ace the final yesterday in Organic Chemistry or what!"* he asked himself. He knew going into the test that it would be 40% of his final grade. Before the test he had a 95.7 average, still unbelievable to him because first quarter in Organic had started with such a struggle and he had pulled a 68 on his first test. This was the first class in college where his study and memorization skills, adequate to make him high school valedictorian, were not enough to master the course work in college. He actually had to study and analyze the material, not just read over it.

He had disciplined himself to reformat all the information presented in lectures into a series of questions. He would create and write hundreds of questions from his course material, and now every other academic course, onto a sheet of paper, with the answers on a separate sheet of paper. When he could correctly answer all these questions unaided, he was ready for any fair test of the material. When fellow students in study hall saw his sheets of questions they were curious and asked about his system, but no one tried his method. Tedious though it was, it worked for him. He was now getting further up the grade point ladder.

The Organic Chemistry final exam was a 200 point test. He calculated before the final exam that he needed 161 points to wind up with a total final average of 89.62, which would round up to 90, an "A". Before turning in his test he added up the points he *knew* he got right, counting 192 points. At worst, he would have a 95.82 average for the course. At that moment he had absolute confidence he would be able to handle anything that stood between him and getting into medical school.

He had exited the exam hall of the University of Georgia Chemistry Building yesterday with the music system in his brain playing the theme from "Rocky". He felt he had trained every bit as hard as a boxer for a championship match, and now after late nights and long hours of preparation it had all paid off with absolute domination of the subject. His body and mind ached from fatigue and floated with elation. He realized that his pre-test jitters had caused him to eat far too little breakfast, and now after two hours of testing he was glad he could walk over to the Bolton dining hall before it closed for lunch at 2:30. As he passed through the food line he was grateful that his meal plan was "all you can eat", and this was one meal where he took full advantage of the offerings.

After lunch he realized just how far behind he was on his sleep, but he wasn't yet ready to nap. As he emerged into the sun, the light seemed even brighter than usual to his tired eyes. He was glad he had opted not to wear his contact lenses today. The sleep deprivation and importance of the Organic Chemistry test made glasses a more reasonable choice for today, and in this sun those hard contacts would have been killers.

He walked on across campus, across the railroad tracks, to the Riverside apartments to drop in on Kay. They had no plans together today, since she would be working at the nursing home that evening on the 4-12 shift, but he felt confident he could walk to her apartment before she would have to leave at 3:45. He arrived at her apartment after a 20 minute walk with a half hour to spare, but to his disappointment, her car was not in the parking lot and she did not answer the door as he knocked. With his head buzzing from too much food and too little sleep, he consoled himself that they had a date already set up for the next day, his birthday. She would cook for him, the first time she had done so, and he couldn't wait to have his own birthday steak prepared by the woman in his life. He took off on foot back toward his dorm on campus. He stopped by his mailbox in the lobby of his dorm and picked up his mail then went up to his room.

In his room he took off his shirt and tossed it over onto his crowded desk, turned on the window fan, thankful that he would soon be home, living in air-conditioning again, and continued to look at the mail he had started reading on his way up the stairs. A birthday card from his parents, saying they were glad he would be home for the weekend, and telling him to call them collect between 5 and 7 pm on his birthday — they had never told him to do that before! A birthday card from his oldest sister Tricia, and a TIME magazine with Jody Powell and Hamilton Jordan on the cover. He kicked off his shoes and pulled off his socks to let his feet breathe as the heat of a warm spring day escaped his body. He stretched out on his single bed to read. The intrigue of these two fellow Georgians and the insight they provided to the newly elected Carter administration was a reading delicacy after the monastic and monolithic devotion to reading exclusively textbooks of the past few weeks. He laughed to read, "At the University of Georgia, Jordan concentrated on having a good time and by all accounts succeeded." Things hadn't changed a lot at UGA for many students! Despite the pleasurable diversion of leisure reading, sleep was what David's body needed, and though he fought to stay awake to read the article the battle was short and the victory complete.

He awoke suddenly in the dark room, with the only light coming from the parking lot two stories below. The TIME magazine crackled as he peeled it from his abs and chest where it had pasted to him as he rolled over it in his sleep. The faintly lighted dial on his clock radio was visible at the head of his bed, but without glasses he couldn't yet make out the time. His watch was similarly dark. So he shimmied toward the head of the bed and extended his head and neck upward to the clock to see the time. It was 5:31. He had slept well over twelve hours, uninterrupted. Now it was his birthday, he was 20, he felt wide awake, and there was nothing to do to celebrate.

He had slept right through supper, but surprisingly he didn't yet feel all that hungry. He wasn't about to go pay cash for a full meal at Waffle House before the dining hall opened, when he could eat for free on the meal plan in a couple of hours. Right now nothing from the vending machine downstairs sounded tempting or necessary, so food could wait.

He could see the form of his roommate across the room, his bed at a right angle to David's. Rex Lee was not a good sport about being awakened and could always exact revenge, so David opted against any early morning trickery. Rex had probably gotten into bed only a few hours earlier, as he had planned to go to the end-of-the-year party that was being thrown by the Phi Mu music fraternity after the music faculty's recital last night. Rex was through with final exams and just hanging around Athens for the Wind Ensemble rehearsals for graduation ceremonies. Whatever time he had finally come home last night, he had probably done so quietly, for which David was grateful, so he would return the favor and let him sleep until noon if he could, which he probably would.

Kay was surely asleep at this early hour, and it would be cruel to call her, even though he felt the egocentric privilege that accompanies a birthday. He would see her for their date at two o'clock this afternoon, and she had to work again tonight, so better to be kind. Instead, he felt around in the dark on the bed for his glasses, then on the floor beside the bed, where he located them. Placing them on his face, he realized that the right arm of the glasses was now deviating downward, which lifted the glasses off his nose and tilted them to the left of his face. Thankful for cheap black frames that were used mainly for late night study, he quickly bent the frames back into shape.

He quietly slipped out of bed and out of his jeans throwing them over to the floor of the opened closet. If cleanliness was next to godliness, the end-of-the-year finals week was a laundry purgatory, somewhere between heaven and hell, but much closer to hell. Clean laundry was at a premium so the underwear would stay on for now in a tribute to economy of time and the realization that his mother would do his laundry tomorrow when he got home.

He stood in front of the dresser that was at the foot of his bed and thus at the entry to his room. The dresser was strategically placed to allow the door to open into the room, barely missing the dresser. On entering the room as the door swung open into the room against the wall to its left, about all one saw was the chest high dresser, as the wall to the right projected into the room to create a small closet for its occupants. Further entrance into the room then required an immediate right angle around the dresser and into the open center floor of the room. Such a furniture arrangement afforded the roommates a little more privacy when the door was opened, and some days this passive form of courtesy was about the only courtesy they remembered to extend to each other.

He silently opened his top drawer and peered intently trying to make out the colorless forms in the darkened drawer. He could feel his keys and wallet in the drawer and grabbed them both, considerately muffling the otherwise jingling keys against the wallet as he placed them on top of the dresser. He located a pair of black UGA gym shorts (not worn in the past ten days, so fairly aired out — "dry cleaned", as Will Rice used to say last year) and a plain white undershirt, only worn once since its last cleaning and thus certainly adequate for the task at hand.

Instead of eating, trickery, or romance, he planned to start his birthday with a jog on the practice track located down Lumpkin Street. He would even splurge and drive there. With gasoline at 62.9 cents per gallon he usually parked his Ford Maverick on Sunday and didn't drive again until the weekend, walking or using the campus bus wherever he went. But today was his birthday and the school year was over. The opportunity to know just how far he had run using the quarter-mile track would be more informative and rewarding than just running around the campus. He knew he had enough gas to get back home tomorrow, and then Mom or Daddy would likely slip him $5 toward his next tank of gas.

He pulled on his second drawer and squinted at the meager contents. He located the white blob and could tell these were the socks he sought. He stepped into his white cotton running tube socks and pulled them up until they covered his calves with their three horizontal red stripes. He sat on the side of his bed as he laced up his worn white Adidas running shoes with the dark blue stripes on either side. The stripes still reminded him of shark's gills. He bought these shoes the summer of his high school senior year while working at Six Flags Over Georgia. Twenty-one dollars seemed like an exorbitant amount to pay for a pair of sneakers, but these shoes had been worth it.

Feeling more than just a little dapper in his color coordinated UGA red and black he opened his top drawer to get the toiletry bag which held his contact lens case and solutions. He could do this part of his day by rote. Just as he had done countless mornings before, he made a trip down the dimly lighted hall to the now very necessary community bathroom, not surprised to find he was the only one using the facilities at this early hour. As per his routine he walked past the first two urinals to use the third of the four urinals available. He was a creature of habit in these things. Even he was not certain why, except that perhaps he had subconsciously noted the third was most often available. He next washed his hands and inserted his contact lenses, then was soon back in his room where he dropped off his toiletry kit and grabbed his wallet and headed for his car, the "Marvelous Maverick", as Kay had christened it.

She had a way of seeing the best in every situation. For David the 1973 two-door Ford Maverick represented, in some ways, a reminder of his dependence and financially undesirable state in life. His father had given it to him last Christmas after owning it for the first four years and putting 100,000 miles on it. It was the sporty line of the Maverick, if such a thing were possible, the "Grabber". It said so, right on the lower panel behind both front wheels in white plastic adhesive that was now beginning to peel after so many miles. The color was a faded yellow, "piyourick" yellow, he had once heard his father say, but he had never taken the time to find out what that meant. Over the years it had lost some of its early glory. His brother, Mark, had once rigged the passenger front seatbelt to clip into the backseat's passenger-side belt clip so that the automatic buzzer wouldn't go off, as it would if the front belt were fully retracted, which was often the case on date night with a bench front seat. But the split back of the front seat had to be flipped forward to allow access to the backseat, which then strained the front seatbelt forcefully. On one occasion, the force of the seat as it went forward had cracked the housing on the backseat seatbelt clip. Now before using the seatbelt the housing had to be aligned just so with itself, which required a brief instructional lesson for each new rider in that seat. Since David had agreed, as a requisite for receiving possession of the car, that all of its occupants would always be belted in, he spent quite a bit of time instructing passengers, of which there could be many for a student with a car at UGA, on how to assemble the rear right seatbelt. Without this lesson the seatbelt housing predictably wound up in three pieces with a firm spring falling out, a booby-trap frustrating its next victim.

Kay acted as though she thought the car were a new chariot. She pointed out the low mileage of only 4200 miles, since the odometer had only five white digits (and a sixth black digit for tenths of a mile) and had rolled over to "00000.0" shortly before David had received the car, unable to display the first 100,000 miles that had now been traveled. She pretended she didn't mind the broken inside grab handle/arm rest on the passenger side, noting that this necessitated David always staying on her side of the car to close her door, making her feel like a princess worthy of this royal coach. (David had once tried to repair the handle with electrician's tape, which only lasted a few weeks before pulling apart. Now any unsuspecting rider trying to pull the handle from its logical mid-point would get a sticky set of fingertips from the leftover adhesive that initially gave the handle the appearance of being a single unit, but allowed it to breakaway with any pulling attempt. The only way now to open or close the door from the inside was by grabbing the door handle much closer to the armrest.)

She made it a game to count quickly to six as David pumped the gas pedal six times the same way each time to finesse one more start out of the car in the fashion that he had learned was the only way to make the car start. Turning the key on the sixth pump and then pumping four more times with the key turned, the key was then released and the engine (usually) ran. To stop the engine, which would otherwise chortle on for thirty seconds or more after the ignition was turned off, David would turn off the engine with the car still in "Drive" and then shift the car back into "Park".

The Maverick was a good reminder that he would have to work in life to have any nice things, and he was appreciative of the fact that his parents had trusted him with a car while away at school.

Now as he ran he approached the trash can on his right coming out of the curve. He followed the second hand and noted it at exactly one minute and forty-two seconds for the first quarter-mile lap as he crossed the point of the barrel. That was eighteen seconds less than two minutes, so four laps would generate seventy-two seconds less than eight minutes, a six minute and forty-eight second mile pace. Not six minutes and twelve seconds, but he could work on this over the summer. This summer...

This summer he would be living with his parents in Fayette County. They had moved there after his ninth grade year, south of Atlanta in the rural wide-open spaces. Now he had a job lined up to be an orderly at South Fulton hospital — the night shift. 11p.m. to 7 a.m. It would be a good experience. Different from the other jobs he had held.

The summer after tenth grade when he was 16 he didn't work because he was selected for the six-weeks long Governor's Honors Program. After eleventh grade he had played trombone with the Lost Safari Dixieland Band at Lion Country Safari. What a great job! Half hour show, then half hour off, six shows a day. At almost three bucks an hour, while all his friends were making $1.85 per hour. It was a stroke of luck that he had such good audition and got the job. He could thank Will Rice for that.

Will was his friend from high school and before. He had inspired David to go to UGA. They had first met when David was in the fourth grade, playing in Mr. Waterhouse's elementary band, composed of students from seven different local Atlanta elementary schools. Initially they were neither very good trombonists, but the nice thing about playing the slide trombone is that you are never very far from the right note. During that year they sat beside each other in the lower end of the trombone section, but each had his eyes on ascending into the ranks of the accomplished.

Although Will was three years older, he seemed to admire something in David and bonded again with David during the time they spent together at Therrell High School during David's eighth and ninth grade years. By then Will had become a first class trombonist and held a job playing trombone in one of the outside bands at Six Flags Over Georgia. For several years Will spent weekends in spring and fall and all summer playing Dixieland trombone for guests at Six Flags while they waited in line. His was a dream job that any high school musician would love to be good enough to have.

One Saturday when Will couldn't be at work he asked David to fill in for him. Nervous and knowing that he was out of his league, David played in the shows that autumn Saturday, having studied the music the week before. He was doing OK until the band went into a parade routine while playing "When The Saints Go Marching In". "Play it in 'F'," Bing, the trumpet player had called over as he announced the next song. Will hadn't said anything about this, and David didn't have any experience improvising musically in the key of "F", or any other key for that matter. But in an instant of musical epiphany, the previous six years of trombone lessons, of playing scales and arpeggios — which to that point had been fairly rote and mechanical exercises — and years of just listening to and enjoying music for its harmonies and rhythms suddenly melded with meaning and purpose. While the trumpet, clarinet, sax, and tuba were playing away, he listened to what they did and added notes of his own, trying to stay within the notes of the "F" scale and/or matching the chords he heard or anticipated. When in doubt, as he quickly learned, a well-placed glissando seemed to be all the audience really expected from a trombonist anyway. It turned out to be a great day for David, and he returned to his high school band with an elevated status, as he could now tout his experience as a paid musician.

The following spring when Lion Country Safari sent out a flyer to local high schools announcing auditions for their soon to be formed Dixieland band, David drove over to Stockbridge High School and auditioned. The sight-reading part of the audition wasn't very hard — he could usually play music that he had not seen before without too many errors. After he completed the piece, the audition judge, a round little man who looked like he should play the tuba that stood on its bell over in the corner, said, "Now I want you to improvise with me. Play 'When The Saints Go Marching In' in the key of 'F'". So while the judge positioned himself on the stool with his tuba, David's mind rushed back six months and tried to remember what they had played at Six Flags. The tubist counted off, "One, two, humpf..." and led in with a bass line. David tried to add some melody, counter-melody, and the requisite glissandos. He was offered the job at the end of the audition, and was always certain it was on the strength of that improvising...improvising that was not at all spontaneously improvised but had been prepared six months in advance at Six Flags, thanks to Will Rice.

It was at Lion Country that he had met Rex Lee, who was now his roommate at UGA. Rex was a talented trumpeter, good enough to make it a career. David was a talented entertainer, good enough to have a summer job. But that was fine with David. He wanted to be a doctor.

After a summer, the job at Lion Country had led to an audition at Six Flags Over Georgia. Will Rice's band was winding down its time at Six Flags as too many of its members were going off to college and needing more time. So the "Lost Safari Dixieland Band" reformatted itself to be "Raz'Mataz" at Six Flags. Another great job and fun summer playing trombone followed David's senior year of high school, learning more Dixieland tunes from their newly acquired and more experienced piano player, Sandy Greene. Sandy was in college, sort of, and older than the rest of the guys in the band, and he did a great job of shepherding the group into a much more polished band. David could also thank Will for introducing Sandy to the band. Will had known Sandy during his Six Flags years, at which time Sandy had been working as a caricature artist, but always wanted to hook up with a band instead of performing solo at an Atlanta Shakey's Pizza Parlor. Sandy's enthusiasm for now being in a working band was to everyone else's advantage. Although he was the newest member, Sandy was quickly handed all the responsibility for managing the group by a vote of unanimous apathy from the rest of the members of the band, who would rather spend time meeting girls after shows than filling out time cards.

After David's freshman year at UGA, Raz'Mataz had an offer to play in a Dixieland nightclub in downtown Atlanta. All the guys quit the Six Flags job, joined the musicians union, worked at Dixie Daisy's for one weekend, and then were unemployed when the club went out of business. David spent that summer stocking books in various stores, enjoying the summer and playing jobs with Raz'Mataz about once a week as Sandy was able to obtain bookings.

So in some respects working in the hospital this summer would be David's first "real" job, not just playing trombone or menial labor. This work was in the field of medicine so he looked forward to the opportunity, and also looked forward to the opportunity for more bookings with Raz'Mataz, because the gigs continued to come in and the money was good when it was there. The adventures of a road trip with Raz'Mataz were always something to which he could look forward. How many more summers could he play trombone? Now he was 20.

As he ran he reflected over his previous birthdays. When he turned 4 he got a card with a dollar in it from Aunt Carolyn, and in fact every year since she had sent him a card and a dollar. But that first card and dollar made a life-long and life-changing impact. He had gone almost immediately to the store with his mother and spent that dollar on a plastic car and truck set. It wasn't very long afterwards that he grew tired of the car and truck and developed his first case of buyer's remorse. Ever since, he had been very careful about spending any of his money, almost to a fault. But he was always more content to have money and know he possessed the potential to own many different things rather than spend the money and be limited to owning the one thing that the money had purchased. This morning he could even laugh that as a result, he had come to have a reputation for being a bit of a tight-wad — his little sister Janet said he called all the girls "chicks" because all they said was, "cheap, cheap."

Now as he again approached the trash can on his right coming out of the curve his mind jumped back to his rate of running. He followed the second hand and noted it at exactly six twenty-one and twenty-two seconds after the first half-mile. That was thirty-eight seconds less than four minutes, so his second lap was two seconds better than his first lap. After a half-mile he was on a six minute and forty-four second mile pace.

His thoughts returned to a review of his previous birthdays. Every birthday seemed to mark a milestone that marked the path to manhood. He had wanted to be a man as long as he could remember. With the passing of each year he was certain that he finally was.

When he turned six his mother filled a small aluminum trash can with ice and buried a watermelon deep within to chill it to a level of perfection. Since that year, his birthday was the unofficial "First Day of Watermelon" in his family. Any watermelon purchased prior to his birthday was at risk of being too early in the season and of poor quality. He eagerly anticipated the first good melon each year, and that usually happened in celebration of his birthday. He felt all grown-up at six, because he was now old enough to sit on the crossbar of the backyard swing-set without adult supervision.

In the last days of second grade he turned eight and his class had a field trip to a local park as part of the end of the year activities. His mother arranged for the neighborhood ice cream truck to stop by the park and give each classmate an ice cream treat to celebrate his birthday. He had been in awe to realize the financial powerhouse that his parents must be if his mother could afford the 10-15 cents per ice cream for twenty-five second-graders, and it made him feel like a royal prince at his coronation to see his parents sparing no expense to so publicly recognize the importance of the anniversary of his birth.

At 15 his full attention was centered on the ability to obtain his driver's learner's permit. It was a Thursday, his father's day off from work, and Daddy let him stay home to miss school long enough to get his permit. Driving was men's work, and the two men set out to get the permit that was the true mark of manhood. On the way back to school from the Department of Motor Vehicles David was acutely aware of how narrow the streets of Atlanta were, how fast the other drivers seemed to be approaching in on-coming traffic, and he wondered how his father could be such a skilled driver so effortlessly. He rode quietly in silent fear that his father would pull over and tell him to drive the rest of the way. But they both had responsibilities to attend that morning and no driving lesson was on the agenda. Fortunately, when that first driving lesson did occur, it was in an empty parking lot, not a narrow city street.

Turning 16 was also a memorable event and milestone in manhood. He got his driver's license, but not until more than two months after his birthday. That summer he was going to be away studying science at the Georgia Governor's Honors Program and wouldn't have reason to drive while away for the six weeks. Since he had to pay for his own car insurance, he decided to economize and wait until he returned in late July to actually get his license. But what made his birthday special was the way his parents treated him that day. It was turning 16 that had finally made him feel like a real man.

On the day after he turned 16 he was due to play at a church softball game. But his parents had insisted that he needed to stay home to be able to go on an otherwise secret surprise outing with his father. David dutifully and respectfully followed their wishes and notified the team he would be unavailable to play that day. He dressed casually as directed by his parents, and he drove off from his house with his father at about 5:30 p.m. to go who knew where. But he knew better than to ask. This was his father's modus operandi on many occasions. As an obstetrician in solo private practice he oftentimes had to leave a family outing in response to the phone call or paging announcing the imminent arrival of a new life — Daddy had recently told David that as many as half of his plans for doing things with the family were sabotaged by labor pains. So to prevent disappointment his father seldom announced family plans in advance. Special events usually just evolved, and David learned to enjoy these surprises as they unfolded rather than trying to coax details out of his father before he was prepared to reveal the schedule.

As they drove away David tried to formulate what this surprise could be. They were heading north toward Atlanta, but then again, that was about the only direction they ever headed. About the only thing to the south was the Dairy Queen in Fayetteville. *Where could he be driving?* Not a Braves' game — they were playing in St. Louis against the Cardinals. He remembered a father-son dinner the Medical Association of Atlanta had sponsored years ago. It included brief talks by Ernie Johnson, the Braves announcer, and Charlie Vaughn, one of the Braves top pitching prospects at the time. It had been a fun night and he still had the autographs he had gotten that night. Maybe tonight would hold similar rewards.

"Drat", Daddy exclaimed when they were about four miles from home. "I forgot my beeper." So they turned around to head back home. As they pulled up the driveway, David recognized Will Rice's car in the driveway. It was not at all uncommon for Will to be at the Patson house. He would often drop in on the family to check in on David, or the rest of the family. But as they pulled up to the house Daddy said David might as well go in to say hello to Will while he found his beeper. And when David walked into the house he was greeted with a "Happy Birthday!" from all his family, Will, and Beth, David's girlfriend for most of high school. They all had a steak dinner there at the house in honor of David's birthday, a literal killing of the fatted calf noted David, and he felt like a real man.

Turning 18, of course, is the real mark of a man. As his 18th birthday approached David had felt a bit pensive. The day before his birthday, Saturday, he had worked at Six Flags. Saturday evening was his high school prom, and he was a senior and would have had a great time with his classmates being there at the prom. But he was still dating Beth, and she had a very important horse show (although he could not imagine such a thing) that she wanted to go to. So they didn't go to the prom. It didn't bother David that much — the amount of money he would have spent going to the prom was more than he would otherwise spend dating the rest of the summer! And since Beth didn't go to his school she probably would have felt like a fifth wheel at his prom. But as he drove home from Six Flags that night he felt a bit alone, turning 18 while his classmates prommed and his girlfriend promenaded. It was thus quite a surprise then when his father awoke him at about 1:30 a.m. in the early hours of his birthday to tell him he had a call. Gena Dean, one of his classmates, who really was "just a friend", but a very dear one at that, was calling. She wanted to let him know he had been missed by "everyone" at the prom, and to tell him "Happy Birthday". As he went back to sleep, he did so feeling like a real man of 18. First, because his father had actually awakened him for a crazy middle of the night phone call without so much as a frown, and secondly because a girl had been the caller. He hadn't really ever considered the possibilities...

His 19th birthday last year had also been a bit melancholy. It had been on a Tuesday in the middle of exam week during his freshman year at Georgia — his first birthday away from home. He turned 19 at midnight while studying for his final exam in chemistry. He stopped studying long enough to splurge for a rare treat purchased from the vending machines: a Coke and a Payday candy bar. That was his peak memory of turning 19, a Coke and a candy bar. But somehow the rugged individuality of being up late studying for a killer test seemed like a test of manhood, and he felt that adulthood had arrived. Oh yeah, and the pizza. Will Rice had ordered in BoxCar pepperoni pizza for a birthday party that night after the chemistry final. Will was great about remembering his birthday that night, despite how busy Will was with the end of his senior year at UGA, finals week, and Will's acceptance into medical school that same week.

David suddenly realized the trash barrel was again on his right and he checked his watch. It now showed ten seconds past 6:23. A little slower pace with a lap of one minute and 48 seconds, or five minutes and ten seconds for 3/4 mile. He could come in under seven minutes for his first mile by running a one minute fifty second pace on his next quarter-mile, so he dug in and kept running.

He had been so deep in thought about his birthdays he had almost missed noticing the trash barrel, and in fact had missed noticing the man who now appeared on the track.

Chapter 2
The Company

As David started the fourth lap on the straight-away, he noticed a man standing on the track on the opposite straight-away. David could tell the man was doing some stretches warming up in anticipation of a run. He could also tell the man was standing on the track, on the inner most aspect of the track, which meant David would have to go to the outside to get around him. This might seem a small point to some, but it would add to David's time. David was hugging the inside of the track as he ran to milk every possible advantage for an optimal running time. Perhaps the man would start running before David got around to the other side.

Or at least David thought the man would be running. But as he looked over to the far side of the track he could tell from the man's morphology he was probably in his forties, about his father's age, although more trim. He had on a pair of shorts for running that were perhaps the most ridiculous that David had ever seen on a grown man. While David's UGA gym shorts were loose but fairly formed and cut high on the thigh, this man was wearing dark shorts that were baggy and seemed grossly oversized, reaching down almost to his knees. He had on a baby-blue short-sleeved T-shirt, a shade of blue that did not suggest masculinity.

While David came around the curve of the track he also noted two other people sitting on rough bleachers along that straightaway of the track. They had positioned themselves about half-way up the six rows of wooden seats, and appeared to be two more men, older than the first. The heavier of the two sat forward with his elbows on his knees, while the slighter figure rested back against the seat behind him, propping his elbows on that seat.

Now as he approached the man on the track David could also see him better. He was facing into the infield area of the track, hands on hips, standing on toes and then relaxing, to stretch his calves. He didn't seem to be aware of David approaching, so David could study him a bit without appearing curious. His socks were white, but only as high as the top of his shoes. The only people David saw wearing these anklets were usually female tennis players. *"With calves that thin I think I'd opt for tube socks,"* David said to himself critically about the man who was rudely blocking his way on the track. He was also wearing the oddest shoes — gaudy white, yellow, black, that looked heavy with an oversized textured black sole which rode up the back of the heel looking perhaps as if designed by NASA.

As David approached closer he veered outward toward the center of the track to allow for socially acceptable passing space when he ran by, and calculated the second or two the wider swath would cost him in time elapsed. Just altering his course made his legs feel a little heavier. The man continued his calf stretching and the men on the bleachers who appeared to be with him watched with what appeared to be a minimum of conversation, but postures that indicated an interest in their surroundings.

David was now only a few yards from the man when he turned 90 degrees thus facing David, as he simultaneously began bending over forward at the waist with his knees straight, grabbing his calves and pulling his chest towards his thighs. As his head rolled forward his eyes met with David and locked for ever so brief a time in acknowledgement by each of the presence of the other on the track. He was clean-shaven with a short, nondescript haircut typical of a TV anchorman. He wore glasses which seemed appropriately athletic, but unlike any David had seen before, with no visible rims and thus almost invisible oval lenses held in place by the nose piece and the side arms. But however cool the glasses were, the shorts would always define this man, David smirked.

In the brief time David had to actually see this man's face he didn't notice much outstanding. He looked vaguely familiar, but David could not think of whom he reminded him. Given more time he might have noted the strong resemblance to the single remaining picture of his maternal grandmother's brother Edward. Edward had died in his 30's in a tragic hotel fire in Europe — the body never identified in the ashes — long before David was ever born, and his picture was on a shelf in his grandparents' home where David had rarely seen or noticed. In the context of the hour and the meeting one could not fault David for failing to identify the resemblance.

Now David quickly shifted back to the inner most part of the track to optimize his time. As he was drawing to the top of the curve of the track he trained his attention on the trash barrel ahead that would mark one mile. David looked to the left to see where the man was. He was no longer standing there. David was startled for an instance to realize that the man was now running just off to his right, stride for stride.

Based on the pace the man was running he must have taken off just after David passed him. The other runner didn't seem to want to go past David, but seemed content to be paced by him.

David passed the barrel and looked down at his watch. It showed four seconds before 6:25. His first mile had been six minutes and fifty-six seconds. But now with this guy off to his right and the distraction of the physical effort now being required, he didn't do the remaining calculations for his split times. Maybe he could remember his numbers and do them later.

For now his attention was focused more on the runner who continued to pace off of him. This irked David more than he might have anticipated, so he decided to pick up the pace just a little as he headed into the straight away. His breathing quickened as his frequency of inhalations to exhalations adjusted to the increase in demand by becoming a 1:1 ratio. The fresher runner didn't seem to mind the challenge of a slightly quicker pace and continued to match him step for step.

Meanwhile, as the runner distracted him to his right, David became aware that the other two men had now stood up and were off the bleachers, standing on the ground between the bleachers and the opposite straight-away. They were offering what seemed to be cheers of encouragement, "Run faster, you can beat him!', but their specific exclamations for the most part went unheard due to the distance from which they stood, the noise of the runners' steps, and David's own increasingly labored breathing. They seemed to be enjoying this spontaneous Roman holiday that he had foolishly generated.

He looked back to the right at the runner, who was now looking straight ahead and devoting most of his energies and attentions to keeping up with David. Sensing David was looking at him, he glanced to his left at David with an intense glare and cocky terse grin that seemed to say, "I can beat you." It now became more of the principle of the matter for David. This guy was violating two of the unwritten codes of the track. He had no right to: 1) block the inner aspect of the track with his warm-up stretches, requiring David to go around him, and 2) establish his pace off of David without his permission. There were just certain traditions of track etiquette that any runner should follow, and this guy demonstrated downright plain rudeness and disrespect. David realized that he would have to back off this faster pace soon, but perhaps he could put some space between him and the challenger before he tired too much. "Just what is this guy up to?" he thought to himself. The thought was interrupted by a vicious "oomph!" as he fell to the track.

Chapter 3
Names

When he went into the curve, the quicker pace of his run had required David to close just slightly the distance between him and the inner boundary of the track. He was acutely aware of the runner immediately off his right shoulder. In his fatigue and with an effort to minimize unnecessary time lost to taking too wide a berth, David had planted his outer/right foot just a fraction too close to the inside of what would be his normal ergonomically best running alignment. As his inner/left foot lifted to take its next step it kicked off the inner aspect of his right shin and calf, which caused David to veer slightly to the right and quickly plant his left foot to compensate. This caused his center of gravity to now be to the left, and he over-corrected this by tilting his upper body to the right, a move that speed and fatigue could not accommodate. He tumbled forward and to the right, just missing the evading runner to his right and tumbling onto his right shoulder before completing the summersault and winding up on his back sprawled supine on the track. The hard impact of the full breadth of his posterior ribcage against the gritty surface momentarily stunned his breathing, but the need to breathe to compensate for the anaerobic results of his just-ended full sprint overrode any other message to his lungs. He lay gasping, more from air hunger than from pain. All was still around him. He wondered if he had knocked himself unconscious for a second, but he discounted this possibility. His head did not hurt, although in a split-second reflex to regain his balance as he hit the ground he had arched his back and thus driven the back of his head into the track even harder than the fall alone would have dictated. He was "seeing stars" but he often did after a really hard run. He didn't recall what he had done wrong in his running, but didn't suspect foul play. His shoulder hurt and he was amazed that at the age of twenty he didn't feel like a man. The birthday boy was scared and wanted to cry.

He had only been on the ground a second or two when he was startled to hear a voice standing near his feet and he instantly remembered the runner who had been running alongside him.

"Are you OK?" he asked, leaning forward with his hands on his knees, drawing deep recovering breaths.

Suddenly feeling somewhat foolish, David was embarrassed by the necessary attention and any thoughts of crying were overcome by the territorial testosterone generated in the presence of another male of the species. Whoever this guy was he would not have the pleasure of seeing David further humiliated.

"Yeah."

"Looks like you tripped. Is anything hurt? That was a pretty nasty fall."

His manners returned to him as his mind cleared. David replied, "No, sir.

I'll be OK. I guess I just wasn't being careful." His gaze continued to be straight up into the rapidly brightening dawn. In his shame he would prefer to be left alone. He would be OK.

"Well let me help you sit up," said the stranger, extending his right hand into David's field of vision. Still heaving large volumes of air, David reached up with his right hand and clasped the hand of the stranger, locking grips firmly as the stranger pulled him into an upright sitting position. Remaining on the ground, David pulled up his knees and folded his arms across the top of them then rested his forehead on his arms as he continued to take deep breaths.

"That's a bit of an abrasion on your shoulder," said the voice from above.

David extended his neck and rolled his head upward to see his rescuer. He wet his lips and tongue to speak, but they were desiccated from the run and the adrenaline surge of the fall. He tried again to speak.

"It doesn't hurt," David replied almost reflexively as the back and outer portion of his right shoulder began to sting. He looked back over his hunched right shoulder to match observations with the runner. Dropping his right shoulder and rotating it inward while straining to twist his neck as far to the right as possible and rolling his eyes as far downward as possible he could see that the back of his shoulder did indeed have a two inch square area of glistening blood, although the dust that coated his arm and shoulder were soaking up the blood as it slowly appeared.

"It doesn't look too bad," David lied.

The stranger peered forward and even placed his left hand on David's shoulder to better isolate his attention to the area by framing it between his thumb and index finger.

"It's dirty and needs to be rinsed off, but I don't think it would benefit from sutures. It's going to leave a scar, though."

David was impressed by the cool manner in which this stranger quickly assessed the situation and recommended treatment. He spoke with authority — he sounded like a doctor.

"What's your name son?"

"David Patson," he replied, craning his neck to look back up at the stranger.

"Are you Patrick Patson's son?"

So this man knew his father. He probably *was* a doctor.

"Yes, sir. And who are you?" he asked to be polite, not intending to interrogate, but interested nonetheless.

"My name is Dave Tew," he heard the man say.

"Do you know my father?"

"Oh, yes indeed."

"Well thanks for your help. Are you a doctor?"

"Yes, but not a trauma surgeon," he panned, dryly.

"Do you deliver babies too?" he asked, unable to think of the word obstetrician in the flush of the moment.

"No, too much malpractice risk there," Dr. Tew chuckled.

Amazed at what a small world it could be, David extended his spine, arching his back in anticipation of standing up. Dr. Tew extended his hand and David again grabbed it. He stood up and started to brush off the accumulated dust and fine grit, doing an assessment for any other injuries as he went. He found no other problems, and again went through the necessary contortions to assess his shoulder and make certain it was no worse than Dr. Tew thought. The blood there was not flowing, just glistening. Meanwhile, sweat, which hadn't really yet started during the abbreviated run, was now flowing from his brow, his chest, and his thighs. His back felt covered with a thousand spots of grime from lying on the track.

"Do you feel like you can walk OK?"

"Yes, sir."

"Let's walk to the water fountain over there and we'll get you cleaned up," he said, pointing near the fountain that was beside the wooden bleachers. As they both looked toward the fountain they noted that the other two men had risen from the bleachers and were walking with determination toward the accident scene, although their pace slowed slightly as they saw David rise and brush himself off.

"He's OK!" Dr. Tew called to the others as he raised his right hand palm forward. "We're going to clean it off at the fountain!" he shouted, as he then pointed twice to the fountain ahead on his right. The heavier of the two men waved back and the two men slackened their steps and waited at the end of the wooden bleachers beside the fountain, sitting on the ends of the first and second rows of bleachers, facing the approaching runners.

"I'm sure they'll want to meet you, too," Dr. Tew started as they continued toward the fountain.

"Yes, sir," David responded as his thoughts focused on how stupid he was to fall while running. How hard could it be — left, right, left, right. Hadn't the joke in PE been that the instruction manual on running was only three words long — left, right, repeat?

"Feels sort of humiliating to fall when you're running, doesn't it?" Dr. Tew asked, rhetorically, seeming to read David's mind. "I tripped once running years ago. Still not sure how it happened, but it hurts no matter what causes it," he noted, stating the obvious.

"Yes, sir," David replied. He just wanted to get to the fountain, get some water, clean up a little, pick up his shirt, and leave these guys and any reminder of his fall.

"Well, I hope I didn't distract you. I thought I'd have some fun to see if I could keep up with a young buck like you. You look like you know what you're doing out there. You must be running close to a six-minute mile."

"Usually," David lied, letting his pride replace the truth. "But, no, I wasn't distracted by you. I was really in a zone, unaware of you or anything else," he further extended the lie.

"Well I'm glad you're OK," Dr. Tew added, sounding almost like an admonition or warning to be more careful next time, as they closed in on the water fountain.

"Hope you're alright," said the heavier of the two men ahead as they crossed into the undefined area that makes conversation appropriate between approaching strangers.

"Yes, sir, thank-you," David replied.

The two men had risen and started walking toward them and the heavier of the two extended his hand as Dr. Tew said, "Gentlemen, this is David Patson, eldest son of Patrick Patson."

"Nice to meet you," was the phrase of convenience as the three shook hands, interrupted by Dr. Tew's call to, "Come over here and get cleaned up," as he stood beside the fountain.

As he eyed the fountain David was glad to recall the full force of water that flowed from it, usually. He had come to appreciate this fountain during winter quarter when his class ran on this track three times a week, and the fountain was very much appreciated, even during the cold of winter. It had been off for about two weeks during a cold snap, and it was not clear to David if the water source had been turned off or if the fountain was somehow broken, but the service had been restored and all had gone well since, as far as he knew. Runners don't ask for much, but they do want water after they run.

It was a heavy, simple three feet tall fountain made of iron or some similar alloy with the appearance that indicated utility and durability that could withstand years of use and abuse. The fountain was anchored with a squared base from which extended a small foot pedal, with scattered remnants of green stains which implied that it had once been painted. Now its pedestal was primarily textured brown rust. A not-so-clean basin was atop the pedestal, but the only feature that mattered to David as he leaned over the fountain and depressed the pedal appeared faithfully. The water flowed up into the air at an angle and with a force that resulted in most of the water squirting beyond the confines of the basin and onto the grass that grew immediately to the side of the fountain, the greenest, thickest grass anywhere along the field that abutted the track and bleachers. David was pleased he had remembered not to lean too close to the anticipated path of the water stream. More than one person had taken a shot of water to the side of the face from this fountain by underestimating the force of the water that streamed forth when the pedal was depressed. And David had already had enough humiliation to last the rest of this year.

After three long draws of water he remembered his manners and asked Dr. Tew if he would like a drink. When this was declined, he went about rinsing his hands off in the streaming water, then catching water in his cupped hands and, hands still cupped, throwing the water over his right shoulder onto his wound. After two such splashes with the very cold water, he then gingerly slid his hand over and around the surface of the abrasion, adding several more handfuls of water until the shoulder felt clean enough, or at least cold enough, to stop rinsing. The three men stood by silently as he completed this task, and David felt awkward in their silence. He didn't think they had said their names as they had been shaking hands. His hands now cool and wet, he used them to comb his fingers through the sides of his hair, momentarily exposing his ears which were usually otherwise covered by hair that was just long enough to do so. He then refreshed his face and upper chest before giving his hands a final rinse. As he dried his hands off on either side of his now wet shorts he actually felt much better.

Only then did Dr. Tew take a brief drink, then once again took control of the situation. "David, I'd like you to meet these guys. This is Doc," he said, motioning to the heavier of the two, "and this is Pops". The informal introduction with no last names struck David as a little odd, but now that he was a man of 20 years he would have to get comfortable calling adults by their first names and their nicknames. Because there was nothing else to do in response as Dr. Tew conducted the introductions, David again shook hands with both of the other men. While he did so he observed a little more about them for the first time.

They were both obviously related to Dr. Tew, maybe his father and uncle. The heavier man had enough of a belly to redirect the descending angle of the red knit short sleeve shirt he wore, tucked into a pair of unbelted and well-worn jeans. His hair was full where it was, but had receded high on his temples and was entirely gray, parted on his right and conservatively styled so as to be unremarkable. He had golden-rimmed glasses resting on a long but thin nose with a size more than adequate to perform its functions, and a full silver moustache with goatee which enhanced his professorial appearance, despite the blue jeans. Although David wore jeans almost daily, he wasn't accustomed to seeing grandfathers wearing them.

He had a high forehead with mildly prominent frontal bone ridging over his eyebrows that made his eyes seem to be placed deep into their sockets on his somewhat narrowed face, a template that was obviously used to create the visage of Dr. Tew, and the other man as well. Apparently not a lot of creativity had gone into assuring variations between these three when they were created, David thought. He briefly recalled his course in biology where he had studied genetic make-up, DNA, and the thousands of genes each human has to determine every possible characteristic. Yet the dominance of particular genes in these men led to obvious familial characteristics that made David wonder what other family members would look like. Did this family all look the same like the famous Hapsburg dynasty profile pictures he had seen in the genetics chapter of his Biology book?

The third man was much tanner than the others, of slighter build but similar height, and with more wrinkles across his face. While browner and more wrinkled, the skin of his face didn't appear overly weathered or dried. He had a full head of light brown hair that might even be blond in the sun, which he wore longer than the other two, although not as long as David's — just full on the sides and to the tops of his ears, parted also on the right and combed over to the left, with bushy sideburns that extended to a full but nicely manicured beard. He wore no glasses, which made his eyes appear even more deeply set than the other two with the trait all three shared. He wore what David figured to be a sweat suit, a lightweight zippered long-sleeved jacket over a black t-shirt, with long lightweight pants that had an elastic waistband, and white shoes that looked like a cross between tennis shoes and dance shoes — unlike any David had ever seen before, but looking incredibly light and comfortable. The material of the sweat suit jacket was what set it apart. It was not like any cloth David had ever seen — a color that seemed to be a blend of orange/rust/gold that looked as though it would feel like satin. But it captured any light and gave a strange effect on depth perception, creating an optical illusion of depth and motion that fascinated David. His pants were a deep royal blue.

David had registered that both men moved a little more stiffly than Dr. Tew while they had been walking toward him. 'Doc' had seemed to walk with a slight limp, or to perhaps be favoring a leg, while the slighter man, 'Pops', had a broader-based and more careful, deliberate gait. It made him appear to be the frailest of the three, but it was hard to peg an age on him because his hair and tan bespoke youth, as did his constant impish grin that was almost a smile, and the twinkle of life that seemed to emanate from those deep set eyes. Now they were standing still, smiling at David while they seemed to be giving him the once over, studying him, politely, even more than he was studying them.

"Do you have a shirt, David?" Dr. Tew interrupted.

"Yes, sir, over there by that barrel," he said as he pointed to the barrel.

"Let's walk over and pick it up. We can use that as a cool down lap before we go."

"We?" thought David, "What's this 'we' business?". Then he realized that Dr. Tew probably meant he and Doc and Pops would be leaving and that was just fine with David. So he responded, "OK".

The two took off around the track with a much brisker walking pace than David would have considered to be a cool-down, but he reasoned that since Dr. Tew was a doctor, he probably knew better about how to do these things. He looked over to Dr. Tew and asked, "Are those men related to you?"

The curt and dismissive affirmative response he received sounded almost as if Dr. Tew was ashamed to be with the other two men, or at least not in a mood to talk about the family bonds, a much different tone than David had felt from him when he was in the presence of Doc and Pops, so David let it drop.

"What are you studying here at Georgia?" Dr. Tew asked, seeming to change the subject. And as they walked around the track, retrieved the shirt, and completed the lap to reunite with Doc and Pops, David and Dr. Tew discussed David's plans for a medical career and Dr. Tew's education history and medical practice. Like many Georgians, they both had gone to the University of Georgia in Athens, and then Dr. Tew had continued with medical school at the state's Medical College of Georgia located 100 miles to the east in Augusta. That was where Will Rice was in medical school now. David considered it as an option, but would also look at other schools before he narrowed it down to just Georgia, he explained politely to Dr. Tew. He told Dr. Tew that while obstetrics — *"Shesh, why hadn't I used that word before?"* — seemed like a rewarding practice, he was keeping an open mind on which area he would chose for a specialty, not feeling pressure to follow in his father's footsteps. Dr. Tew agreed that was the best way to pursue the future. David enjoyed hearing about Dr. Tew's internal medicine practice in Atlanta and getting his honest advice about the future of medicine. He asked Dr. Tew what he enjoyed most about his practice— the 'front row seat' of watching people as they go through life and being a part of somehow enriching someone else's life experience as they enriched his— and the thing he enjoyed least about medicine — increasing expectations of perfection and the seeming anticipation of a (fortunately) very small percentage of patients that he could be better than human.

The lap around the track passed much too quickly, not because of the pace, but because David would have enjoyed discussing becoming a doctor more with Dr. Tew, nervous though he was to be around a real adult and doctor who wasn't his parent.

"Well, you're hogging the boy to yourself," chided Pops in his good-natured call to Dr. Tew as they returned to the bleachers.

"You didn't spoil the surprise, did you?" asked Doc, seemingly almost child-like in his enthusiasm.

"What surprise?" thought David, almost defensively. Did these guys have something to do with UGA? Were they going to award him a prize for doing so well on the Organic Chemistry final?

And with that, in a bizarre and unexpected change of atmosphere, the three men stood together with Pops in the middle, framed on either side by Doc and Dr. Tew with their arms on both of Pops' shoulders, and standing as a trio, they sang "Happy Birthday", starting off in unison. They divided into harmony and slowed when they reached, "Happy Birthday dear Da—vid", and ended in a wonderfully harmonized, "Happy Birthday to you!"

David couldn't help but be overwhelmed with surprise and the combined sense of pride and embarrassment that comes from having others acknowledge one's birthday. And hey — these guys sounded good together. Not that they were polished vocalists, but the genetic blend of their voices smoothed the edges off one another's tones, with Dr. Tew singing an adequate tenor, Doc singing the melody, and Pops working devotedly to assure a rich bass line.

"Wow!" was about all David could say, otherwise speechless as they concluded. *"Who are these guys? And who set them up for this? Is this the parents' present? Wow!"* were some of the thoughts as they raced through and collided in his surprised brain. Then with the conclusion of the song all four erupted into a deep long cathartic of howling laughter that made David feel truly comfortable and accepting of these strangers for the first time.

A passerby would have wondered what all the laughter was about at such an early hour, and assumed the four were all closely related, the only differences in appearances seemingly due to the result of being members of different generations of the same gene pool.

Chapter 4
The Maverick

"Y'all sing really well!" said a genuinely grateful David.

"Thanks. We're for hire, if you ever need a group. But we only know one song," teased Pops.

"No, I'm serious," said David, hoping he would spontaneously come up with a better way to voice his sincere appreciation. He couldn't help asking, "Who put you up to this?"

"Who do you think?" replied Doc, curiously.

"Well, you do know my parents, so I'd guess that they arranged this. Although how, I don't know. How did you even know I was here?"

"Trade secret," taunted Doc, playfully.

That tipped his hand. Whenever David's father had a secret or a plan he wasn't yet ready to reveal, as was so often the case, rather than give inquisitive children any information, he would simply reply, "Trade secret." Whether intentional or not, Doc had conveyed the identity of the birthday planners, but he was thus also implying that he wasn't going to, or wasn't ready to, reveal the source. David was familiar with this strategy after years with his father's methods, so he decided not to push the point further. It would come in due time, when his father wanted to announce things. Perhaps that was part of the plan for the collect call David was supposed to make to them this evening between 5:00 and 7:00.

"OK," David smiled, knowingly.

"So how about you let us join you for a birthday breakfast? It's not every day you turn 20. Do you have any plans?" asked Doc.

"Well, no, I don't have any plans," said David, scrambling to process the effect this offer could have on the rest of his day. He certainly needed to shower first, but then he didn't need to be anywhere until he went to Kay's at two o'clock this afternoon, so things should work out time wise. "I would like to go shower first," he said, again brushing off his forearms as he spoke.

"Good idea," winked Pops.

Perhaps on another day David would have exercised more caution in choosing whether or not to join a group of three men he had never met before. His concern for his own safety did not enter his mind at this point, distracted as he was by the birthday glee. They claimed to know his parents, and knew it was his birthday, so whatever the plan was, he would go along with it for now.

"Where are y'all parked?" There was no evidence these guys had come in a car.

"Well, we thought we might hitch a ride with you. Do you mind?" asked

Pops.

"Not at all, as long as you think we can all fit into my Maverick," David replied. "It's right over there," pointing past a grassy strip to the dirt parking lot with the single car occupying it. He finished his sentence as he stepped to the fountain to grab one last drink, and then took a few quick strides as he joined up with the other three who had already started walking the few yards toward the parking area.

"It's the yellow car there, my dad says it's 'piyourick' yellow, whatever that means," added David, further identifying the car in the event they needed additional clues to help them locate the only vehicle in the lot. Trying to slip into his shirt without causing disruption of the forming crust over his right shoulder, he looked a little ataxic working to keep up with the group with his shirt temporarily over his head obstructing his vision, all the while yearning to carry on an intelligent conversation.

"Pyuric — it means 'infected urine'," said Dr. Tew, flatly. The other two chuckled at this coarse characterization of David's car, and he didn't know if Dr. Tew was making a joke or telling the truth. He would now be sure to look it up.

Dr. Tew continued, seemingly enjoying the opportunity to demonstrate his knowledge to the easily impressed student: "'Py-' from the Latin term for pus, and 'uric', also Latin, the adjective form for urine."

That seemed plausible. It *was* a weird color. David's father had purchased the car off the lot while wearing his sunglasses, unaware of how the exact true color was being modified by his tinted shades. Daddy liked telling that story, perhaps to offer an explanation in his own defense. Nevertheless, David would look it up.

"A Maverick," Pops mused, almost wistfully, stroking his chin as he contemplated the ride. "Do you mind if I drive?"

This request caught David a little off guard. He had already tried to start figuring out how to best arrange the seating, since the back seat was so cramped for anyone taller than a third grader. His younger brother, Tim, had once cracked that they should have a measuring stick painted on the outside of the Maverick, analogous to one of the signs posted in front of some of the thrill rides at Six Flags, which would state, "You must be *under* 42 inches tall to ride this ride." Being a younger brother and thus being relegated to the back seat when three or more were gathered did have its drawbacks.

David had calculated that Doc's knees might do better by being able to stretch out in the front, leaving Dr. Tew and Pops with the short end of the deal and a seat in the back. David would drive, since he always drove. Another agreement with his father when he first received the Maverick had been that none of his friends would be allowed to drive the Maverick. There had been no discussion of that point; it had simply been handed down from Mount Sinai, along with the edict to have all passengers wear seat belts. That absence of a discussion or request for clarification now served to David's advantage, he reasoned. Since Pops wasn't *his* friend, and was more likely his father's friend, Daddy would certainly not mind if Pops drove the Maverick. So on the grounds of this technicality and feeling generous, wanting to return a favor on his birthday, David replied, "Sure." He was reassured that neither Doc nor Dr. Tew spoke up with a counteroffer, their silent endorsements confirming his confidence in Pops' driving abilities.

As they now approached the two-door Maverick, Dr. Tew and Doc assigned themselves toward the passenger side of the car, so David followed Pops to the driver's side, flipped the driver's seatback forward and quickly slipped into the backseat. Meanwhile, Dr. Tew and Doc held a polite discussion of seating arrangements with Dr. Tew offering to sit in the back and Doc accepting his offer. Dr. Tew then mirrored David's entrance into the backseat, with a minimal struggle to contort himself into the confined space, and then the seatback came to rest against his knees as Doc less gracefully slid into his space on the front seat. Doc reached for and almost tugged on the broken and thus useless plastic door handle but somehow saw that it was broken, grinned, shook his head, then closed the door by holding onto the opened window frame.

David, realizing he hadn't told Pops where the key was hidden under the floor mat, was a little chagrinned to see that Pops had already retrieved the keys from under the mat and placed the key into the ignition. He made a mental note to come up with a better place to hide his keys while he jogged. The under-the-mat location was too obvious, after all, in an unlocked car with the windows left down.

Pops then did something David had never seen done before in his car, or any other car. Pops reached up over his left shoulder and deftly retrieved the separate shoulder strap accessory, which was clipped in its original factory position along the left border of the car's ceiling, and skillfully slipped it into the appropriate notch in the seatbelt before clicking both into the receptacle. *"So that's how that works,"* David thought. He had never seen anyone use that cumbersome feature, not even when he took Driver's Ed in high school, although it did make sense. He had always been a little bit afraid that if he had taken it out of its original position that he might never get it to go back into place, the proverbial "folding road map" challenge of restoring something to its impossible-to-achieve original perfection. So he had just left it alone. Now he was reassured to see that Pops, despite his years, valued safety. People of his parent's generation and older oftentimes seemed to view seatbelts as an afterthought, an option, since wearing seatbelts had not been the habit, or even standard equipment, in earlier times.

Pops gave a quick 6 pumps to the accelerator, followed by four more pumps while turning the key. The Marvelous Maverick rumbled to life. He called over his right shoulder to David in the back seat and grinned, "I used to have one of these Mavericks — best car I ever had. Wish I still had it. We had a great time together, but I drove it into the ground before I sold it."

Hearing this eulogy for the deceased Maverick, Doc turned his head toward his left shoulder, dipping it a bit to look over the rims of his glasses while looking at Pops from his position in the passenger seat, simultaneously lowering the inner aspect of his right eyebrow as he raised his left eyebrow in a mime of disbelief. A small smile crept across his face as he made a slight but perceptible shake of his head.

David heard a "click" and looked down to his right and was impressed to realize that Dr. Tew had just mastered the engineering problem of fastening the seatbelt in the backseat without much difficulty. Meanwhile Doc was now repeating the example of Pops in fastening his seat and shoulder belt.

Pops placed both hands on the steering wheel, raised his shoulders slightly, extended both elbows fully, closed his eyes and slowly took a deep breath as a dreamy smile came across his face while he caressed the wheel. David admired his jacket and wondered where he had bought such a cool looking outfit. Not wanting to interrupt Pop's meditation, David remained silent. Pops exhaled, opened his eyes and announced, "Reed Hall?"

"Um, that's right!" confirmed David, surprised that Pops would know the name of his dormitory. But if they had planned this surprise birthday greeting in advance, how difficult would a little more reconnaissance be to learn the name of his dorm? Whoever put them up to this certainly knew where David lived.

He put the car into reverse. "Best car I ever had," he repeated, to no one in particular as he put his right arm over the seatback to improve his view while he looked backward. He put the car in drive and headed toward Lumpkin Street where he would then make a right turn and head north toward Reed Hall.

"Hmpff," pronounced Dr. Tew with a head bob. "I think I would hold out for a Mercedes." He smirked as he looked over his hunched and confined right shoulder at the passenger side window immediately beside him. The almost triangular rear side window was actually designed to serve only as a small vent. It did not roll up and down, but rather popped out a few inches to allow air to circulate, hinged at the front portion of the window. But the clamp that allowed this window to shut and lock had been forced too far by one of David's passengers a few weeks ago during the first heat wave of spring. The window now stayed neither opened nor closed, but flapped in a dysrhythmic tempo determined by the airflow into the car. Air from inside the car pushed the window open until the angle of the hinged window increased to a critical point against the outside wind pressure which would then override the outward motion and pat the window shut. With Doc's open front window, Dr. Tew was now getting a full stream of wind, and the window to his right was opening and closing in a distracting pattern with a patting sound, as if willfully taunting him. The only thing that kept the flapping from being worse was the moderate speed limit of Lumpkin Street. The ease with which he was perturbed by such a situation was more a testimony to his temperament than the amount of irritation the flapping should cause an individual possessing greater equanimity. "Roll up your window!"" he barked to Doc, who elected not to hear him.

"Do you think you'll ever buy another one?" asked David, optimistically, as he looked forward into the rear-view mirror to see Pops' response.

Pops' vigilant eyes connected briefly with David's in the mirror before he looked back to the roadway. "No, I think one Maverick in a lifetime is probably enough. Ford isn't going to make them after the 1977 model — they halted production of the 'Grabber' version after 1975 —, and who's to know what I'd get if I bought one used. But it's a good line. It broke the '65 Mustang first-year sales record," he lectured enthusiastically as he drove, adding much more about Mavericks and telling David more than he knew or wanted to know about Maverick history.

Part way into his dissertation, Pops paused long enough to ask, "Do you want to know something more about the Maverick?"

With this Dr. Tew rolled his eyes with a grimace that bespoke, *"I'm beside myself in anticipation,"* but David politely answered, "Sure."

Even more paragraphs followed with information about production numbers, engine sizes, Falcons, Comets, Sprints, and Stallions, monopolizing the conversation for the moment. Doc occasionally nodded as if reminded of something he already knew. David listened good naturedly, glad there was not going to be a test after the end of the monologue.

"Where would you like to eat breakfast after you clean-up?" interjected Dr. Tew, perhaps in an effort to ignore the window that continued its syncopated tapping, obviously in an effort to change the topic, which he did not deem to be worthy of quite so much time.

"Well my meal card at Bolton Hall is good through the end of the week, so why don't we go there?" he suggested, recalling they had offered to *join* him for breakfast, but had not specifically mentioned *treating* him to breakfast. The food at Bolton dining hall was good enough, especially at breakfast, and he did not want to waste any meal money that had already been paid. He did not start working for another week and right now every penny counted.

"Revoltin' Bolton," mused Dr. Tew, "Ah, yes, I remember it well. That should be a wonderful place for re-discovering the finer cuisine that Athens has to offer —"

"If you'd like to go someplace different —" David interrupted.

"No, it will be good for nostalgia if not for nutrition," Dr. Tew replied as he took control of the conversation. He reported an event to David which only a doctor would enjoy but which kept Pops and Doc amused, laced with some medical terms which David didn't understand, about an episode of diarrheal illness that had gone through Dr. Tew's dorm one year. A brief summary of the longer version told is as follows:

Students kept showing up at the student health department with diarrhea that was initially blamed on eating at the dining hall. Ultimately the source of a bacterial infection was traced back to a pair of gerbils, Harry and Chopper, which were kept, against dorm rules, as unofficial mascots within the community of dormitory residents. The asymptomatic gerbils were very popular with dorm residents and were shuttled from room to room, infecting and re-infecting students who handled them as they went. No one revealed the presence of the gerbils until a Resident Assistant (one of the students assigned to live on the floor as a hall monitor of sorts) confessed to their presence when asked about any animals by health authorities brought in by the Center for Disease Control to investigate. After a few more days spent in hiding with sympathetic students in the spontaneously formed underground resistance, Harry and Chopper were turned over to the health authorities. Their autopsies (the results of which were part of a report published in a medical journal advising other doctors of the risks of rodents as pets) confirmed the infections, which then immediately ceased in the student population. Outraged students held a protest march at the student infirmary, demanding the return of the bodies of the martyred gerbils for proper burial. No bodies remained for such a tribute, so a memorial service was organized to be held on the large grassy quadrangle to the north of Reed Hall. Hand-printed then Xerox copied handbills started appearing all over campus inciting students to get involved. The UGA student newspaper, *The Red and Black*, dutifully reported on the upcoming event, an item which was picked by the Associated Press on what must have been a slow news day. Students from all over UGA came to pay their respects to the two critters, overwhelming campus security with the size and ultimate boisterousness of the overflowing demonstration of support and supposed grief, egged on by the electrifying presence of news crews. Coeds cried while many guys, and some girls, felt beer, and lots of it, to be the most appropriate form of tribute to the honorable decedents. Music provided by the Gerbil Jam Jazz Band, which Dr. Tew sheepishly implied he had helped form, eased the pain for mourners. Of the songs the band played, the most popular was "Oh, Didn't He Ramble", a song that starts as a funeral dirge and then picks up to a simple but infectious Dixieland sound, with lyrics including, "*He rambled all around, in and out of town,...'til the butcher cut him down.*" For the rest of their academic careers at UGA the members of the Gerbil Jam Jazz Band were folk heroes among a few of the crowd there who always wanted to hear that song again.

The music was followed by the formal program of spoken recollections of the fallen heroes which dissolved into a spontaneous series of chants and two arrests which would have been even greater in number were it not for the great restraint exercised by UGA campus police. Overall, quite a memorable evening was inspired by the furry fomites with the sophomoric intensity that can only be found on a college campus.

The most remarkable thing about Pops' short drive back to Reed Hall was how unremarkable it was. Pops took a longer route than David would have chosen, going all the way north to Baldwin Street before turning east, then taking Baldwin Street the necessary three blocks east until he turned south on East Campus Road for two more blocks to arrive alongside of Reed Hall. He appropriately chose the smaller but more convenient lower parking lot available to Reed residents behind the dorm — not the side lot that was more often used by residents of the adjacent Milledge or Payne Halls — and even selected a parking space in the half-empty lot that would be amongst the first shaded from the afternoon sun. Once stopped, he smoothly pulled out the hand parking brake with his left hand as he immediately silenced the obedient engine when he turned off the ignition with the car still in drive.

Chapter 5
Reed Hall

The most prominent feature on the campus of the University of Georgia was Sanford Stadium, bordered to the east by East Campus Road, beyond which were the famous railroad tracks upon which students could sit and peer into the open-ended stadium to watch the Bulldogs play whomever on autumn Saturday afternoons. To the west of the stadium was Sanford Drive as it crossed an elevated bridge which spanned the valley between the south campus with all its science buildings and the north campus and its arts and humanities related facilities. The Bridge thus provided an opportune vantage point for viewing the stadium from its open west side, or, looking west from the other side, down over the expansive parking lot that served as Mecca for tailgate partiers from all over the Southeast any weekend there was a football game.

To the immediate north of the stadium, even closer than either East Campus Road or Sanford Drive, stood Reed Hall, a large building roughly in the shape of a blocked letter "C". Separated from the north entrances to the stadium by only a narrow alley, Reed's backside, left and right wings seemed ignobly squashed up against the stadium, as if ignoring its proximity. The more proud front of Reed Hall faced northward as a wide stately four story brick building with a columned central entrance, its roof studded across its length with more than a dozen dormer windows looking out on the large grassy Reed Quadrangle shaded at its borders by massive water oaks. Reed was flanked on its right by the smaller and less impressive three-story residence hall, Milledge Hall, and on its left by Memorial Hall, a multi-purpose student center, concert hall, and café which in its original plans was designed to be none of these things.

Reed Hall was built 25 years earlier, the namesake of Thomas Walter Reed, a UGA alumnus and subsequent registrar and university historian who died in 1950, but not before writing the monumental "History of the University of Georgia". To honor his eighty years of life the new dormitory was named for him. Reed Hall opened in 1953 with a capacity for 500 male students coupled in individual rooms which utilized large community bathrooms at the north end of each wing and the west side of the main hall . Now one of the older dormitories on campus, it held a personality not found in the newer sterile high-rise dorms named Russell, Brumby and Creswell off to the west, with their cookie-cutter designed rooms, furniture bolted to the walls and floors. Those dorms seemed to be the default rooms given to entering freshmen who did not request a specific housing assignment. Unlike the high-rise dorms, Reed Hall had been transformed to a coed dorm during social progressions of recent years. The women lived to the west of the heavy fire doors that demarcated the 10 p.m.

curfew zone, but the presence of females seemed to have both a maturing and stimulating influence on the male side of the dorm.

One flaw in the original architectural design of Reed Hall had been the stairwell at the unattached south end of the men's wing of Reed Hall. In an effort to squeeze the most room space out of the available floor plan, the corner rooms of each floor of that end of the wing were located alongside the stairwell which ascended through the southernmost aspect of the wing. Each corner end room was thus "land locked" by the stairwell, with no designed space for a door to open into the hall, since the hallway ended at the two heavy fire doors that opened into the landing of the stairwell. The architects had solved this problem by designating the last two rooms on either side of the hall to be suites for four people, connecting the corner room to the adjacent room with a doorway, allowing both rooms to use the last room door on the hall to exit into the hallway just before the fire doors.

The unintended consequence of this solution was that now four university males were confined to the same living space, proving the hypothesis that testosterone has a multiplier effect on behavior of young men. As an experienced mother once observed, "One boy, one brain; two boys, half a brain," and thus with four men in one room, behavior was less often influenced by forethought than by impulse. Predictably, these end suites, which were unfortunately the farthest away from the watchful eye of the Resident Assistant's room at the other end of the hall, were the rooms most likely to be reported to the Campus Housing Authority regarding infractions of housing policy.

The previous year, David's freshman year, suite 270/272 had been occupied by Will Rice, Rex Lee, "Mad-man" Madison, and David. The creative mischief that emanated from that room had been for the most part coarse in content but benign in intent, beneath the radar of the Campus Housing Authority, and stress-relieving as all four members of the room were actually very dedicated and hard-working students. Mad-man, for instance, could generate a blood-curdling scream that was something like a cross between the laugh of Cheetah the chimpanzee in the old Tarzan movies and a loud long "whoop." When properly directed out the back windows of room 272 the vocalization could be bounced off the tall concrete walls of the adjacent Sanford Stadium, and while the original scream was an impressive 15 or 20 seconds, its reverberations between the stadium walls and the back wall of Reed Hall lasted much longer. For reasons that likely mystified the otherwise sleeping residents of Reed Hall, Mad-man never really seemed to be inspired to give a performance until after a long night of studying into the early morning hours. Without fanfare he would enter suite 270 and go into the back room where all four men slept, although even at that late hour only one or two of them may have yet gone to sleep, most predictably Rex. Mad-man would turn off the light if it were on, open the back window if it were closed, spread his legs to the width of the window standing far enough back from the window to then allow him to bend forward to assure full projection out through the screened window. After his most amazingly loud display of his version of the primal scream — which started with a soft, low pitched "wu, wu, wu" and then crescendoed into a horrific laughing yell, the origin of which was hidden by the immediate echoes off the stadium walls — without further ado or comment he would silently crawl into his upper bunk over Rex, and feign immediate sleep. Faithful to the code of comedy, Rex never once complained about being startled awake, in part to retain the creed of manhood which demands never admit to being frightened, and in part out of sheer admiration for the brilliance of each performance. Without fail, such a nocturnal event would be the topic of discussion the next morning as students brushed their teeth and showered — "Did you hear it last night?...Who do you think it is that does it?..." Certainly much less complementary discussions were held on the women's side of the dorm.

The first opportunity Rex had to experience a Mad-man prank had been the night before his first day of classes as a freshman at UGA, and he had been the target. By 11:00 that evening David, Will and Rex were all moved into Reed Hall and settled into their beds for a full night's sleep to start the quarter off right. One gargantuan task earlier that day had been to dissemble the heavy metal bunk bed in room 270 and move it into the corner room 272 where the other bunk was. The cast iron construction of the beds and the rusty bolts which held the upper and lower beds together required all three men lifting together to move each half bed through the door into room 272. They then had to work in concert to reassemble the bunk and then reposition both bunks along the walls at right angles to each other, the beds growing heavier with each relocation. But the effort was worth the result. They now had a "parlor" in room 270, where they would later place a couch that Will found along a road, along with two of the four university issued metal desks. Both of the university-issued four-drawer-high dressers were placed side-by-side in room 270, on top of which went a collection of Rex's and Will's audio equipment. Room 272 would contain both bunk beds and the other two desks. Not a bad set up, they observed proudly.

As they went to bed that first evening, the only evidence of Mad-man was a single extra-large duffle bag which had appeared while they were gone for dinner. The duffle bag, overstuffed despite its size, was in the middle of the top bunk he would claim, over the bottom bunk which Rex had made-up earlier and now occupied. Not much speculation had been made about Mad-man's whereabouts at that point. There were so many things to attend to the first day back on campus that his absence seemed necessary.

David had met Mad-man the previous spring when he visited Athens and stayed with Will one weekend to get an advance look at college life. He talked with Mad-man only briefly, and he had seemed very polite, articulate, and interested in encouraging David in preparing for the beginning of his college career. His casual manner set David immediately at ease. Nothing of the antics Will had previously described about Mad-man had occurred, and David left the encounter almost disappointed.

James Ambrose Madison, III, was known as "Mad-man" to most, "Jim" by a few. So few people knew his real name, or contemplated American history adequately, that the fact that he shared his name with a founding father was rarely noted, and that was fine with him. Just to be certain, he introduced himself only as Mad-man.

Mad-man was the only child of a loving couple in Charleston, South Carolina, born to them fairly late in their lives. His father was a surgeon, very well respected, and already retired. His mother was very proud of her boy who wanted to be a doctor.

His first year at college had been at the Citadel. For reasons that were never clear, and that seemed to change every time David heard the story, Mad-man had transferred to UGA at the start of his second year. During that year he had impressed Will with his late night study habits – many nights Will and Mad-man were the last two students to leave the study hall room at Milledge Hall where they had both roomed for that year only.

At that time Will and Mad-man had separate roommates, and the acceptance of Will's good friend David and David's good friend Rex to UGA made it reasonable for Will to suggest Mad-man as the final piece that would allow all of them to stay in one of the Reed suites. On paper Mad-man had a pedigree that made him look like a good match for the other three.

As they prepared for bed that evening before classes started David was glad he had already spent a weekend on campus. He seemed to feel more at home and to be having fewer jitters than Rex, who would never have admitted to such, but did seem a little anxious. The business-like approach with which Will and presumably Mad-man were beginning the start of the year had a calming effect on both of the new freshmen. Throughout the evening several of Will's friends had dropped by to welcome him back, and he had introduced each to Rex and David, so they were already feeling like they were getting to know a good number of people and enjoying the prospects of the social life that they were certain would develop. Even a couple of girls had passed by, and Will had introduced them also. Almost without exception, every drop-in guest asked about Mad-man, or upon hearing who the fourth roommate would be, already knew Mad-man. David was impressed by the respect and awe other students held for Mad-man as they briefly told their favorite Mad-man story or just said "Wow!" knowing he would be living on their hall. Rex, who had not yet met this living legend, was even more impressed. Rex was particularly captivated by the response of the women, because he fancied himself to be a ladies' man, too, and had great plans for the next four years. He could learn a lot from this upperclassman.

As 11:00 came about, a reasonable time for lights out, it was with a sense of mild regret that the boys of suite 270/272 went to sleep without their fourth roommate, represented in absentia by a stuffed duffle bag in the middle of an unmade upper bunk. But the need for a good night's sleep before the first day of class dictated, especially for David and Rex, a proper bedtime. The truth be told, Rex was accustomed to a 10 p.m. bedtime at home, so he was all the more tired after the events of the day and the anxiety of the impending first day of college. Will did not seem too worried about the absentee so neither would David, now settled into the other upper bunk over Will. Rex, solo on his side of the room, did not voice any concerns he might have been thinking about the importance of sleep or self-imposed curfews.

With the lights out Will pronounced it a good day, as only he could without sounding corny or maternal, and it was with this reassurance that the entire room was soon asleep with little other discussion, first night jitters overcome with the fatigue of a long day of preparation.

Their brief sleep was gently nudged awake with the tinkling sound of keys clinking against the outside hall door of the adjacent room 270. The holder of the keys fumbled with them for quite a long time, keys dangling free and swinging against the door as a succession of unsuccessful keys were tried and rejected in search of the necessary one. By the time the door was opened, Rex, David and Will were all awake in the dark of room 272. That darkness was pierced by the shaft of light that poured in from room 270 as the light was turned on, but then quickly turned off after no new or large obstacles were identified.

In the dark of room 270 stood Mad-man, singing to himself the song that was still reverberating in his brain, still dancing the one unfinished dance that his feet couldn't resist after an evening of release from pressures which did not yet exist. He cocked his head to the side as his body swayed unsteadily, repeatedly singing only, "Yow....yow...," the background vocal to the Earth, Wind and Fire hit "The Way of the World" with the grace and balance of John Travolta on Benadryl. He progressed in the dark towards the doorway into room 272, first slamming into the wall beside the door with an "Oomp," and then into the doorframe with a polite "Pardon me," before successfully passing through the doorway into room 272 on only his third try. Here was prima facie evidence that the Georgia State Legislature should raise the legal drinking age from 18 to 21 years of age, as it one day would.

"Oh, I'm sorry, I didn't mean to wake you," he slurred loudly to the darkened room, which had not yet given any evidence of being awakened. He was fully aware he had an audience, however.

Without moving out of bed, Will, who knew how to have a good time himself, paternalistically scolded Mad-man for partying so late on the night before school started. Mad-man countered with defenses that made it obvious he was not in the state of mind to receive instruction.

Will, still not otherwise moving, then told Mad-man that David and Rex were also in the room in their bunks. Following Will's example, they both simply said "Hi, Mad-man," and left it at that for the time being. There would be time for more complete introductions tomorrow.

"Yeah," was all that Mad-man replied. His responsibilities to continue providing background vocals and dance persisted with a greater urgency than any need to be sociable. David, lying on his left side could now see his undulating form as he stood in the middle of the darkened room in no particular hurry to go to bed. His was a short, stout frame with broad shoulders that lessened the visual impact of an abdomen of sizable girth. David correctly attributed at least a portion of his apparent inebriation to theatrics performed as an initiation for the new rookies. David, whose motto was "I'll sleep when I'm old," and would always choose to be entertained when given the choice of entertainment vs. sleep, rolled his face toward his pillow and stifled his laughter. He did not want to disrupt the comedic performance being so seriously portrayed by Mad-man and absorbed by Rex.

Feigning an inability to find his bed in the dark, Mad-man stumbled with the full force of his weight against the length of the heavy iron bunk, displacing it an inch closer to the wall. He cried out in supposed pain, and punched out at the bedrail of the upper bed with his open hand, moving the entire bed a final inch closer to the wall in a violent outburst that emphasized how angry a drunk can be and how much strength was contained in his upper torso. He then stabilized himself physically and emotionally while holding alongside the length of his mattress. He began to undress standing beside the bed, and thus right beside Rex, continuing with occasional vocalizations and gyrations, punctuated with an occasional scratch, smack of the lips, snort, belch, hic, or otherwise, unmindful of the rest of the world and its proprieties. He removed shoes and clothes, dropping them in a pile as he did that accumulated on the floor directly in front of Rex's bed. When only an undershirt and underwear remained, he attempted to climb onto the bed. He neglected to use the rails at the end of the bed, electing to use the most direct path. Stepping clumsily onto the side edge of Rex's mattress, almost standing on Rex, he tried to hoist himself up onto his bed. The series of unsuccessful attempts that followed were a display of gymnastic maneuvers worthy of a gold medal as he repeatedly bent himself over and under his mattress, legs and feet oblivious to the contained sleeping space over Rex's bed but never coming in contact with the freshman who lay petrified, not wanting to provoke anyone strong enough to move the heavy bed with him in it. At times his rotund posterior swung precariously closely to Rex's head, but no foul was ever committed. Mad-man's commotion eventually resulted in him knocking the overstuffed duffle bag off the top of the bed, which careened off his body laterally and landed with a heavy thud on Rex. Still in awe that this legend was now home, Rex said nothing.

"Sorry," said Mad-man, retrieving the duffle bag so he could throw it on the growing pile in front of Rex's face on the floor.

With the unsuccessful completion of the side-mount portion of his program, he continued his preparation for sleep by going to the end of the bed, attempting to climb up and over the foot of the bed. As he neared the top bar he appeared to slip. As he fell backward he adroitly grabbed that bar, jarring the bed viciously, pulling the front two legs of the bed briefly off the floor as though performing a wheelie. His second attempt was more successful and he was soon lying flat on the bare mattress with the comforts of neither sheets nor a pillow. Rex remained deathly silent. All remained quiet for about a minute while David waited for the other shoe to drop. And it did.

Mad-man rolled halfway over the edge of his bed and directed a loud whisper at the bed beneath him, "Rex...are you awake?"

"Yes, Mad-man," replied the plebe below.

"Oh, sorry...I didn't mean to wake you up, man," sounding emotionally labile as though he might cry in disappointed shame.

A few seconds of almost silence passed as Mad-man rolled over flat on his back, this silence interrupted when he completed the final chorus of "Yow's". He smacked twice and sniffed, then rolled back toward the edge of the bed again.

"Rex...are you awake?"

"Yes, Mad-man."

"I'm sorry I didn't take the proper amount of time to introduce myself. I'm Mad-man." He spoke louder now than was necessary, even with the droning of the two window fans.

"It's very nice to meet you, Mad-man," said Rex, trying to sound more grown-up or formal than was necessary for the current situation.

With this David was now straining the muscles of the back of his neck as he stifled his laughter into his pillow. College was fun!

Mad-man rolled onto his back and the room was again quiet for about a minute.

Mad-man stirred. He rolled onto his left side once more, hanging his head over the side of the bed for further conversation.

"Rex... she wanted me," opening a new can of worms that by its very introductory sentence told David that the show was far from over. Not waiting for or needing a response from Rex, Mad-man continued with speech that was less slurred, more intense in its narration with well-placed emphasis on selected words to further enhance the already enhanced story.

"I went down to 'The Other Place' — that's a dance club downtown. There was a *beautiful* blond pouring drinks at the bar. She was trying to get me drunk. *She* was trying to get *me* drunk."

"Rex, she *wanted* me," he moaned deeply, a brief shiver simultaneously running through his body and voice.

He rolled on his back, to allow more effectively those words to marinate silently in the fertile imagination of his young listener. Then, still on his back, for added emphasis, he repeated, "She *wanted* me." His emphasis on "wanted" further raised the temperature in the room, already warm in the late summer despite the two window fans. This unforgettable euphemistic use of the word "want" would become a part of Rex's lexicon for years to come anytime he felt, justifiably or otherwise, that he, too, was irresistible.

Another moment of silence, then Mad-man repeated, this time angrily, "She wanted *me!*"

Another pause followed, each sentence punctuated with just enough silence to give any listener the false hope that conversation had ended and sleep could resume.

Mad-man, now confident he had full control of Rex's imagination looked down over the side rail again and continued,

"She was trying to get me drunk. I had about, I don't know, maybe 8 or 9 beers,"

David felt his bunk shake as Will now convulsed silently in the bunk below him.

"She wanted me. But then her boyfriend, a *frat-boy*," he emphasized with a contempt which was based on having failed to be accepted into any fraternity last year, "a little *punk*, came in and told her to knock it off. He tried to pick a fight with me, but I didn't want to fight. It wouldn't have been fair. I would have *killed* him."

After the outburst he had just witnessed, Rex didn't doubt this assessment.

"She told him he was drunk, to go home. She kept hitting on me. She wanted *me.*"

That thought permeated the silence in the room. Rex, now wide awake with anticipation about what unfulfilled female appetites wandered the campus of UGA, couldn't think of sleep, his tortured libido abuzz, his ego eager to go on the prowl.

"Yow," drifted softly, musically, from the top bunk. Smack, smack... scratch... belch, and then Mad-man breathed a restful sleep.

The room remained silent for a few minutes save an occasional sigh, now from Rex. As if to punctuate the end of Mad-man's performance, David rolled over onto his right side and was now facing the wall, turning his back on any further activity, ready for sleep.

After another couple of quiet moments, David could hear Rex's bed squeak faintly, and he became aware of increasingly deep, rhythmical forceful breathing coming from the general vicinity of Rex's lower bunk. Almost fearing what he might see, David rolled back over onto his left side and peered over the side of his bed. He censored a laugh and then watched Rex complete an additional forty or more push-ups, slowing and straining with great effort as he completed the final push up, collapsing briefly onto the floor and then quickly scampering up into his bed.

"You OK?" David queried down to him innocently only after he was done.

"Oh yeah," replied Rex quickly, as if caught doing something wrong. "Just clearing the brain before sleep — a little trick my grandfather taught me," he replied, sheepishly.

"Uh-huh," said David. "Good night."

The room was again silent for only a minute, then the supposedly sleeping body of Mad-man shuddered as if in pleasure as he mumbled, "She wanted me..." followed by a somnolent high-pitched squeal of delight.

David suppressed a laugh, then rolled back over only to hear Rex mutter "Dang you Mad-man!" under his breath, followed by an additional fifty-two push-ups as best as David could tell from the breaths he counted.

More quiet moments followed, but just a few. Then David flipped back over to watch the encore when he heard Mad-man, who was again leaning over the edge of his bed. He whispered loudly to Rex in a voice that dripped in its earnestness, "Rex, man, she really, *really wanted* me!" Rex almost instantly got back down on the floor for another set of push-ups, and the still awake Will cried out, "Dang it! Cut it out Mad-man, you're going to kill him!"

Mad-man's retort will not be repeated here, given the anatomic impossibilities involved.

Satisfied this was likely the end of the show, David closed his eyes and quickly followed Will and Mad-man into a deep sleep, as Rex stared up at the bottom side of Mad-man's mattress, trying to comprehend the mysteries life, unable to return to sleep. When sleep finally did come to Rex that night it was fitful, interrupted too soon by an alarm that announced the first day of school. Peaceful sleep would not find Rex for two more hours, not until he was fifteen minutes into his first class of his first day of college.

Even during the regular hours of the day, the residents of suite 270/272 provided huge amounts of comic relief for any of the dorm residents who might be in on whatever plots were being hatched from those quarters. What fun they had was usually intended to bring pleasure to themselves or others, rarely inflicting pain or hurt in the process. Overall, they were good boys. They didn't smoke or (for the most part) drink. Drugs were a definite no, and they were (for the most part) gentlemen when around the ladies. Perhaps their greatest fault was in not more actively admitting to their own standards of goodness and setting a more mature example to which others would aspire. College did not seem like the time in life to get *that* serious.

The younger team of Rex and David were always ready for a good escapade to show they were cutting-edge comedians willing to risk whatever necessary for their art. Will had few inhibitions when it came to a performance that might make others laugh. Above them all, the man who needed no supporting cast was always Mad-man. He seemed to be in a league of his own. Like the others, he knew how to study. He just didn't seem to think that the slave driver of education should inhibit or restrict the muse of entertainment.

On many occasions David had seen Mad-man leave the Reed Hall study at the urging of some lesser student who stuck his head into the study, saw Mad-man, and beckoned him to join or become a group that would be doing something other than studying. On other nights when Mad-man entered the study, it soon became evident he had no intention of studying. David first witnessed this on an evening early in his first quarter at UGA.

The spartanly furnished study held tables in addition to several padded chairs placed against the walls of the room which provided more comfort but no desktop. The door of the study hall was in the near corner. The opposite wall was lined with windows that looked out eastward onto the Reed Hall parking lot, the shorter left wall windows looked out to the north onto the corner of the Reed Hall quad, and the wall containing the door continued on the other side as the hall that led out the main door. As a result of this strategic placement, any student who so choose could monitor the comings and goings of a large portion of the Reed Hall residents, or be distracted by these activities instead of studying.

This evening the scholars would not have to look beyond the study for a distraction from their studies. The room was full of students with good intentions during that first week of school, all fulfilling their self-made promises to themselves or their parents of how they would study their new school material every night, prepare for class the next day, each with a perfect academic record so far in that early vestige of a school year.

Mad-man entered the full but quiet room carrying a single book, apparently a U.S. History book from the appearance of the U.S. Presidents on its cover. He sat down at one of the two open table seats which remained at the four rectangular tables that each sat eight students — the second chair from the corner at the back corner table, mutely positioning himself between two other students, making eye contact with neither. He placed the book unopened on the table in front of him with a sigh that was louder than necessary in the otherwise silent study. This sigh caught David's attention, and while he wanted to study, his eyes instead trained on Mad-man, realizing that the sigh was possibly just the overture to an act like many that Will had previously recounted. Several other knowing and more senior pairs of eyes were similarly already looking up from their books, not wanting to miss anything Mad-man was about to do.

Seemingly oblivious to all, Mad-man just stared intently at the thick full-sized but paperback book lying unopened in front of him, hands folded in his lap, his quiet form motionless. After another 30 seconds he gave another heaving sigh — almost as though a concession of defeat, then opened the book to the first chapter, pressing the book fully open with the base of his right palm to assure the book would remain open. His hands then returned briefly to his lap. He soon cocked his head to the right with a rolling motion of his neck which resulted in three audible pops of his cervical spine, drawing further eyes away from their books and to his attention. He next placed the outstretched fingertips of each hand along either side of his head, thumbs at the base of his neck, firmly holding his head in place while he made a final, more fine adjustment of his head position so that his visual line was now directly on the left-hand page of text. He lowered his hands so his arms were resting on the table on either side of the book, his rigid gaze still fixed on the book. A faint whirring noise drew the attention of anyone who was not already looking as his right arm robotically bent upward to 90 degrees at the elbow, its hand cupped with fingers apart, pointed at the book. With the sound of a "poof" as his fingers quickly flared then returned to their original shape, his mime of an old-fashioned photographer was thoroughly remarkable. He turned the page, flattened it out, then repeated the sequence two more times, ignoring the cackles that filled the room.

Not satisfied that his photographic memory could be trusted to get him an "A" in the history course, he flipped through the first quarter of the book, stopping at a large picture. He scratched rapidly at the picture with his right index fingernail for a few seconds, then held the book pressed up against his face, drawing in a deep nasal breath, followed by an audible, "Ahhh..." Another photo was located, and "scratch and sniff" learning was repeated.

He next opened the book to its center and gripped either side, rotated it counterclockwise 90 degrees as he held it in front of him, arms held away from his body with elbows locked, eyes half-closed, head slowly shaking left to right as he murmured, "Mmm, mmm, mmmph...", leaving the uninitiated viewer to wonder if perhaps Miss September wasn't staring back at him. His eyes became glazed as he smacked lightly while his mouth filled with saliva, a strand of which spilled over the right side of his lower lip to a length of almost six inches. Just before the drool reached a breaking point he skillfully slurped it back up like a piece of spaghetti. This drew more laughs from the male portion of the crowd, the females for the most part trying to act unaware of what he was doing, although certainly a few of them had to be laughing on the inside.

Ready now for his big finale, Mad-man turned back to the introduction section of the book. He tore out a page from the book and tried to push it into his skull, first flatly against his forehead. Seemingly unable to comprehend why this study method was not successful, and with vocalizations of consternation, he wadded the page and unsuccessfully tried forcing the ball of paper into his left ear. Unfazed by continued failure, he opened the ball of paper back up, studied it momentarily, tore off what seemed to be the vital portion, and popped it into his mouth as coeds voiced "ooo...," in disgust and guys slapped the table and laughed aloud. As though unaware of his audience, he sat back in his chair, hands again folded in his lap, head tilted back at a 45 degree angle, eyes closed. He slowly finished chewing, face now relaxed with teeth apart and lips together, his eyes rolled back under the lids. He dipped his chin during an audible "GULP," that silenced the room. He smacked his lips twice while licking them, then uttered an unbelievably long and loud burp, far louder than any sound of the last 5 minutes. As he burped he also spoke, "The 19th Century of the United States provides the historical perspective from which we come to understand the events and actions of the 20th Century." With this, a deafening roar arose from the audience, hoots of approval and howls of disapproval. Mad-man's expression did not change during this time, not even a slight smile to acknowledge his appreciative fans, which he had worked like a professional.

One student needing no better reason to terminate his studies rose and took his books. He left shaking his head with awe and disbelief, tossing a quarter on the table at Mad-man, saying, "Thanks for the show." Mad-man, feigning anger, batted the still spinning quarter away on the floor. He refused to accept any reward for his study efforts which had now been so rudely interrupted by this entire room of raucous students who were making far too much noise to allow anyone to concentrate.

On another evening, late in the same quarter, he wandered into the study hall during final exam week, and sat beside a fair young miss whom he estimated to be a sorority girl who had likely spent the entire quarter doing anything but studying, but had now decided to get serious about her grades. He had seen this story before: young girls leave home, spend all of Daddy's money partying with other sorority girls, and then feel like a victim because, they report back to Daddy, their professors are unfair and the tests are impossible. As already evidenced, Mad-man had Houdini-like control of every aspect of his body and its activities and this unsuspecting member of the PanHellenic community would suffer from the disdain and contempt he held for the organizations which had previously failed to accept him for membership.

After all was silent he suddenly raised his head, lifting his nose into a sniffing position, furrowing his brow, a concerned look in his narrowed eyes. His head scanned around the room in quick jerking motions, his eyes darting about with his upper lip furled. His mouth remained slightly opened with his bottom lip flaccid, his tongue barely visible but quivering. He surveyed the area while he made short rapid sniffs. The only way he could have performed a more convincing imitation of a vigilant lab rat sensing a threat in its environment would have been to rise up on his own hind legs. She continued to read unaware of his attentions, as he froze his gaze on her. He muttered in her direction, much louder than would have been necessary if his comments were intended only for her hearing, "That's *disgusting!*" and rapidly stood up, took his books and left the room. The swath that his girth cut through the air as he exited, fanned by the door as he pulled it quickly shut behind him, only served to distribute that air throughout the study hall, so that all present would agree, and mistakenly assume the innocent Miss as the source of the acrid sulfurous fumes that wafted through the increasingly malodorous study.

Will Rice was also capable of some fairly outlandish things. His style of comedy was different from Mad-man's. Mad-man's act was for a small, intimate audience. Will performed hoping the entire world would see. One prime example of just how far he would go for a stunt occurred at UGA the spring Will was a sophomore. That day alone would have been enough to secure his induction into the International Collegiate Prankster Hall of Fame.

Thursday, March 7, 1974, started in Athens like any other day with the first rays of light streaking across the morning sky. There was a unique energy buzzing on campus as winter quarter drew to a close and final exams approached, an energy fueled by the warming trend of late winter that promised spring would soon arrive. For reasons that future generations will never be able to understand, the rays of light weren't the only things streaking across the college campus that week.

"Streaking", as it was known, had become quite a fad at colleges across the country, and UGA was no exception. While various techniques for streaking existed, a common component was the element of surprise where one or more individuals exposed as much flesh as they dared for a brief instant in time while running past unsuspecting onlookers. Variations in style allowed for wearing masks or strategically placed props, and sometimes even remaining relatively over-dressed for such an event by sporting a pair of BVD's or, in the case of the gentler gender, a bikini. Whatever the costume, any event was certain to be the talk of the campus. And there was a lot of talk on campus. The talk was usually secondhand reporting of streaking events. Most UGA students had not yet seen a streaker, although everyone knew someone who had seen one.

To see a streaker, one had to be in the right place at the right time, since these things occurred unannounced, like a shooting star. Just the possibility that the next streaker could appear from around the corner kept everyone on edge, wondering if they would be fortunate enough to witness a part of history that would certainly soon fade away as streakers regained their sanity and ended this inexplicable lunacy. The news media seemed to report every streaking event no matter how minor, anywhere across the country. The frequency of such reports and the growing number of students involved held the country's attention and fueled more frequent and larger gatherings. A national record of sorts had recently been reported at the University of South Carolina where police estimated 500 streakers had appeared en masse.

Local police were feeling on edge, too. Police and UGA administration officials were not humored by the recent dress code violations. On one occasion police had even used tear gas on a trio of streakers and the rabblerousing crowd they had aroused. Another student streaker had the misfortune of falling and fracturing his leg while running from authorities.

In an attempt to prevent an escalation of events and even more tragic outcomes, UGA authorities, police and student representatives had met earlier in the week and reached a truce of sorts. An agreement was announced. The students agreed that there would be no further streaking. In exchange for this concession by student representatives, authorities responded with a sage compromise that could only exist on a college campus by agreeing that police would exercise great restraint should any further streaking occur. The table was now set for Will.

His plan was to wait until the cover of darkness and to dash across the grassy Reed Hall quadrangle. He did not want to waste such an appearance on just whomever happened to be lucky enough to be looking out the window when the moment arrived. His ego imagined appreciative spectators cheering him from their dorm windows. He would give advance warning of his trek. That would be a good way to break up some of the pre-exam jitters that existed in the dorm this time of year, a good way to blow off some steam.

Tuesday morning Will made a sign on a sheet of notebook paper and posted it on the bulletin board beside the Reed Hall mailboxes. It said:

STREAKER
REED QUAD
THURSDAY
9 PM

Finally everyone would be able to say they had seen a streaker, although he planned to run far enough away from the building so most would not know who that streaker was, or at least miss some of the finer details.

He was a little disappointed when he stopped by to check for mail Tuesday afternoon and found his sign had been removed. Since no one was looking, he posted an identical sign, checked his mailbox, and headed for Calculus class.

The sign was missing again that evening, so when hall traffic died down a bit he replaced the sign again. The sign disappeared again overnight and again on

Wednesday. Undaunted, he continued to post the sign, wondering if anyone had actually seen the sign.

Thursday morning as Will stood shaving at the sink in the third floor dorm bathroom, Greg Farr, one of the first people he had met in the dorm, came up to the sink beside him. Before he started brushing his teeth, he said to Will, "Did you hear there may be a streaker in the Quad tonight?"

Will did not speak with the razor at his neck, but caught Greg's eyes in the mirror and acknowledged his question with raised eyebrows. Somehow Greg sensed Will knew something.

"Rice...are you going to streak?"

Will, wishing to maintain the element of surprise but thankful that someone had at least seen his sign, paused just long enough to confirm Greg's suspicions.

"You crazy wild-hair!" exclaimed Greg.

Will's eyebrows knit together deeply as he stopped shaving and warned Greg, "Sshhh!" There were too many ears in the stalls and showers to risk discovery. "Don't tell anyone!" Will added. He could trust Greg. He was a good guy; he knew how to have a good time.

Without further thought, which was probably the sign of a character flaw, Greg decided, "Rice, I'm going with you!"

This created an unexpected dilemma for Will. Another streaker might slow things down. Greg had a more athletic build than Will, so more eyes might be on him. *"That might not be such a bad thing,"* Will reasoned with himself. He was willing to share the glory with Greg.

"Are you sure?" Will asked Greg.

"Heck yeah," replied Greg. "Some of us were talking about streaking last night and I said I would do it, and I meant it. I didn't plan to do it, but I don't intend to let this pass me by."

Will briefly explained his plan and the two agreed to meet in the bathroom at 9 p.m. that night for their run. They would leave their clothes on the hangers by the showers and be that much closer to the Quad than if they started in either of their dorm rooms. Besides, neither could quite picture taking off their clothes in the other's room. That would be too weird.

Will stayed in his room 364 that evening to study. At about 8:45 there was a knock on the door. It was Greg, wearing a cowboy hat. He was not alone. He piled into Will's room with five other men in tow, some of them swigging from their liquid courage.

"Rice, I recruited some of the other guys who said they wanted to streak the other night."

Will knew Boss, Brad, Big-un, and DW. He had seen Steve before, but did not know him. They were all so excited and crazy it almost made Will nervous, but now he started to get excited too. Seven streakers at once would probably be some kind of record, if anybody cared.

"Let's go ahead and do it now!" shouted DW while he waved his Atlanta Braves ball cap. From appearances he might not remember the event if he did not do it soon.

"No!" said Will above the din of the group. "We've got to wait until nine o'clock so people will know to look. Are you guys all sure you're not going to wimp out?" asked Will.

"Every time I talk with my brother he asks me if I've seen a streaker," said Steve, who was holding a gorilla mask. "Now I can tell him I have!"

Will explained to the group, or at least that component which cared to listen, his plan to use the dorm bathroom as the home base. At nine o'clock they would go from the bathroom, cross the hall into the stairwell, go down to the first floor, go right past the study and exit onto the Reed Hall Quad. Once on the Quad they would blast straight down the unlighted sidewalk in front of Milledge Hall toward the big oaks, do a sweep around the oaks and run back across the Quad into the dorm and up the stairs into the bathroom. They would be in the dark and shadows most of the time. The whole trip would take less than two minutes. Then Will could study for his Calculus test, which was tomorrow afternoon.

In the few minutes that remained the seven gentlemen spent the time hurling various insults at each other, giving rebel yells, and finishing their libations. As the hour approached, Will, who was already wearing gym shorts, put on a pair of socks and laced up a pair of hiking boots. He grabbed a ski mask from his closet shelf and a parade whistle he had used in his Six Flags band. He had originally planned to use the whistle as a noisemaker to draw attention. (He would have preferred to use his trombone, but was uncertain about the possibility of trying to run and play at the same time.) Now with a group of seven he was not certain he would need any additional noise, but he decided to stick with his initial idea and take the whistle. There had been enough deviations from the original plan already. He wanted a smooth operation and did not need any more surprises or last-minute unexpected changes from his plan, which he knew would work. He grabbed the doorknob and said, "Let's move out!" to the rest of the rowdy crowd of six.

The gang proceeded down the hall, into the bathroom, and in no time at all appeared outfitted for the task. Will had elected to leave his watch on as though it were a necessary item for this precision commando strike mission, and when all were ready he looked at his watch then shouted, "Let's go!" He led the way, out to the hall, into and down the stairway, followed by four men and one gorilla (at the last minute Brad bailed out and did not go) all hollering "Streak! Streak!" at the top of their lungs, ear-splitting whistle blasts sounding all the louder in the echo chamber of the stairway.

They poured down the three flights of stairs, burst onto the first floor hall, turned to the right past the study, still yelling at the top of their lungs, Will blowing the piercing whistle, in the otherwise still and quiet building, giving no regards to the students who might be trying to study. Will blasted through the exit door onto the Quad, propelled forward by the five screaming crazed wild men behind who gained energy and momentum from each other. They pushed into each other as their forward progress was temporarily slowed by the opening door, all shouting "Streak! Streak! Streak!"

Up to this point in time, Will's plan had gone very smoothly, exactly as he had envisioned. What he had not known, and what Greg had not told him, was that the reason Greg had known about the streak was not from having seen the posting at the mailboxes at Reed Hall. He had first read the posting on the bulletin board at Bolton Hall (a place not often frequented by Will, since he was not on the meal plan). If either had looked, he might have also seen the same sign posted on the jobs-interview/magazines-for-sale billboards on north campus, or in the library on north campus or in the science library on south campus, as some well-intentioned streaking enthusiast had assisted in dissemination of the information regarding this event. And what an event it promised to be!

Very few students had anything else to do on a Thursday night in Athens, GA, so they started to congregate in the Reed Hall Quad around 8:30 for the only game in town. Some brought lawn chairs, others stood around as if they intended to be there for some other reasons, pretending to be unaware there was about to be a streaking event. Predictably, refreshments were the only thing some students brought with them. An amateur DJ on the fourth floor of Reed Hall opened her windows and put her stereo speakers on the window sill, pumping music out across the Quad over the increasing crowd. She first played "Crocodile Rock", followed by "The Night the Lights Went Out in Georgia" to entertain the masses which by nine o'clock had grown into the thousands, all hoping to see their first streaker. It appeared that everyone at UGA knew about the event and was there. Everyone except Will and his streaking team, who were joining the party a little late, unannounced, without reservations... running into a festive, energized crowd that filled the Quad and now with standing room only.

The six screaming streakers were so closely packed together that at first only Will could see there was a crowd as they burst onto the sidewalk outside Reed Hall. Initially confused by the presence of such a large gathering, he was afraid there had been a fire drill or other unannounced catastrophe, and for a split second he considered aborting his plan and going back upstairs. But the sudden appearance of six screaming and whistling streakers was instantly noted by the energetic crowd which was there for one distinct purpose. For an instant there was a hush across the outside crowd so all that was heard were the voices of five maniacal men screaming over the background music of "Let's Get It On" by

Marvin Gaye and one very loud parade whistle. The quiet lasted only a second, and then a roar arose from the crowd with chants of "Streak! Streak! Streak!"

The sidewalk in front of Milledge Hall was so packed with lawn chairs and observers that Will's original route had to be altered. He headed off into the crowd that filled the grassy lawn, faithfully followed in a compacted single-file by the five panicked runners behind him, now propelled by beer and fear. What also surprised Will was that while everyone seemed to want to see a streaker, no one wanted to be touched by one. The crowd parted like the Red Sea wherever he turned to run, making navigation across the Quad much easier than he had initially anticipated. The advantage of having all eyes on him was that no one was surprised he was approaching, and all gave way to his progress.

Will was amazed by the massive cheering crowd — he had expected some cheers, although he would have preferred them from a distance. What Will had given no thought to was just how much pent-up enthusiasm there was for streaking, and not just as a spectator sport. The entire campus had become a tinderbox of kindling wood just waiting for a spark to set it ablaze. There were many students who were not willing to be the first or only streaker, but who did want to be able to say they had participated in the craze. The appearance of Will plus five more streakers ratcheted up the frenzied crowd which realized there were now six streakers where only one had been promised. These six were the catalyst that ignited the campus into a spontaneous combustion of insanity. Before he and his men made it halfway across the Quad they were joined by a few, then dozens, then hundreds more streakers in a once-in-a-lifetime chain reaction that made even Will think, *"These people are crazy!"*

Having accomplished his goal and so much more, Will completed his run unscathed. He returned to the door as planned and quickly ascended the stairs, returning to the bathroom. Greg and Boss followed, but the others were not to be seen.

Brad was still in the bathroom, waiting for them. "How did it go?" he asked the laughing, gasping trio, as they grabbed their clothes and started dressing.

"Oh man! You didn't go?" asked Greg, disdainfully. "You (expletive deleted) loser. You could have made history. Just go look. There may still be time if you aren't too chicken."

Greg and Boss congratulated Will on such a great plan, slapping hands all around. Will gave one more "Streak!" scream for old times' sake and to deplete whatever compressed fuel remained in his tank, and then told them he had to go study. He really did have that test tomorrow.

Having enjoyed his 20 minute study break, Will headed back to his room to study Calculus for an additional five hours.

History will not remember Will's efforts that night. History will remember that the spark he lit continued to burn late into the night. Unfettered from their cares and concerns, students spread the streaking party southward to the Myers Residency Hall complex. There an even larger crowd assembled outside the dorm, and once again streaking broke out. Some of the more competitive and compulsive students, probably Political Science majors, set up a chute and announced they would begin counting streakers as they passed through the chute beginning at 11:00 p.m. Their goal was to break the unofficial world record for 500 streakers which had been claimed by the archrival University of South Carolina.

Over the next few days newspapers across the country would report that on the evening of Thursday, March 7, 1974, students at the University of Georgia had established a world's record for the largest group streak with 1,543 simultaneous streakers. Not reported, but definitely more significant, was that Will Rice scored a 94 on his Calculus test.

Sometimes the Boys of Rooms 270/272 worked as a team to pull off a practical joke, at times at the expense of another roommate. One such example occurred in honor of Will's 22nd birthday.

On the eve of Will's birthday, Rex and David had returned to their dorm after dinner at Bolton Hall. As they were collecting the items they would need for their evening responsibilities of practicing trumpet or studying Biology, Will entered the room, grinning from ear to ear. He was dressed in faded jeans and a previously white T-shirt, now stained with the same grease that covered much of his hands and forearms.

"Where have you been?" asked David.

Will smiled with a swagger as he almost sang, "I'm going to have a birthday supper cooked for me by Marilyn Danner."

"Whoaaa," replied Rex and David simultaneously. They both knew Marilyn and that Will had his eyes on her — so did half of Reed Hall for that matter, and for good reasons — but neither realized there was actually anything going on between Marilyn and Will.

"Doesn't explain the grease," David pointed out quickly.

"Well, she asked me if I could look at her car. She offered to cook me spaghetti if I would check it out. Turned out she needed a little tweaking. And her car needed some work too," said Will, who was not very good at delivering a punch line. Maybe that was why he so often relied on more outrageous stunts to get a laugh. Having elicited the predictable feedback from Rex and David, he continued.

"She needed a couple of belts replaced. Dang Cutlasses. I could have rebuilt an entire Volkswagen engine in the time it took me to get to those belts. So I've got to get showered off while she's cooking supper."

This explanation occurred while Will quickly undressed. He threw his soiled clothes into the knee-high olive-green trashcan he had requisitioned from room 270 and used for his laundry hamper since an identical metal circular can had also been issued for room 272. One trashcan was more than enough for the four roommates. He wrapped a white bath towel around his waist.

"Not much of a birthday present if you have to work for it," observed the jealous Rex, throwing cold water on Will's impish enthusiasm.

"Well, technically, I guess you're right. She doesn't even know that tomorrow's my birthday," Will admitted, "but I'll tell her at supper. Who knows? Maybe she'll want a little Rice-aroni for dessert!" he said as he proudly headed out and closed the door, unable to hear their insults targeting his attempted wordplay.

"Well," said Rex, now alone with David, "I guess that only leaves one thing for us to do."

"What?" asked David, not certain he wanted to know.

"Carwash!" shouted Rex.

"Happy Birthday, Will!" said David in agreement. Biology would have to wait.

"Carwash" was a term that Rex and David had heard discussed only once. On the day they moved into Reed Hall and were moving furniture around their suite, Will had introduced them to Greg Farr who stopped by to welcome Will back for another year. While Greg was there he and Will told a few stories of the two previous years' adventures to the two freshmen. Greg started with the streaking escapade, corroborating a tale David had heard before but had assumed was exaggerated. As David learned it was not, with Greg adding even more details that Will had previously omitted. Another story was about the stunt they had pulled known as "carwash". No one was certain where the trick originated or who named it, but Greg had recruited Will last year to help him perform it on Greg's brother when he had come up for a weekend visit. The trick, as they explained it, was to catch an unsuspecting bather exiting the shower and douse him with a large bucket of cold water, or with Will's help, two large buckets of cold water, shouting "carwash!" as the water met its mark. "Good clean fun," Greg had explained, laughing.

Rex went over to the trashcan full of Will's dirty clothes and dumped them out onto Will's bed. David grabbed the room's trashcan. They waited a couple of minutes to make certain that Will had time to begin showering as they reviewed their plan, and then headed down the hall to the bathroom. Half-way down the hall David emptied his can into the larger community trashcan in the hall. He was now ready for action.

When they arrived at the bathroom, David held Rex's can and waited outside the door while Rex went inside and casually scouted out the bathroom. Will was in the shower and didn't notice Rex as he washed his hands in the sink to justify his reconnaissance mission. Rex quickly returned to David and said, "He's the only one in there, let's go."

They went to the far sinks, not visible from the showers, and both filled their cans with as much cold water as they could lift, surprised at how heavy the cans became with the large volumes of water. They positioned themselves on either side of the exit from the shower stalls and waited, David on the right closer to the hall door, Rex to the left near where Will's towel was hanging. Seeing the towel, Rex tucked it into the back of his waistband, hoping to stall Will's eventual pursuit.

In about two more minutes they heard Will turn off the shower as he sang *"I wish I had a pencil-thin moustache..."*. With that prompt, Rex and David each readied their trashcans, arms trembling in anticipation and under the weight of water which each held, cans swung back and cocked for delivery. They moved a little farther away from the exterior wall of the shower, careful not to be seen by Will. In doing so they created a more direct line of fire into the showers that would assure they did not splash each other.

In another second or so Will approached the exit from the shower. He saw Rex to his right the instant Rex was delivering his torrent of cold water as both David and Rex screamed, "Carwash!". In a reflex Will was able to spin just enough to his right so that Rex's water hit him in full profile, even as David's freezing flood came pouring onto the back of his head, his shoulders and his arching back. It was a direct hit from both barrels.

David instantly broke for the door and headed down the stairs across the hallway from the bathroom, Will's howls then threats echoing in the bathroom. Despite slipping on the wet floor he helped create and dropping his can, Rex almost beat David out of the bathroom and took off to the right, back down to the dorm room, Will's towel still tucked into his waistband.

David blasted down the stairway and onto the first floor hall, trashcan still in hand. He immediately slowed his pace to a respectable walk when he recognized Helen Henderson and her roommate Mary Ellen McClendon walking into the building. David was buddies with both of them in the Redcoat Band. He had gone out with Helen a couple of times and they were rapidly becoming a couple. She looked so good attired in the pale yellow cashmere sweater she had donned anticipating the nippy night air that it almost seemed a shame that autumn had not arrived earlier.

He stopped and talked to them both, but Mary Ellen, sensing her exit cue, kept walking and said, "Helen, I'll see you up in the room. 'Bye David."

"So where have y'all been?" David asked Helen, now in no particular rush.

"Mary Ellen and I went over to the Baptist Student Union for their

Tuesday night fellowship. Now I've got to get my flute and head over to the practice rooms. How about you?"

"Oh, I'm just about to get started on some Biology," said David, holding the still dripping can. Helen did not want to seem too inquisitive, but she stared at the can long enough for David to realize an explanation was due.

"Just rinsing out my trashcan. They get dirty after a while, you know?"

"Yes," she responded, hoping he was not obsessive-compulsive. She was studying that in Psychology this quarter.

"Do you mind if I walk with you up to your room?" asked David, hoping to change the subject. He really did want to be able to spend some time with Helen, who lived on the girl's side of the second floor. Conveniently, she could also temper Will's revenge in case they ran into Will upstairs. Will had already met Helen and seemed fond of her. Certainly he would not do anything too outlandish in her presence. After all, David reasoned, Will knew that her brother was a Southern Baptist preacher and her father was a retired FBI agent. That, she had previously reminded David, had moral and legal ramifications if he did not treat her like a lady.

The couple headed up the stairs together, Helen to David's right. No longer feeling the need to embrace the trashcan with both hands, David lowered the trashcan, carrying it by its rim in his left hand off to his side. They chatted about nothing in particular as they climbed the stairs up to the second floor, where David held the door open for her. He nervously peered over his left shoulder at the closed bathroom door which was harmlessly still as they proceeded to the right. It was only a short distance down the hall that would then take them to the left turn that led down the hall to the ladies' side of the dorm.

Unbeknownst to David, and especially unbeknownst to Helen, was Will's response to the carwashing. He had been so crazed by the shock of the cold water and the need for revenge that he scooped up the trashcan that Rex had dropped, hurried back into the shower, filled it with as much cold water as he could manage, then decided to go hunt down Rex or David. His desire for retaliation was so strong that proper hunting attire seemed unnecessary at the moment, given his limited options. He rapidly carried the can of water to the door and stuck his head out the door. Seeing no one in the hallway but hearing footsteps in the stairwell, he decided to stake out the area by hiding in the janitor's closet, just up the hall by the corner that led to the ladies' wing. He quickly opened the closet door and, still dripping, stepped inside, pulling the door closed behind him. With not much time to think, he realized just how cramped his quarters were, shared as they were with a rolling bucket and mop. The floor space remaining was adequate for only his feet, so he was left holding the cold trashcan against his wet shivering body as he waited for payback time. He could see just a little area of the hallway carpet through the slanted ventilation slats at the bottom panel of the heavy wooden door, limiting his ability to monitor hall traffic. That did not matter, he reasoned. He would remain here until tomorrow if need be. Dinner would have to wait. He demanded vengeance.

Will heard the heavy fire door at the stairwell open. He couldn't hear much more, but perhaps that was David and Rex talking. He squatted down, uncomfortably backing against the rough wooden mop handle to try to get a view through the slats at the bottom of the door. He recognized David's left Adidas shoe and the trashcan swinging by his side a yard down the hall. His plan had worked but now there was not a second to spare!

Using the element of surprise to his greatest advantage, with a great shout and in one mighty move Will burst out of the closet. The contents of the trashcan were already halfway out of the barrel before the door had fully opened or before Will had time to refine his aim. With the adrenaline that still remained in his veins from his earlier confrontation with Will, David abandoned any pretense of chivalry and leapt back, plastering himself against the wall on tip-toe, avoiding any and all water.

Helen the Innocent was not so fortunate. She was so horrified by the blood-curdling scream, so mortified by the wild-eyed assailant, so disappointed by the effect of the cremaster after prolonged exposure to cold, that she was paralyzed in her tracks, unable to move as the entire trashcan full of cold water cascaded down on her as David watched the surreal event.

Will stood equally horrified and mortified. (He would not have been so disappointed by the role of her pilomotor reflex, but he was otherwise distracted. David, of course, was too polite to notice.) In the half-second that Will had to decide his next move, he weighed his options. He could tuck his tail and run back to the closet, or to the bathroom, or all the way down the hall to his room. None of these plans sounded like the end to the story he knew he would have to listen to David tell for the next fifty years. He needed an escape that would make him look like a performing genius willing to suffer for his art, going to any length to get a laugh. He hoped to salvage something from this embarrassment that would allow him to tell the story his way with pride. So he stood his ground.

In no particular hurry, he rotated 90 degrees to his left, bowing like a butler, giving a smooth sweeping motion outward with his left arm as he positioned the trashcan with his right hand to take advantage of whatever screening benefits it had to offer. While bending over he said, with a blended Groucho Marx-French accent that was not a very authentic replication of either, "Madame, walk this way to your room," pronouncing "room" with a nasal "hhrhum" in an attempt to imitate Inspector Clouseau from *The Pink Panther* movies. Remaining bent over, he then began to slowly shuffle back into the closet, holding this posture that offered at least a semblance of modesty.

The stunned Helen, not able to think on her own, did as he instructed. She started with a slow foot-dragging zombie-like gait as if maintaining constant contact with the carpeted floor would somehow keep her feet from getting wet any more quickly than they were as sheets of water coursed down her pants legs, wicking from her socks into her penny-loafers. To conserve heat and preserve decency she folded her arms across her chest and hunched forward, turning her head away from Will.

David, relieved to have a temporary reprieve from the wrath of Will, quickly regained his chivalry and splashed up alongside Helen, taking her by her left elbow. He hoped to offer whatever support, apology, or encouragement seemed appropriate. In her most vulnerable moment Helen looked back up into David's face, her hair plastered against her head and dripping, her body shivering, her lips trembling as though she was about to cry. As she sloshed forward and Will blindly shuffled backward, David thought they looked like a lumbago-plagued coachman with an oversized specimen cup trying to get alms from an unfortunate, destitute waif. Funny though it seemed, his thought was poorly timed. David looked back down into her dazed eyes, her mouth open but not speaking. He burst out laughing.

Her gaze became even more stupefied as her eyes narrowed and her head tipped slightly to the left as her bottom lip began to tremble uncontrollably. He quickly and wisely regained his solemn composure. Her eyes reflected a look of hurt and betrayal. Her upper body shook twice as she emitted two pitiful silent short huffs. She closed her eyes. David prepared himself for her imminent breakdown. Then came what was the defining moment that endeared her to Will and David. He heard a third huff that was a giggle. Then she giggled again, bending over at the waist, arms still wrapped around herself, splinting her chest tightly as she erupted into laughter louder than David's had been.

She realized she had just been smack-dab in the middle of the kind of a prank that David had told her about as he entertained her with stories while they rode back to Athens on the band bus after the UGA-Florida game last week. She had found most of those tales so outrageous as to be unbelievable, but now she was convinced. This was something she could tell — or categorically deny — to her grandchildren someday. From what she already knew of Will she did not think that he had a cruel bone in his body. She concluded there was a good reason that David had been walking around with a wet trash can. He had seemed just as surprised by Will's ambush as she was, so she did not think David had set her up for this. Certainly Will would not have gone through such humiliation if she had been the original target of this practical joke. Regardless of whatever was supposed to have happened, she felt a sense of pride that her involvement had somehow made it even better.

She looked over to her left as she saw the closet door silently pull closed.

In her mind's eye she could picture, perhaps even better than she wanted to, Will standing inside the dark closet, soaking wet, shivering, cold metal trashcan pressed against his chest, waiting for the coast to clear. She stared up at the ceiling and closed her eyes, water dripping off her hair down her neck. Embracing herself, embracing life, she declared happily, "You guys are *crazy*!" and then laughed again.

A more detailed complete listing of the further exploits of Rex, Will, Mad-man and David might serve to besmirch the otherwise fine but unmerited reputation of this scribe and will thus be foregone, irrelevant to this chronicle as they are.

Across the hall in suite 271/273 had resided four other even less subtle pranksters, including the guy Mad-man had nicknamed "The Baby Sampson". A huge brute of a man who at first glance appeared to be from another branch of the evolutionary chart which David had studied in biology, James Sampson was actually a fairly benign guy. He took easy classes and was shy, choosing to spend an unhealthy amount of time in his room where his favorite occupation was to listen to country music and drink beer directly from the gallon jugs in which it could be purchased from Jumbo's package store conveniently located just off-campus up Baxter Street. Not one to waste much effort, the Baby Sampson would keep his previous gallon jug as an item of convenience. While nothing was ever proven in the investigation by the University Campus Housing Authority, the residents of suite 171/173 complained that periodically a golden mist would be blown into their room through their window fan, the origin of said mist a mystery to the Baby Sampson whose open window was only one floor up.

As a result of the many complaints over the years that seemed to arise from the activities behind the doors of the suites, the University Campus Housing Authority finally decided over the summer of 1976 to do away with having any more than two males in one room. The doorway connecting room 270 and 272 was sealed over, and a new door was cut through the wall of room 272 directly into the stairwell opening onto the landing. This resulted in a dorm room door that was separated by two heavy fire doors from the rest of the hallway which all the other residents of the floor shared. This door sealing and cutting was repeated in all the suites, so that when David and Rex returned in the fall of 1976 for the beginning of the sophomore year, they were now alone in room 272, with a door that opened into the stairwell. The foursome of Will, Mad-man, David and Rex wouldn't have been possible that year anyway, since Will had graduated and gone on to medical school, but Mad-man had become the odd man out since David and Rex had a longer history together. Mad-man had elected to stay on the same floor, but now had a new roommate.

For David and Rex, the trade-off for being in a room that opened directly into the stairwell and thus limited some of the casual contact that comes from being on a hall where a bunch of rooms have the doors open, was the distinct advantage of having windows on two sides. The two windows were nice for the view but far nicer for the cross breeze allowed during the hot days and nights of early fall and late spring. No one gave much thought to the uniqueness of these rooms. Other rooms in Reed Hall were also compromised in one way or another. The fourth floor "dormer rooms" had low angled ceilings and yet other oddly shaped rooms had been reconfigured to accommodate three women in the basement level, so David didn't give his room situation much thought until he viewed it through the eyes of others, like the three guests he was about to entertain.

As Pops turned off the Maverick, Doc reversed the process of his buckling-up and Pops then followed suit. After the shoulder straps were quickly and correctly back in their retainer clips, the two men got out of the car which allowed Dr. Tew and then David to unfold themselves from their backseat positions. David retrieved his wallet from under the seat and pocketed the keys as Pops returned them.

The older three looked upward and visually scanned Reed Hall from its rear side. It was even taller from this side, as the natural south-sloping topography had been preserved during construction so that access from the front of the building was at the first floor, but from the rear one entered at the basement, which was one floor below the ground floor, which was the floor below the first floor. The first floor was actually the third floor when viewed from the rear.

There were several other students in the parking lot and going in and out of the building and packing cars, some with older people one would assume were their parents — willingly or unwillingly recruited to help move them out of the building for the summer or forever. Excited parent and reluctant offspring, or vice versa, moving out of the dorm and back into the more traditional confines of the homes they had left last fall.

Even from the parking lot and at this fairly early hour one could identify at least four different songs being enjoyed by the remaining occupants of the open windowed rooms of Reed Hall: "Make Me Smile" by Chicago, "Whipping Post" by the Allman Brothers, a third song that David would have recognized as being something by Gino Vannelli, if he had given it a conscious thought, and a fourth song that sounded like a whining female vocalist that David had no knowledge of. All in all not a bad background soundtrack to amplify the emotions of those students still occupying Reed Hall — those fortunate souls who had already finished their final exams but had not yet moved out of the dorm for the summer, and those pitiful beings who still had exams to take between now and when the dorm closed on Saturday.

"Looks like it should be a fairly warm day," prognosticated Doc as the four walked up the short tiered sidewalk toward the backdoor of the east wing. David led the way, closely followed by Dr. Tew, with Pops and Doc taking up the rear in no particular hurry, enjoying the morning atmosphere.

As they reached the solid metal door David grabbed its silver handle and heaved the heavy rusty door open, politely allowing Dr. Tew the opportunity to be the first to enter the stairwell that it opened into. Unbeknownst to either of them, however, was that at that very instant Vicki was using that portion of her anatomy best designed for sitting to push open the door, intending to back against the horizontal aluminum push bar to open the door and proceed through backwards since her hands were full with the load she was taking down to her car.

Vicki Post was an attractive sophomore childhood education major from Bainbridge in south Georgia. To say "attractive" in describing her does not adequately capture her being. Sensuality came as naturally to her as breathing does for other people, a constant in her life that occurred whether she willed it or not, but, like taking individual breaths, when she thought about it she could dictate to a degree. In her innocence she did not fully realize the allure she held over the truly weaker sex, and thus much of the time her body broadcast messages that her brain did not intend to radiate. Today, however, she was exuding the message intentionally.

She lived closer to the west end of the building, so when exiting the building she would have more naturally left from the western side doors. Today she had chosen to walk the full length of the front main hall and then down the east wing, the men's hall, before going down the steps and out the door. Her attire for moving day consisted simply of a pair of cut-off shorts that were certainly that, and a form-fitting tank-top style white ribbed undershirt, an outfit her mother would have deemed more appropriate for pajamas than a parade through the men's dorm. She was definitely trolling, using bait that gave her a markedly unfair advantage over her prey. If this were fishing, the Department of Natural Resources would have outlawed the use of such a highly effective lure.

David had first met Vicki during fall quarter of their freshman year. They had even gone out, once. She had been one in a series of girls he had dated almost half-heartedly at times during the first couple of months his freshman year while he tried to keep fanning the embers with Beth back home. But time and distance change relationships, and David had not really impressed many other girls — until he met Kay.

One date with Vicki was more than enough time for each of them to realize the other was not the person they had come to college hoping to meet, but they remained pleasant acquaintances. She had a manner of tilting her head to the side, shaking her full head of hair styled to copy the look Farrah Fawcett had just made world famous, but with a few more curls. She utilized the tools nature had given her, pouting her lips and batting her eyes whenever she wanted to feign ignorance. This had been a turnoff to David, she did it so often, and he had quickly grown disinterested because of the fool's gold that was her intellect, despite the Fort Knox that characterized the rest of her package. She was attractive in a very fundamental way. Her's was an image that would burn itself into the mental scrapbook that exists either as a cultivated guest or an unwelcome intruder, permanently hardwired into each male's brain.

David had just pulled away the heavy door the instant before Vicki would have thrown her weight against it to open it. Instead she backed full force and off balance into the unprepared Dr. Tew. Her backwards momentum overwhelmed his forward progress and they both fell backwards onto the hard sidewalk. He landed in a sitting position of sorts with her in his lap. While either could have been sorely injured, neither was. David quickly released the door as soon as he realized what he had caused, and lifted her and the plastic crate she was carrying off Dr. Tew. Fortunately, the crate contained only two pillows, further evidence she was not yet actually doing any hard work.

"Are you OK?" asked David, urgently, his comments directed to Vicki, not Dr. Tew.

"Oh, I'm fine," was her demure response, staying in character as she stood with his assistance. How convenient for her that she had run into David ... uh, what was his name?

Still sitting on the ground with the same angle of perspective that makes viewing Mount Rushmore or any well-created edifice even more awe-inspiring, Dr. Tew seemed momentarily stunned. He started, "Vi...Very unfortunate tumble we had there..." a sentence terminated with a couple of huffs that could have been either short laughs intended to emphasize his comedic wit demonstrated by such a spontaneously ad-libbed understatement, or maybe he was just catching his breath. Overall, it was not one of his finer moments. She seemed to ignore his presence and his remarks and continued with David.

She wasted no time getting right down to business. "I don't suppose you could help me move a few things to my U-Haul?" She nodded over at the white pickup with a U-Haul trailer with its yellow lights flashing. It was parked parallel but nonetheless blocking half of the unnamed narrow alley that separated Reed Hall from Sanford Stadium. David doubted she knew how to back up with the U-Haul attached, and could see quite an adventure ahead for Vicki.

"No," he only partially lied. Pity the poor fool who she recruited for that task. She lived in one of the fourth floor dormer rooms. With no elevator, each load would have to come down five and a half flights of stairs before exiting through the sub-basement doors. And Vicki had lots of stuff. David had seen her room and was amazed how important it seemed to some girls to so personalize their dorm rooms with unnecessary items — throw rugs, foot stools, coat racks, wall hangings, ceiling beads — as if to make it look more like a boutique store at the mall than a college dorm room.

"Oh, well... it doesn't hurt to ask. Have a good summer," she said, quickly dismissing him as she turned to carry her pillows to the truck. Dr. Tew maintained his vantage point until she had taken several steps away, and then redirected his attentions to standing, his baggy shorts doing nothing to enhance the image to which he aspired.

"So you know her?" he queried voyeuristically, dipping his right eyebrow and raising the left.

"Sort of," he only partially lied again. He was embarrassed by the fact he had once been trapped by her powers, at least long enough to ask her out, and now wanted to appear stronger than that. Dr. Tew did not appear to be concerned with his own demonstration of such fortitude.

"She didn't even acknowledge me!" he complained in disbelief to the other three. "She looked right through me as if I were invisible."

"To her you are," jabbed Doc. "It just doesn't pay to be forty."

"At least that tells how old he is," David thought. *"Who is this guy? Who are these guys? What did he expect, her phone number? Girls that good-looking learn to ignore guys they don't want hitting on them."* He had learned that lesson well from personal experience.

They resumed their journey to David's room, scaling the stairs and arriving at the landing in front of the never-painted smooth wooden door with a plastic black "272" bolted to it.

"My roommate is probably still asleep, so we'll need to be quiet," David said in a lowered tone of voice as he pulled his keys from his pocket then opened the door.

As the four entered the room, David motioned them quietly into the center of the room, where they stood on the tile floor ringed by the university issued furniture which was pushed against most of the three walls not consumed by the entry door and closet. Rex Lee's bed was against the far wall with its head pushed flush into the corner to the right. Rex slept soundly in the bed. At the foot of the bed was a metal desk. To their left was David's bed with the dresser at its foot, the dresser they would have walked into if they hadn't made an immediate right turn upon entering the room.

David returned to the cramped entryway and opened the top dresser drawer, depositing his wallet, watch and keys. David took one of the last remaining pairs of clean underwear from the drawer and his toiletry bag. As he did so Pops and Doc stepped over the few items of mail and a wrinkled magazine on the floor beside the bed and sat silently on the unmade bed that was David's.

Dr. Tew remained standing in the center of the room surveying the room. He did not find much to catch his interest. In contrast to the boutique-like room of Vicki Post, the boys of 272 had done nothing to decorate their room. A small handwritten note was taped to the wall beside Rex's desk, which was along the wall opposite David's bed, the surface of the desk at the same height as the window sill that it abutted against. That note was the sum total of things taped or tacked to their beige walls. Half of Rex's desk top area was dedicated to a cassette deck and two shelf-sized speakers. A sizable stack of sheet music was weighted down with a marble paperweight which looked like some kind of award in the shape of a treble clef sign. A closed shoebox rested alongside the cassette deck. David's desk was along the window at the foot of Rex's bed, piled high with books, papers, a few *Time* magazines, yesterday's shirt and an assortment of other items which, in toto, eliminated any usable working surface. A black telephone hung on the wall to the left of the door, adjacent to a second door that was the closet, its door painted, long ago, an industrial light blue. The closet door, half open, hid a phone booth sized area for hanging clothes on a rail and a pillow case on the floor which served as Rex's dirty laundry bag, amongst the few pairs of shoes also on the floor of the closet, and a single pair of discarded jeans. A red duffle bag with hand-drawn black block "P" hung from a hook on the inside of the closet door, overflowing with David's dirty laundry. Two white towels also hung on two hooks inside the door. The outside of the closet door had a small mirror bolted to it at eye level.

David stepped over to the closet and carefully removed his shirt which stuck, just a little, to the crusted abrasion on his right shoulder. He crammed the shirt into what little space remained in the hanging red duffle bag, kicked his shoes off into the closet and put his socks into the same dirty clothes bag. He took his towel off his hook and draped it around his neck.

Dr. Tew came over and whispered, "Do you have a clean towel I could use?"

"Yes," he whispered, eyeing Rex's towel on the hook, thinking, *"...sort of. It's the end of the quarter and end of exams. I don't have anything clean. Rex won't care...if he doesn't know. I can take all mine home tomorrow and get Mom to wash them."* He loaned Rex's towel to Dr. Tew. The two of them headed out the door to the hall, David catching the door as it closed itself to prevent a loud slam that could awaken Rex.

From the stairwell they opened one of the two fire doors which entered into the long hall of the second floor that led to the bathroom, the last door on the left before the hall turned left to go across the front section of the building. The sound level went up a good 30 decibels as they had opened the door, due largely to the Pink Floyd fans somewhere down the hall. Demonstrating one's musical tastes by playing it loud in Reed Hall was an unwritten right exercised by many.

Doing so was in part an elitist statement to demonstrate how much wattage any particular individual could afford to purchase. Providing one's music to others also fulfilled a responsibility some felt to offer a music appreciation course, allowing others to learn about their favorites. It would have been childish to complain about such loud music this early in the morning, so few had the insight to exercise common courtesy or expect it to be exercised by others.

Half-way between them and the bathroom was large barefoot Rocky Jaworski slowly walking toward them wearing a pair of black gym shorts with a towel draped around his nape, thick black hair bushy and wet, carpeting him almost head to toe.

Jaworski was a senior who lived in room 269. He was one of the few people in Reed Hall who didn't have a roommate, his roommate having left school after mid-terms in spring quarter. Jaworski had been in Poli-Sci 101 class with David last year and was a slacker who tried to get David to somehow help him out before tests. Fortunately for David, there really was not much he could offer. But the attitude had irritated David. Jaworski had a poor work ethic. Not that he would tell Jaworski that. But it was heart, not size, that had hurt Jaworski's efforts to play football as a walk-on with the Dawgs when he came to campus as a freshman. Jaworski was now considerably bigger, but slower, than the aspiring offensive lineman who had come to Athens four years before. Because he had a reputation for being a troubled loner, people just gave him a wide berth and he had few friends. His college years had been a bitter disappointment.

He moved as if only half awake despite his recent shower. He stared at the worn blue carpet as he progressed toward them, silent while walking between David and Dr. Tew when he reached them, actually brushing against Dr. Tew just a bit.

"Good morning," called Dr. Tew as he passed them.

As morning conversation was optional according to the Unwritten Code of Conduct adapted by the male residents of Reed Hall, David didn't think it odd that this didn't elicit a response. Apparently not having read The Code, Dr. Tew did find his behavior lacking. Dr. Tew stopped walking and turned around to watch Jaworski.

"Who was that?" asked Dr. Tew in a voice louder than David would have suggested, but in a volume required because of the Pink Floyd which blared out through the closed door of room 263, beside which they now stood. "He acted like I wasn't even there!"

"Oh, that's Rocky Jaworski. He's a jerk," said David, softly, his eyes trained on Jaworski.

And in a moment that froze in time for David, Dr. Tew then bellowed out, "YO, RO-CKY!"

David flinched in part due to the sheer loudness of the sudden outburst but also in equal measure from dread of what Jaworski might do. With the release of the blockbuster movie by the same name last year, Jaworski had rapidly grown tired of this greeting. His retorts threatened enough violence that anyone with an inclination to taunt him with such a greeting had long ago given up any such thoughts.

Jaworski stopped, turned around and faced them from ten feet away.

"Funny as a crutch, Patson," he said, his sarcastic eyes burning a hole in David. And then the senior, defeated by four long years, turned around and went to his room to hope before his last final exam.

Relieved to still be alive, David, with Dr. Tew at his side, resumed his trek toward the bathroom. "You could have gotten us killed!" said David, half-jokingly. "He thought I was the one who said that."

"He's a jerk," reiterated Dr. Tew.

As they approached room 257 Dr. Tew stopped again.

David started to wonder if they would ever get to the shower. Dr. Tew asked, "What is that um..., 'music'?"

David recognized the sound which was coming out of Mad-man's room.

"That's Jim Madison's room," explained David, realizing the use of Mad-man's more proper name did nothing to legitimize the fact that Native American war chants and drums were coming from the other side of the door.

"He likes to listen to that specific record before exams," not adding that at this very minute Mad-man was sitting on the floor, trance-like, cross-legged, arms folded across his chest, eyes closed, in his underwear — briefs, large, very large, always white. Before going into the test Mad-man would also apply his version of war paint across his chest, sight unseen under his shirt, but granting the wearer an added ferocity in battle against his professor.

This was how Mad-man had prepared for every final exam last year. The record, *Sounds of Americans, Volume II*, had been purchased on a family vacation out west when Mad-man was 12 years old — the kind of trip that families in the 1960's used to take their kids on hoping for a fun and educational experience but getting neither. Last year Mad-man told David a memorable story about how he thought he just had to have that record when his parents offered to buy him a Western souvenir. He bought it and then he spent the next eleven days trying to keep it from melting in the hot car, unable to play it the entire time since he hadn't thought about the fact that he would have to wait for a turntable to listen to his purchase.

David hoped this method of test preparation worked. Mad-man had been a little up-tight at times this quarter waiting to hear from med schools. He was an alternate at South Carolina, and would have to continue to wait to see if someone backed out of their position there to open up a spot for him. He had already been rejected by the Medical College of Georgia, which was not surprising since 95% of

MCG students came from in-state and Mad-man was still officially a South Carolina resident.

Dr. Tew stroked his chin as he paused and listened to the lone male voice chanting in a foreign language and rhythm, accompanied by only a beating tom-tom with an occasional metallic "clank". His eyes narrowed and a smile spread across his face, as if propagated by a distant association with Native American chants, but he remained silent.

They resumed their walk to the bath and after a few more steps David made a left hand turn and pushed the door open into the large bath then held the door open for Dr. Tew who followed.

The room they entered looked like the large community shower and bathroom that might typically be shown in prison movies. Four individual toilet stalls were off to the left, where, had time allowed, David might have sat and read the newest graffiti postings, some of the most creative writings — paragraphs at a time — coming from the pen of Mad-man. But he only needed to utilize one of the four wall-mounted urinals which were off to the right, against the ¾ high wall that opened on its far side into the open shower floor with two shower heads on each wall. He lay his toiletry bag and clean underwear on the shelf over one of the white sinks lining the center of the large room, then he reflexively headed to the third of the four urinals. He bumped shoulders with Dr. Tew, who was also headed to the same urinal, both men moving as if drawn by a homing signal to a beacon. Embarrassed by his clumsiness and awkward closeness, David muttered an "Excuse me," to Dr. Tew, who was simultaneously muttering the same. David deferred to Dr. Tew and used the fourth urinal to right the balance of fluid intake and output.

David then stepped back to the sink, washed and dried his hands, re-examined the now drying crust on his shoulder as reflected in the mirror in front of him, and plugged in his electric razor. In what was more of a perfunctory ritual than necessary hygiene, he quickly shaved what scant whiskers there were to be found on his chin. Since Dr. Tew was watching, he did not want to appear he had missed any areas, so he shaved his entire face whether he needed to or not. He had tried to grow sideburns during the winter quarter but had abandoned that project when he realized there was more than a full vertical inch of space in front of each ear where sideburns should be, where absolutely no hair, not even fuzz, had appeared after three weeks without shaving. His fair complexion just was not going to sprout a lot of beard. He knew lots of girls with better sideburns than he had. It was hard to be fashionable with no hair growing in front of one's ears, but he had contented himself with letting his hair remain stylishly long enough to cover the offending areas. He was just thankful that muttonchops were not the current rage. The fact that Kay did not seem to care one way or the other was what put his mind at rest over the matter.

Dr. Tew came alongside him at the sink to his right, and removed his shirt, folding it neatly and placing on the shelf that ran along under the mirror. David made a mental note not to get old — he didn't like to see older guys without their clothes — pale, too many moles, love handles whether merited or not, and in Dr. Tew's case, an unattractive flat broad scar over his somewhat boney right shoulder. As Dr. Tew set about using Rex's towel to rinse and dry his face and upper body, David grabbed his soap and shampoo then stepped over toward the showers, slipped out of his shorts and hung them and his clean underwear and towel up on a hook on the outer wall. He felt a little self-conscious as he noted Dr. Tew's eyes seemed to be tracking his activity in the mirror over his sink.

David had quickly learned last year he had nothing to be self-conscious about when he first adapted to the community shower concept as a freshman. Nevertheless, the Unwritten Code for the bathroom (which Dr. Tew apparently also had not read) was that you looked a man in the eyes. Save comparative anatomy for the classroom. Unless, of course, you were making an intentionally crass joke about a fellow bather. Most men at Reed did a pretty good job abiding by The Code, but not that creepy guy last year, Myron Medville, a senior English major from East Cobb County, who always seemed to be looking everywhere but your eyes. He was about the only resident David had met who actually seemed to enjoy the community shower arrangement.

Myron created annoying nicknames for everyone on the hall, although to his dismay no one else ever used the names he so proudly culled from great writers and their characters. He called Rex "Oedipus", and Mad-man "Pickwick". Will was "Pinch" and David was "Wadsworth". David did not know or care enough about any of these names to learn why they were selected. His interest in literature in high school only extended as far as was necessary to go to earn an "A" in the class. He had no desire to waste the time going to the library to look up the names. He just avoided Myron. David's roommates each reciprocated with their own made-up names. Will called Myron "Twinkie". Mad-man called him "Horatio" and left a wickedly funny limerick, even more profane than it was clever, about "Horatio" in the second bathroom stall. Rex did not exercise as much creativity and simply called him a coarse phrase that does not bear repeating. (Ironically, David later came to realize that same name was a more accurate description of Oedipus than of Myron. This enlightenment did not come until he was a first-year medical student. During an otherwise soporific psychiatry lecture David laughed out loud when he suddenly made the association. The lecturing psychiatrist was not amused.)

David did not bother to make up a nickname for Myron. He figured being called "Myron" was punishment enough.

David turned his back more toward Dr. Tew as he stepped toward the shower. *"Probably jealous,"* thought David about Dr. Tew snidely, in an attitude that surprised him. *"Wishes he could run like me, wishes he had ever had a body this good,"* as he then stepped onto the shower floor and turned on the water from the best flowing shower head in the left corner, out of view from Dr. Tew.

    The warm water felt refreshing after all the events of the past 24 hours, removing a layer of grime that seemed to hold the layers of testing anxiety, early summer heat and humidity, prolonged sleep, exercise, and his fall at the cinder track. Part of him wished he could stay in the shower all morning, but he realized he needed to get on with the day and he was conscious that he was keeping his guests waiting — but who were these guys? His thoughts were temporarily interrupted by a sudden reflexive step to the right out of the shower stream as he heard a toilet flush, and he sensed the temperature of the mist rise about 50 degrees as the water became transiently scalding while the toilet monopolized the flow of cold water. He used the interlude to lather up with shampoo, and then stepped back in the warm shower, only mildly inconvenienced by the sense that it was quickly too cold to be standing naked outside the shower of water, but not wanting to get burned by stepping in too quickly. Since it was only a single flush, he would not let this aggravate him on his birthday. He did realize that he felt a little irritated not to know who had done it or how this trio of strangers had been set up to surprise him, but as he rinsed the soap from his body he resolved to be a good sport about this surprise and let it play out.

    David turned off the shower, shook and fluffed the water from his hair and whisked off his upper torso. He exited the shower to his right just as the markedly corpulent and only half-awake Baby Sampson, probably still sleeping off the effects of whatever he had done the night before to ward off pre-exam jitters, simultaneously attempted to enter into the shower area from his left. The slippery entry to the shower through the passage in the wall was the width of a standard doorway, and was not at all designed for an encounter with the Baby Sampson. Before either of them was aware of the other, the huge and nude Baby Sampson collided up against the nowhere-as-huge but equally nude David as the men were but for an instant squeezed into the passageway together. In a much quicker instant they were both aware of their circumstance. Both quickly tried to step back out of the shower together, but not before the initial reflexive attempt by the Baby Sampson had only served to throw himself off balance on the wet floor and shift even more of his weight and accompanying greasy body grunge, stubble, fur, and morning breath onto David who was being compressed, to the degree that such was physically possible, against the side of the entry.

    David did not fall as he was being pressed up, held up against the cool damp beige wall, still holding his shampoo in his left hand, his soap box in his right hand, arms outstretched to clasp from either side the front wall of the shower, the right side of his face pressed against the tiles. Baby Sampson did not fall, in part because he had grabbed either of David's upper arms from behind to steady his surprised self, and in part because what balance he could not achieve was compensated for by supporting his weight leaning against the wedged David. Both remained standing as they fell out of the shower back into the sink area, David spinning back around toward the Baby Sampson, each momentarily stunned as he tried to figure out what had just happened. As they stood there staring at each other, they realized the extreme closeness they had just unwillingly shared and each shuddered as if that might somehow help erase the memory, if not the actual event. An observer would have seen Dr. Tew shudder also.

The Baby Sampson was not humored but did not want to be close enough to David to hit him, so he resumed his trudging to the shower as he warned, "Watch where you're going!" David, thankful his rib cage was evidently compressible enough to absorb the thrusting weight of the Baby Sampson without fracture, was at a loss for an immediate retort, so he elected to say nothing. He stepped over to where his towel and underwear were hanging on the wall and welcomed a few seconds of quiet to dry off and compose himself. He shuddered again and felt unclean at the thought of having his fresh and pristine flesh pressed between two such unclean objects. He needed to get back into the shower and start over, but the last thing he wanted at this moment was to be in a shower with the Baby Sampson. He stepped into his underwear and toweled off extra briskly as though friction had a cleansing effect, then wrapped the towel around his waist before he returned to the sink beside Dr. Tew who was now dressed again and combing his hair.

"Friend of yours?" mused Dr. Tew, with the slightest smile, admiring his parted hair in the mirror.

"Dweeb," muttered David in reply, not loud enough to be heard in the shower. Realizing that he was speaking to an adult, he sensed the need to say something more responsible than simply call names, to say something that an adult might say, and without further thought, he straightened up a little and added, "He could put somebody's eye out!"

"Not from that angle," observed the still smiling Dr. Tew.

As David tried to forget that encounter, he again assessed his shoulder scrape in the mirror. Dr. Tew put the comb back into David's toiletry kit, and apologized, "I hope you don't mind that I borrowed your comb."

"Oh, no," lied David, now realizing the breech of property rights, reaching instead for his brush. *"Just make yourself at home. Would you like to use my toothbrush next?"* he thought to himself. *"Geez!...I guess that's my payback for letting you use Rex's towel. I don't want to use the comb after you. How can I part my hair without a comb?!"*

A few quick brushes were all that were necessary for the temporary styling that would have to do until he could dry his hair in his room. He packed up his toiletry bag and headed toward the door, Dr. Tew following his lead silently.

He pulled the door open, and then let it close, remaining in the bathroom with an afterthought. With a sly grin, he nodded to Dr. Tew with a look that said, *"Watch this,"* and walked back to the urinals. In what filled the cavernous bathroom with a sound effect not unlike that of a well-synchronized torpedo bombing run, he pulled the handle of the first urinal, waited two seconds, then flushed the second, then the third, then the fourth. He and Dr. Tew then quickly left the bathroom and headed back toward the dorm room, never certain if the cursing now echoing from the showers was because the Baby Sampson was too hot or too cold.

Chapter 6
In Room 272

Doc and Pops sat together silently on David's bed watching Rex sleep. The droning hum of the window fan gave them confidence that a whispered conversation would not disturb Rex. The hushed tone of their speech in deference to the sleeping roommate might have given the appearance of a sinister plot to a suspicious observer, if such were present. Pops leaned sideways to close the gap between him and Doc.

"Do you have any cash for breakfast?"

Doc stretched out his left leg as he reached into the left front pocket of his jeans and withdrew several neatly folded new bills. They both looked briefly at the money, smiling.

"I don't think you'd want to have to try to get that past anyone with a sharp eye," stated Pops, shaking his head.

"This from a guy with a jacket that keeps turning heads," replied Doc.

"You're right," said Pops, as he took off the jacket and stuffed it under the bed between his feet.

"He's probably got some money in his top drawer," whispered Doc, fashion no longer an issue.

"Nah, he doesn't carry enough money — he'd notice any was missing as soon as he went to get it. Why don't you walk over to the Instant Banker? We don't need much and he's always got at least twenty in his checking account. His card is in his wallet. You know the number."

"I guess that's why they say you should change your PIN periodically," said Doc softly, smiling, then admitting, "but I've never changed mine."

"Neither have I," grinned Pops as Doc stood. He walked over to the dresser, quietly slid open the top drawer, quickly located the wallet and then the ATM card, and then exited into the stairwell, mindful to catch the closing door to preserve the silence for the still deeply-sleeping Rex.

Pops watched Rex sleep for a few breathing cycles, a little jealous that young people can sleep so soundly. When younger, Pops hadn't given sleep much thought, seeing sleep as an intrusion to the fun that was life. But now he appreciated the restoration and escape that quality sleep afforded when it presented itself, which it seldom did.

His eyes veered further to the left, off Rex and over to David's desk. With a twinkle in his eye he arose from the bed and quietly lifted the desk chair back and then pulled open the thin drawer under the desk. He located what he hoped to find, and walked cautiously over to Rex's bed. Rex's face-up supine position and David Cassidy hairstyle that parted in the middle, layered back over his ears, perfectly exposed the forehead that would be Pops' canvas.

Holding his breath he unscrewed the cap from the bottle of Wite-Out and knelt beside Rex's bed. Starting on his forehead as far to Rex's right as hair would allow he painted a large block "W", always intently watching his closed eyelids for any telltale flutter that would signal an awakening. But the early morning bedtime Rex had chosen proved to be far too great a sedative to allow him to be disturbed by such a light touch. Emboldened by his initial success, Pops admired his work, then added an "I" to complete the right side of the forehead. The remainder of the signage was quickly finished with the addition of "M" and "P".

Pops stood back and assessed his accomplishment. Rex continued in the deep slumber that favors youth. Pops walked back to David's desk and carefully returned the Wite-Out to its original location. He watched Rex a minute more, passing the time looking out the window to his left at the increasing activity in the other Reed Hall parking lot as students began their day and ended their year. When he felt certain the Wite-Out had experienced adequate time to dry fully in the light breeze of the fan, he reopened the desk drawer and then forcefully slammed the drawer closed with a bang intended to be loud enough to awaken Rex, which it did.

Rex sat up in bed and immediately asked, "Who are you?" He looked surprised but not threatened by this old guy looking through David's stuff, the Wite-Out message on his forehead bringing out the whites of his eyes and making them appear larger than they had actually become when startled.

"Hi, I'm Pops. You must be Rex."

Rex nodded as Pops continued, "I'm up here to help David out on his birthday. You know he turns 20 today."

"Yeah, I know," Rex lied, involuntarily twitching his nose as his subconscious tried to identify the faint smell of Wite-Out which lingered. *David hadn't said anything about family members coming in for his birthday — oh yeah, David's birthday had been during exam week last year.* He relaxed a little, looked at his clock and fell back onto his mattress.

"It's too early!" he croaked in a morning voice.

"Sorry to awaken you. You go back to sleep. When you wake up I've got a message from a girl, I believe she said her name was Vicki... yeah, that was it. Her name was Vicki Post. Sleep tight."

Rex lay on his back, his body energized by the mention of her name, his mind even more so. *Vicki Post!? What could she want? She had probably just stopped by looking for David — she paid David more attention, especially last year. The old geezer probably just got a message wrong.* She had never responded to any of the many suggestions Rex had made, subtle or otherwise, that he'd like to get to know her better. *No, he said she left a message for me. She has probably realized she's going to leave Athens real soon for the entire summer and after playing hard-to-get all year she's afraid she's missed her chance to be a "Lee-She"*, a term for his female playthings that Will Rice had invented last year to describe a series of women Rex Lee had gone out with during year. Will had meant the remarks to be disparaging critiques of the manner in which Rex selected women and the unifying characteristics they possessed, intellect not appearing on the list, but Rex had liked the term. It was an emblem of honor to have Will Rice recognize his women with a brand name created for his various conquests, and he had stuck with it.

He sat up in bed again. *She was probably about to leave this very minute, heartbroken that she had missed her big chance and would now have to live a summer in regret, longing for what might have been.* The song "See You in September" involuntarily began to play in the back of his mind.

"What did she say?"

"Oh that's alright. I'm sure it can wait. You go back to sleep now. I'm very sorry to disturb you. We've been trying to be so quiet to let you sleep."

"No, really. What did she say?" he persisted, with a pressured rapid speech that almost sounded like one long word.

Pops pretended to search for the phrase that he knew Rex could not resist and started slowly,

"She said she needed you,…no, no that's not it, she said she wanted you, and to be sure to tell you that exactly. She said she 'wanted you'. But that's about all she said to tell you."

His imagination already stoked beyond full with no remaining room for any rational thought, Rex threw his feet over the side of the bed onto the floor and brushed his hands down the front of his well-worn green t-shirt, small holes at the unraveled front neck seam. In his maroon gym shorts with the silhouette of a cardinal mascot and the green shirt, which sported a faded logo that once advertised an Irish bar over the left chest, he endorsed nothing more so than poor fashion taste. He rushed barefoot out of the room and up the stairwell, the door slamming behind him, ignoring the mirror that might have otherwise spared his impending embarrassment. He felt no need to further analyze her message, or even wonder how she could know how to use such a term. Wasn't it true that all women were just waiting to be dominated by the right man? Now her time had come. How he loved assertive women!

Pops shrugged with a smile, almost disappointed with how easily his plot had come to fruition without a hitch and with such predictable results. Some things never changed.

Now alone in the room Pops looked around for further distraction while he passed the time awaiting the return of the others. He stepped over to Rex's desk, opened the shoebox and flipped through a number of cassette tapes with handmade labels. He selected one and popped it into the cassette player, lowered the volume, and then pushed play.

When I Fall In Love flowed through the room. The classic version by The Lettermen had never sounded better. Hearing this music, a soft smile filled Pops' face. He closed his eyes as he gently swayed and took a few small steps to its slow rhythm, his arms folded across his chest. After a few steps more, he sat back down on the side of David's bed, covered his face with both hands and sobbed low and mournfully.

The phone interrupted his thoughts, ringing harshly. He ignored it at first, then ignored his initial inclination, hit rewind on the cassette deck, sniffed, cleared his throat, and picked up the receiver. His side of the conversation follows:

"Hello, this is David Patson..'s room"

"Yeah, hi. That would be OK."

"No, I just woke up with a little frog in my throat."

"See ya."

As he was saying "See ya," Pops heard the handle of the door turning and he jumped back away from it just as it opened. David was opening the door for Dr. Tew, but neither could come in very far because the telephone cord stretched from the side entry wall to where Pops stood alongside the dresser. Pops hung-up the phone and stepped back. In walked David, who exchanged his toiletry kit back into the dresser for his watch, then proceeded past Pops into the room toward the closet, followed by Dr. Tew who elected to hang his towel to dry back on the hook David had taken it from rather than put a wet towel into a clothes bag where it might gather mildew. He then headed to the center of the room.

"Oh, you're back — what's been keeping you?" asked Pops, not expecting an answer, but getting one, nonetheless, from Dr. Tew.

"He ran into the Baby Sampson in the shower and had some catching up to do."

David shuddered involuntarily.

Realizing that David would expect to know why he was talking on the phone, Pops looked toward David and said, "That was some kid named Jerry. He said if it was OK he wanted to bring his trombone by now. I told him that would be alright. He thought I was you, but that your voice sounded just a little funny, in case he asks. I didn't want to go into an explanation so I just let him think that."

Gerald Barstow was a freshman from Valdosta, Georgia. He was a trombonist majoring in music education, and a very fine technical player. But he tended to be a bit irritating, anxious and unaware of his effect on others. Time spent with Jerry often seemed longer than it really was. He and David both played in the trombone section of the Redcoat Marching Band and so a friendship, or at least an association, however taxing, had developed. He meant well, but just seemed to most folks to be a bit of a nerd. As Rex had immediately observed to

David the first time they were introduced to Jerry, "Regrettably, trombonist and nerd are all too often redundant."

"Where's Rex?" asked David, as almost simultaneous Dr. Tew asked, "Where's Doc?"

"Doc's gone to get some money," said Pops, but before he could continue to give an accounting for Rex, David continued, almost thinking out loud as he processed the news of Jerry's call.

"Yeah, he lives upstairs," said David, stepping back over to the closet and opening the door for a full view of its contents. Speaking more into the closet than toward Pops or Dr. Tew, he continued, "He has a trombone he wants me to take into Jackson's Music for an overhaul and repair, and I told him I'd do it. Claims he wants it in good shape, but it's his marching horn and there's not much wrong with it. I told him to save his money, but he wants the dents out for marching season next year, at which time he'll probably get more dents. He lives down in south Georgia and had heard Jackson's did the best job, so he nagged me into taking it there."

The room door opened and in walked Doc. David looked around the closet door to see who had come in as Dr. Tew asked from the center of the room, "You're back?"

"I just went down to the Instant Banker to get some money," with a wink and a nod to Pops. With the closet door open and Pops standing at the dresser Doc was screened from David and he took the opportunity to stealthily open the top drawer and silently return the ATM card to David's wallet. In the process of closing the drawer he pushed it harder than necessary and it closed with a bit more noise than necessary or anticipated. Pops, standing closest, was caught off guard by the unexpected sound and was startled, fearing Doc would draw David's attention from the closet.

"Smooth," murmured Pops to Doc.

"What did you say?" asked David from the closet, oblivious to the events at the dresser.

"Oh, nothing," said Pops, looking up at the ceiling. "Just talking to myself."

David looked back over his right shoulder at Pops, establishing real eye contact with him for the first time since he had come back into the room.

"Um...are you OK?" asked David, noticing the redness now fading from Pops' eyes, "Your eyes look a little bit irritated." He didn't want to say it, but it seemed like Pops had been crying. But he appeared otherwise fine. *What could be the problem?* thought David to himself, hoping his inquiry had sounded casual enough not to be accusing.

"Oh, I'm fine," proclaimed Pops with a scripted chuckle. "I've just been talking to Rex. He's a very funny fellow, made me laugh so hard it must have brought tears to my eyes. But I'm afraid I may have misled him a little bit about that young lady out back, and before I knew it he was running out of here like a rabbit."

The analogy, both in terms of speed and otherwise, seemed to fit the situation so David shook his head and gave a laugh too, satisfied with Pops' explanation.

David turned back to the closet and located the jeans he had discarded on the floor at the start of the day. He picked them up and took a blue Izod golf shirt off its hanger, tossing both over to his bed. He wanted to wear something nice for Kay today.

"Nice color," said Dr. Tew.

David agreed. Blue was his favorite color and Kay thought this shirt, a gift from his parents last Christmas, brought out the blue in his eyes.

He stepped back and closed the closet door, which allowed him access to the mirror attached to the back of the door. Pops and Doc sensed he would need to be at the dresser so they returned to their default position sitting on David's bed, and Dr. Tew sat in David's desk chair.

Realizing that he was now the rate-limiting step in the process of going to breakfast, he said, apologetically, "I still need to dry my hair, but this shouldn't take long."

He moved again to the dresser and retrieved his hair dryer from the top drawer. Standing in front of the mirror with his towel wrapped around his waist he felt a little self-conscious as three pairs of eyes now seemed trained on him, but what else could they look at? The loud volume of the hairdryer intimidated any other conversation, so they said nothing. *"They do seem to be staring"*, thought David. *"Who are these guys? What are they up to? Is this a little weird that I'm standing here in a towel and three grown men are ogling me, studying my body?"*

A loud knock on the door interrupted his thoughts and hair drying. He turned off the dryer and shouted, "Come in!" Pops moved toward the center of the room as he and Doc stood from the bed to greet the anticipated entrant, whoever that might be.

The door pushed open halfway as a short stocky male whose most obvious sign of puberty was his acne stepped into the room, but as he did the brown trombone case he carried in his left hand slammed nose-first into the door, halting his progress. Pushing the door open wider with his right hand and then restarting his entrance without much apparent thought, as if this were not an unusual event for him, Jerry Barstow entered the room.

"Hi David," he whined affectionately, looking around the room through large brown-rimmed glasses that made his round face appear to be just that. "Oh, I didn't know you had company," he said, more as an observation than an apology.

"I'm sorry your throat feels a little sore. Is Rex here?" he asked in a series of continued remarks that typified his conversational skills.

"Hi Jerry," interrupted David, without putting down his hairdryer or stepping to face him except to turn his head in his direction. "Rex isn't here," he stated succinctly, without further explanation to limit any ongoing conversation. After all, breakfast wouldn't wait forever. Then he couldn't resist adding, "Thanks for your concern, but my throat is already feeling better." The chance to be on the inside of a joke against Jerry Barstow, however small, in the presence of the other grownups, somehow made David feel more like one of the guys. Jerry's personality just begged for it, as if that was the price he would have to pay to enjoy the company of others.

Remembering his own manners, for the sake of the adults if not for Jerry, David realized introductions were in order. "Jerry Barstow, this is Dr. Tew," he said, now pivoting around the cord of the hairdryer to nod in the direction of Dr. Tew. As they were shaking hands, David realized he didn't know exactly what to call Doc or Pops. He hadn't really called them much of anything yet, but he didn't want to look ignorant or clumsy himself, so he continued smoothly, "and this is Doc and Pops. Just stand it up in the corner there by my desk." "*Sheesh*," David thought, "*why didn't I think to ask their last names when I first met them. I sound like I'm introducing the seven dwarfs.*"

But Jerry, just glad to be treated like an adult, gave it no thought except to hope that none of the adults would ask him anything. To his horror, Dr. Tew did.

"What are you playing there?" he said, referring to the contents of the case in his left hand.

"Oh, it's an old Olds pea-shooter I used in high school. I now use it for marching band, and have a Bach 42B that I play for symphonic band."

"Olds made a fair trombone, but it's hard to beat the Bach," observed Dr. Tew. "Marching season can be rough on a trombone," he continued, not adding what everyone knew, that it was the player, not the season, who had abused the trombone.

Uncomfortably turning his attention to David, Jerry disengaged from Dr. Tew and said, "I really appreciate you taking care of this. I won't need the horn over the summer, so I'll just get it back from you when you come back in the fall. And my mom has already mailed Jackson's a check for their standard overhaul estimate. They said they'll bill me for the rest before you can pick it up, but there should be plenty of time. Thanks for doing this. My mom's helping me pack, so I've got to go. Nice to meet you all," he said walking toward and then out the door.

"Well, let's take a look at the damage," said Dr. Tew, as he lifted the brown hard trombone case with multiple scuff marks, which would have been even greater in number if it were not for three different stickers for the University of Georgia and the Redcoat Marching Band plastered on its sides. He placed the case lengthwise on Rex's bed then opened the three clasps on the side and carefully flipped the top half up and back.

The interior of the case was lined with a velvet-like brown material that was loose around the edges and needed to be re-glued to the case. Dr. Tew lifted the slide portion of the trombone, which separated from the bell component to facilitate storage, and moved the slide back and forth slowly, assessing it for any imperfections that would interfere with the smooth interface which should exist between the silver inner sleeves and the outer brass slide. He then looked down the slide as he slowly extended it. His appearance was not unlike that of a trained marksman checking the sites on his rifle to be certain they were true. David was initially a little surprised that he would be so bold as to open another person's instrument case, a musical instrument being a fairly personal, and many times expensive, piece of equipment. But David remembered Dr. Tew had said something about playing in a band with that gerbil story.

"Do you play trombone?" he asked, anticipating the confirmation.

"It's a nice distraction," said Dr. Tew, not taking his attention away from the slide. His use of the word "distraction" and his frown as he was viewing the slide made David decide to pursue that line of questioning later when there was more time. Maybe Dr. Tew was a little grouchy in the morning before he had his breakfast. At any rate, it looked as if he could be trusted with Jerry's trombone, so David returned to drying his hair.

The narcissistic attention to which David paid himself when styling his hair, which in the finished result would show no style at all except for the over-the-ear length which was the fashion of the day, distracted him from observing what was going on behind his back but could have been easily observed if he had changed his viewing angle in the mirror only slightly. He stared at the mirror and daydreamed just a bit about this afternoon's date with Kay. He thought how great she would look, how great he would look, and how great the steak would look. One could understand and forgive a young man in love on his 20th birthday for being oblivious to the world around him.

So it was with a complete surprise — the kind of surprise that might have made him drop the hairdryer except that he had paid $16.99 for it and would keep a death grip on its handle rather than break it — that his styling session came to an abrupt end.

Chapter 7
In a Jam

The startling suddenness with which the sound started from behind his back came so totally unexpectedly that it took a six or seven beats into the first verse before David recognized the usually instantly familiar melody of "Happy Birthday" being played by a trombone trio.

What David had not seen while he stared into the mirror was that Dr. Tew had frowned at Jerry's assembled trombone and passed it off to Doc. As if rehearsed, Dr. Tew then reached under David's bed and pulled out two more trombone cases. He gave the larger concert trombone, a very fine nearly new Bach 42B trombone, to Pops who had it put together in less than 30 seconds, then effortlessly connected the slide and bell of David's smaller Conn marching trombone. Almost in unison each rubbed his mouthpiece on his thigh as if to hope this ritual would actually decrease the user's risk of germ exposure, and then placed the mouthpiece into the shank that connected it to the slide before quickly blowing through the horn to clear the spit valve. In under a minute, start to finish, they were ready for Dr. Tew's whispered instructions of "Happy Birthday in B-flat."

When David heard the first note he immediately froze, holding his hairdryer pointed at his head. He realized the volume bouncing off the plaster ceiling and competing with the noise of his hair dryer was music. Seeing the flash of brass in the mirror behind him he spun around, dryer still running, to see his serenade.

He turned off the dryer and set it on the floor beside him, never taking his eyes off the spectacle in front of him. He stood there absorbing the verse, filled with amazement, surprise, sheer pleasure, and definite curiosity and puzzlement. A thousand questions collided with ideas in his mind as the realization that these guys had gone to all this trouble for his birthday cast a warm glow on any thoughts that surfaced in his consciousness. *Who arranged this? How long did they have to plot and scheme to coordinate this? Certainly Will Rice had to be in on this, or maybe Rex through somebody he knew in the music school. Is Will Rice here? Or maybe Will and Rex, and even Jerry. Hey, those are my trombones! But they look like they are careful with them. Pops looks like he's having the most fun, and he's stuck playing the bass line. They are playing really tight together. But even if Rex and Will did this, they would probably have to spend some money to put these guys together. Maybe my parents helped pay for this. Wow! What a great birthday surprise! They sound really good. Wait until Kay hears about this!*

They started Happy Birthday in march tempo, a very strict 3/4 time with

Doc playing the melody, Dr. Tew matching his rhythm with a tight but predictable harmony, and Pops playing a bass line on the Bach. As they approached the line in which a singer would sing "Dear David" they slowed together in a grand *ritard* and then played a long, drawn-out, "Hap-py Birth-day....To....You............".

Hearing the end of the verse David said, "Wow," and then realizing this was not enough he added "Bravo!" and started clapping. But the group was not through. They all sustained the final note a slow three beats, and then Pops started playing an alternating bass line, "boom, boom, boom, boom..boom..boom..boom.." He continued with the new tempo established and the other two came back in using this new more relaxed beat as their guide for the next verse. Doc still played the melody, but this time it was more a combination of jazz and swing. He didn't veer far from the original melody, but did alter the rhythms, creating gaps and pauses. Dr. Tew loosened up quite a bit, however, and no longer played the tight harmony matching Doc's rhythm. Instead he played a jazz line that was everywhere Doc wasn't, filling in Doc's pauses and gaps with his own brief licks, connecting them all with a countermelody or dancing descant part. He seemed to be enjoying himself more than David would have imagined. "*Maybe he's not quite as irritated as he seemed,*" thought David. They continued for several verses, connected together with glissandos and an occasional flutter-tongued growl as the verses continued and the improvisation intensified. Pops held the beat true, Doc's line always at least suggesting the melody, and Dr. Tew filling in the meat with a fine seasoning of jazz in a Dixieland style. As each played, his eyes studied the other for clues of where the music was going as it developed, and they also watched David for his reaction. Hard though it is to smile while playing trombone, smiles were evident, and larger as they all heard Pops throw in a line from, "Mammy's little baby likes shortnin' bread," as part of the bass line he created.

"*This is impossible. How could they do this? Who coordinated this? Is this part of a TV show? Is there a hidden camera somewhere? Hey! I'm still in a towel — there better not be a camera here somewhere! Man, is this cool or what!*" were some of the thoughts that continued to race around David's head.

After milking the chord changes of "Happy Birthday" for all it was worth for several minutes, they ended their song on a long chord, then brought their horns off their faces as they burst into a combination of laughter and cheers for the new 20-year-old.

David started to talk despite his awareness of the inadequacy of any ability to express his feelings, but his words were interrupted when Dr. Tew once again held his trombone to his mouth and started playing a march-like fanfare that was joined by Doc and then Pops in the song that David readily recognized as "Bourbon Street Parade". The three trombonists held true to their roles as delegated for the previous song, with Pops laying out a steady tempo in his bass line, while Doc played a line that was usually melody or reminiscent thereof. Dr. Tew continued to handle the majority of the improvisation of rhythm and countermelody, but on occasion would also play a fairly strict harmony to Doc's line when it seemed musically appropriate.

David had played this song countless times at Six Flags with Rex and Sandy Green. Sandy had taught it to the band and it became an immediate standard part of their repertoire. They even taught it to Will Rice one day when he sat in with the group and it would forever be one of his all-time favorites. On the second verse Pops continued to play a playful bass line while Dr. Tew and Doc held their horns down and moved closer together to sing the words, *"Let's fly now... or drive down... to New Or-leans...."*

David absorbed their performance and thought, *"They sound good singing together...Pops still looks like he's having the most fun...Dr. Tew is not nearly as uptight now as he seemed to be...This version sounds a lot like ours — they are singing the same harmony Rex and I made up, and they changed the last few words like we do!"* The trio continued into the third verse on their trombones. *"That's our arrangement. Did Sandy coach them on this? No — this has Will Rice's fingerprints all over it. Rex couldn't have coordinated this, could he? My parents don't know enough about Dixieland to pull this off, they'd think this was crazy. This IS crazy. I love it!"* And the band played on.

The fourth verse of "Bourbon Street" was building to what would surely be a climactic finale when the door flew open and in rushed Jerry. His shocked expression brought an immediate halt to the music.

"What is this?" he demanded to the suddenly quiet room.

Aware he had overstepped the boundaries of musical ethics by playing Jerry's trombone without first asking permission, and that now he had been caught red-handed by this over-possessive lunatic who seemed ready to take his case to court over a trombone that would be cleaned and polished before he'd ever see it again, Doc tried to defuse the situation.

"Uh, we're sorry Jerry. We just wanted to surprise — "

Jerry cut him off, "You don't need to apologize! That's the most incredible that horn has ever sounded! That was great! What was the name of that song?"

"Well thanks," said Doc. "I do apologize for being so presumptuous as to use your horn without asking. You're sure you don't mind?"

"Not at all!"

"The name of that song was 'Bourbon Street Parade.' Would you like to play one with us?"

"Oh, no, sir. Y'all are doing just fine without me. I don't know how to play that kind of music."

"Not even 'Bill Bailey'?"

"No, I don't even know that song."

"Well let's see if your trombone does!" said Doc, itching to play more now that he was warmed up and having fun. With that he played the familiar first line of "Won't You Come Home Bill Bailey," while he held up one finger to Pops and Dr. Tew to signal one flat, the key of 'F'.

Jerry and David both stood entranced. David continued to have a flurry of thoughts at multiple levels, enjoying the individual performances and the sum they created. Jerry tried to grasp the individual lines of each horn player, but this was a new concept for him, and his ear was more attuned to the whole result. He was enthralled by this style of music and how well they played it together. As the group roared to a rousing conclusion of "Bill Bailey" David and Jerry clapped and cheered their appreciation.

"Man, y'all are unbelievable!" proclaimed Jerry, who seemed too naive to be insincere. "How much do you rehearse?"

Almost offended, Doc replied, "You can't 'rehearse' jazz, because then it has a pre-rehearsed feel and doesn't sound spontaneous when you play it. The most fun jazz to play always has that sound of originality that makes it fun to listen to and play — never exactly the same way twice. My word, Jerry, what are they teaching you in that school of music?"

Unaware of the gentle jesting that was intended, Jerry's ears burned and his acne glowed as he looked toward the ground and started to stammer an apology not yet formed when Doc continued the lesson.

"All these years you've been practicing scales and arpeggios, learning the relationships of every note within each key and where it naturally leads. But you don't practice scales so that people will come to hear you play scales. You learn scales so you can be familiar with where each note is on your horn so that you can access it instantly within the key you're playing. When you were a baby you learned to speak so that ultimately you can now select the most appropriate words in real time, almost without effort. You should learn to play in the same fashion — playing the notes your mind hears that will sound like the music that your brain creates. Just like learning to talk, it takes a little while to learn. But ultimately you learn to talk with great precision, selecting just the right word to define very subtle differences in meaning. And the great players, and by that I certainly don't mean us, can do that as if music were a second language, and the really great players do it as if music were their first language."

David almost felt sorry for Jerry as Doc tried to explain jazz. He was coming across almost as if he were sounding critical of the year that Jerry had just spent learning music and music theory. Had that year been a waste?

But something that Doc said resonated in Jerry's brain so that, despite the overwhelming self-consciousness he felt at the moment, he had a new appreciation for what music, any style of music, should be about. He had even played in the school's large jazz ensemble, but he had never thought about how music was created in both an objective and subjective fashion. He listened to the next songs in a whole new light, and it changed the way he heard music.

The lecture over, Doc turned his attention to David.

"How about playing one with us?"

"I don't know..." said David, wanting to play.

Dr. Tew offered him the Conn, prompting David to say, "I don't think I can improvise as flawlessly as you're doing."

"I wouldn't expect you to," said Dr. Tew. "I know I couldn't when I was your age."

"Oh, come on! It's not like you'd be playing by yourself. We'd be playing too," offered an encouraging Doc.

"Well I'm hardly dressed for it...What should we play?" he asked, taking the Conn being offered from Dr. Tew's outstretched hands, wiping the mouthpiece on the towel at his thigh and quickly clearing the spit valve off to the side of the room.

"How about 'Jada', in 'F'?" said Doc.

"Great!" said David, and with that they were off for another song.

David felt immediately comfortable playing the tune he had learned several years ago from his grandfather. Jada was a cheerful simple song that gave him plenty of opportunity to throw in playful countermelodies to the music Doc created as the melody. As they played more verses, Doc got sassier with the melody, taking liberties to reshape it that he had not taken in earlier stanzas, but always faithful to the chord patterns as indicated by the steady bass line created by Pops. At the start of the fourth verse Doc nodded to David to indicate that David should play more of a solo part, which he did while Doc simplified his own part to playing longer notes that simply established the background accompaniment. The fifth verse David and Doc reversed roles. Meanwhile, Jerry sat in deep study of what Doc was doing in light of what he had just said. Jerry's hands were clasped together as he stood motionless, as if moving might break the concentration he was devoting to this newfound art form. The song was over much too soon for David or Jerry.

"That sounded great, David," said Pops. "Makes me wish I was twenty again."

"David, all the times I've heard you play in marching band — I had no idea you could play so well," said Jerry, and immediately upon recognizing his backhanded compliment, he added, "I mean to stand up there and make it up as you go and all that. You sounded great," he said, echoing Pops' complement.

"Oh y'all are all great," replied David to Pops and Doc, ignoring Jerry's clumsiness but unable to improvise a new adjective himself. Then handing the trombone back to Dr. Tew, he said, "Now play something more. You didn't come here to hear me play!"

So Dr. Tew led into the slower "Basin Street Blues", as David and Jerry relaxed a little more — Jerry relaxed a lot more — and discussed some of the techniques the trio employed as they played the song.

"Listen to how they do that question/answer pattern between themselves," Jerry whispered. "Ooh... that was nice, they all used a staccato ending on that phrase...the two of them are playing a three beat chord pattern with a fourth beat rest while he plays a solo on top of their chord line...Now those two are doing the same three beat while he uses the Bach to really play some fat low notes...," and then he squealed, giggly with nerdy glee, "There's a pedal B-flat!" at which time David told him to be quiet and just listen, so he tried, squirming as he did.

As the "Basin Street Blues" continued, maturing into a more raunchy bump-and-grind feel with each passing verse, a hot and sweaty Rex stormed into the room, then stopped almost immediately in the doorway for but a second to assess the situation. His immediate facial response did nothing to mask his displeasure. He was judging the group at one level with the natural disdain for trombonists that exists among trumpeters in the wild, rather than by the station in life of the more senior men present. Obviously hot, frustrated, and distracted by something other than good music, he didn't say anything as he walked determinedly over to the closet, requiring David and Jerry to step forward just a bit to avoid his physical and emotional space. He grabbed his towel off the hook, looking suspiciously at it for just a moment as he squeezed it for dampness, and grabbed a pair of jeans off a hanger in the closet. He moved gruffly over to the dresser to locate his toiletry items and underwear, opening the bottom drawer as the last note of the song was finished. He did not join in with Jerry and David's applause.

Then there was quiet except for the hum of a window fan and the clinking of Rex rifling through his metal drawer.

Pops dared to break the silence.

"What did that girl need?" he asked innocently, intentionally substituting "need" for "want".

Not sure if he'd been taken and unwilling to be further ridiculed Rex shrugged him off, "Not much."

But then raging with the anger of the realization of the advantage she had taken of him, rather than vice versa, he continued, "She wanted me to help her move. I've been lugging these two different seventy pound marble end stools down six flights of steps. And her carpet — a 12 foot roll of itchy wool carpet I wrestled with all the way down the stairs and to her truck. And nine months of hanging clothes. And...sheessh." Then he stopped and looked at Pops again, wondering if he'd been taken, but afraid to ask, not wanting to let on to such a possibility.

"What's that white stuff smeared on your forehead?" asked Jerry, unknowingly.

The Wite-Out had started to run with sweat down his forehead, but had been smeared by the act of Rex's rubbing his forehead against the left shoulder and sleeve of his shirt, as evidenced by the white splotches that he had still not noticed on the green shirt that was now wet with sweat.

Pops coughed to afford himself the opportunity to mask what would have otherwise been a laugh, and in the process was able to cover his mouth and thus his smile.

Rex wiped his forehead upward with his right hand, in the process smearing the Wite-Out upward in the opposite direction it had been running, now creating a white forelock, producing an appearance with his black hair that was not unlike that of a skunk.

Not wanting to appear surprised, and thus un-cool, which would only add to the victory of anyone who was attempting a prank against him, Rex sneered at Jerry and said, "Don't worry about it." But Rex did then wonder if that white stuff could have in part explained the smile that hadn't left Vicki's face the entire time he had been with her this morning. Or maybe she hadn't noticed it, and she really did just want him.

"We're playing a little music here. Would you like to join?" asked Dr. Tew, who had still not been introduced.

"Oh, yes, would you pleeeeeease," urged the sycophantic Jerry, who had long heard of Rex's ability to play many styles of jazz, but hadn't really heard much of it to this point. Jerry had always admired the ease with which he had seen Rex handle music and women.

"Yeah, I heard it in the stairway," said Rex to Dr. Tew, ignoring Jerry, still hacked-off at the world and thus unable to synthesize any courtesy. "I'm gonna take a shower." And then he gave Jerry one last suspicious glare and headed back out the door, declaring to no one in particular as he left, "There's enough trombonists in there to build a geek factory!"

Hearing that and watching the door slam shut behind him, Pops rolled his eyes up and to the right shrugging his shoulders as Dr. Tew and Doc, unimpressed by Rex's command of the metaphor, both looked toward him for any sign of explanation. Realizing the nonsense of his exiting remark and the overall silliness of his situation the room filled with laughter, primarily for the fact that Rex was angry because a girl had outwitted him. That was funny enough. No further details were really necessary.

Inspired by the moment, Doc started playing again and was quickly joined by Pops and Dr. Tew on a tune that David, laughing again, pointed out to Jerry was called "Angry".

David decided to take advantage of the moment and finished fluffing his hair in the mirror, all the while his facial expressions demonstrating a great appreciation for the birthday concert. He next slipped into his shirt, briefly checking his shoulder abrasion. He was reassured to see that the distraction of this morning's music had allowed the scrape adequate time to crust over. There should be no further bleeding.

He nonchalantly dropped his towel. Trying to appear casual, yet standing in his underwear, he wanted to get dressed as quickly as he could without appearing to be rushed. Almost immediately he heard Dr. Tew veer off onto a new melody line, "The Sheik of Arabi," a humorous little ditty known in jazz circles for its repeated background chant:

"I'm the Sheik of Arabi,
- without no pants on
You heart belongs to me,
- without no pants on,"

and on it goes.

His quick change had not gone unnoticed.

Now more comfortable and less self-conscious than when he was standing around in his underwear with a towel, he continued to enjoy the incredible birthday surprise that was his. *"I'm not even hungry. They didn't seem to connect too much with Rex — I don't think he had anything to do with this. I guess that leaves Will and my parents."* In the presence of Jerry he elected not to ask these guys who they were or who set them up. Jerry would grab onto something like that and not let go, and possibly create such a disruption with incessant questions fueled by an aroused curiosity that he would ruin the whole thing. David would just continue to play along. These guys would probably finish soon, tell him who set them up, and then call it a day. *"The whole thing at the track and talk about breakfast had just been a set-up to get them here so they could play,"* he reasoned.

When "Angry" had been musically mined for all it was worth, including a triple repeat ending, the music halted once again only long enough for Pops to observe, "Basin Street sounded really good. Let's do another blues, how 'bout 'Tin Roof'?" and without delay Dr.Tew got things started off with a raunchy lead that was about as raw as where they had left off with "Basin Street" as they played an extended version of "Tin Roof Blues".

Jerry's sincere and enthusiastic applause greeted the end of the piece and he said, "You've been playing all this time and you haven't played 'When the Saints Go Marchin' In'. Why is that?"

"I guess there are just too many good songs to choose from," said Doc. "But you know, if you go to Preservation Hall in New Orleans, there is a sign that advises you how much to tip when you make a request. For 'Saints' it's $25. But we'll do it for free." And with that they were off and running with the most famous song in jazz.

David listened closely as he recognized some of the tricks and licks they threw in Saints as being the same as what Raz'Mataz had done at Six Flags — there was the verse in a minor key with a real bump-and-grind feel — *"Will Rice must be behind this!"* but they did even more playful things with 'Saints' than David had ever heard. There was a chorus of "Jingle Bells", then a lick from "Joy To The World"; a humorously attempted and self-accompanied belly dance with hips swinging by Pops, then a phrase borrowed from "Dixie" by Doc as the schizophrenic collage of sound continued. The tempo picked up, they changed keys up a step, and then Dr. Tew stepped forward as if to sing, but instead vocalized a scat-sing solo, *a la* Louis Armstrong, but in a Donald Duck voice. Jerry and David bent over with laughter that the sometimes so serious and even dour Dr. Tew could let go with music. They went up one more key as Rex reappeared in the room and started unloading his toiletry items and hairdryer at the dresser before moving back to the closet. They finished 'Saints' as he returned his towel to its hanger. His face was clean, his hair clean and dry in a style exactly like he wanted it, and he looked fit and trim in just his jeans, with biceps bigger and shoulders broader than might be expected of a trumpeter, his back to the group as he inspected the closet.

"So Rex, are you ready to sit in for one?" asked Pops when the sound cleared the room.

"Oh, yes, would you pleeeeeease," added the voice Rex had learned to ignore.

In spite of, not because of, the groupie looking at him with such rapt admiration, without speaking Rex went over to his bed, lifted his black leather gig bag, pulled out his silver trumpet, placed his mouthpiece into the shank, mindlessly tested the keys, and looked at the other three. Introductions were not yet a priority. They knew who he was and he assumed he knew who they were. He judged them more by the instruments they held than their appearance.

The compulsion to play drove Rex today, as every day — an obsession that could not be ignored without causing him unrest. His only escape was to play. He had tamed his demon with a relentless pursuit to improve on a daily basis. While others jumped through the hoops set up for them by their teachers without thinking of the goals before them, Rex had known from the beginning he could be the best; he wanted to be the best. He worked to be the best and as a sophomore, in his musical community he was the best.

He had already heard the trombonists and sized them up while he was going up and down the stairwell for Vicki. He could hear them while below their window in the parking lot. He could not hear them in her room where a neighbor was listening to a Carol King album. And on the way to and from the shower he had heard that stupid Indian record that Mad-man liked to listen to before a test.

He had heard the flaws that would be imperceptible to most, sometimes assuming these were willful choices, not understanding the flaws as being the evidence of limitations in skill which they were. Why did the guy playing the bass line choose to play that "A" a little flat? Why didn't the melody play that triplet more evenly? Why not play the sixth tone of the scale there instead of the third? And on and on. Not obtrusive to his other thoughts and only barely brushing his consciousness, this was merely a long accepted ongoing surveillance of any music in his environment, assimilating the information in the manner others might be aware of the temperature or time of day.

This ability was part of what made Rex unique. But he had taken this talent and disciplined himself to add to it the skills that only come from repetition through laborious hours spent in a small practice room repeating and repeating notes, sometimes an entire page, or he might spend 30 minutes just perfecting a seven-note sequence. And so he would join in now, at a different level of ability, silently tolerating the human imperfections of others as he often did, even when invited to sit in with the elite faculty ensemble. He performed at a level of perfection beyond that demanded of any musical genre other than a classical symphonic orchestra which was a style of music and culture he did not enjoy.

Without playing a note he pulled his tuning slide out just a bit, realizing the trombonists were tuned down just a hair from where perfect intonation should be found, but then he was always making adjustments to the musical shortcomings of others.

His businesslike approach removed some of the silliness from the atmosphere, but increased the electricity, not unlike the silencing of the crowd in the gallery before the final putt on the 18th green on a Sunday afternoon in April at the Masters Golf Tournament. Or so he thought. He enjoyed the adoration of his audience, no matter what size, although he seldom acknowledged that. And David was a good audience.

In the love-hate relationship that exists between most young males in any culture or any species, the need for companionship and competition can be incompatible. Theirs is a world where a putdown is a sign of affection, the most open display of caring routinely allowed.

Fortunately for David and Rex, theirs had evolved into a relationship where Rex acquiesced to David's academic accomplishments while downplaying but not frankly disparaging David's obviously lesser musical abilities. Meanwhile, David was effusive in his praise of Rex's musical talents, usually. To deny Rex's talent would only make David look ignorant. He was, however, less genteel in overlooking any flaws that might exist in Rex's intellectual pursuits. They both felt comfortable, in ridiculing the other's efforts to woo women.

With his greatest supporter present and feeling charitable because of the birthday, Rex stood ready to impress anyone within listening range.

"What should we play?" asked Dr. Tew, seemingly a little excited over the realization that the ante was being upped by the addition of a trumpet sound to the group.

Now going into a zone of concentration and focus in the cocoon that enveloped him when he performed, the selection did not matter to Rex, but he did not say so.

"How about 'That's A Plenty'," suggested Pops, "in B-flat?"

With the trumpet now to his lips Rex breathed "OK" out either side of his mouth through the same channels that he would inhale through when he played.

Dr. Tew counted off a moderately fast "1,2,3,4," and they were off.

Chapter 8
Rex

The modern day trumpet is a descendant of the shofar of biblical times. Over the centuries the material used has gone from such natural materials as bone, shell, or wood, to metal. The shape has gone from straight to curved as tubing length has increased. Valves have been added. Despite these improvements, the fundamental principles of the laws of physics have always dictated what sound could be generated by a trumpet.

When the air in a hollow tube is vibrated, a standing wave of sound is created with a frequency inversely proportional to the length of the tube. Depending upon the length of the tube, the diameter of the tube, the air temperature, and the manner in which the air is set to vibration, a sound is created with a specific frequency — its "pitch" — measured in cycles per second, or hertz.

The sound wave created is a vibration. Two separate materials, be they solids, or in the case of columns of air, gases, vibrating at specific different frequencies may conflict with each other and cause cancellation and interference with each other's natural frequency. When this occurs with sound the result is discordant, which is unappealing to the ear. At other frequencies two separate vibrations may reinforce each other and resonate, creating relationships between various sounds that are pleasant to the ear.

The best known and most easily identified relationship between two pitches occurs when one note's frequency in hertz is an exact multiple of another note's frequency. These two pitches will always share such familiar vibrations and harmonics that although they are many notes apart on the musical scale they are given the same letter name. This name identifies the special relationship they share. A pitch created with a frequency of 110 cycles per seconds is called an 'A', as are its multiples, any note of 220, 440, or 880 hertz. The distance between any two consecutive "A's" is called an "octave".

Employing similar mathematical analysis, the relationship between other notes can be determined, and the spacing between these notes, the "interval" between these notes can be defined.

The average human ear is able to discern at least twelve distinct and separate notes in the span of any one octave. These pitches are evenly spaced at predictable intervals which are each spaced approximately 1/12th octave from the next, going from low to high pitch. Unaware of the science of sound but utilizing the patterns they heard, musicians have named these pitches over the centuries, arriving at the current day system whereby these 12 notes are given letter names. There are seven distinct named notes in the span of any ascending octave consecutively named "A" through "G", after which a new series of notes begins with the next octave using the same letter names for frequencies that exactly double their namesake. By a process of raising or lowering the pitch of any note slightly, known as adding a sharp or flat, respectively, another distinct five tones are produced, in a redundant system in which one note's sharp is the next note's flat, or sometimes the note itself. For example, the note named "E sharp" is the same frequency as "F", and "F sharp" is the same frequency as "G flat". Hence twelve tones, evenly spaced along the span of an octave, are the sum total of pitches available to the musician for use in that octave.

To exploit the laws of physics to produce music, a trumpet is created by creating a cylindrical tube 58.3 inches long that begins with the mouthpiece and ends at the flared bell. Three spring-piston valves are available which when depressed allow the air to be diverted through three separate paths of tubing which are 7.0, 3.4 and 10.9 inches in length.

As predicted by the rules of binary mathematics there are eight different combinations of up or down fingering positions for the three trumpet valves. When used alone the third valve creates notes that are less well tuned or can be fingered using other combinations, so the fingering position of third valve by itself is not routinely used. Thus, seven different valve combinations are learned that open access to or leave closed the connected tubing that can vary the length of the distance the air must travel before exiting the trumpet bell, from 58.3 to 79.6 inches. Depending on air current speed, lip tension, and the amount of pressure the musician uses to hold the mouthpiece to his lips more than forty specific pitches spanning over three octaves can be created by a talented trumpeter.

Rex wasn't thinking about physics or any of the aforementioned science as he played.

For him music created a kaleidoscope of the senses, individual notes evoking colors, smells, emotions and textures that made each individual note unique and readily accessed.

The first verse through "That's A Plenty" Rex established a crisp staccato melody line that was, by the very nature of the piece, fast and biting. He did not embellish the melody very much initially, but did end some of the phrases with flourishes of rapid notes that hinted of things to come. By the time they were into the second verse, he was at full stride, playing with an effortless intensity where perfectly crafted notes poured forth out of his horn.

If plotted out on a linear graph, the note sequence which Rex played might look something like a rollercoaster track, but with many more numerous and abrupt ups, downs and turns that for an appreciative listener was every bit as breathtaking as an amusement ride. Unlike a physical ride Rex was not confined by the laws of gravity. As a result high speed abrupt vertical leaps and drops were possible without the impediment of gravitational forces, an auditory experience as thrilling as a high-speed ride for the musicians listening. Watching their body motions one would see the listeners and performers posturing with subtle but very real movements of their entire bodies as if they were on this rollercoaster of sound, rising with an ascending scale, dropping back down as the line dropped a sudden octave, leaning to curve around a particular inflection. Eyes narrowed in the wind as if to improve hearing capability, or at least to reduce unnecessary visual distractions that might detract from complete focus on the music being created. An experienced jazz musician once observed that good jazz is impossible to listen to with fully opened eyes or a totally straight spine. Musicians listening and playing will, without thinking, turn their head a little to the side, raise one shoulder just a bit, or bend forward at the shoulders ever so slightly, all in response to the improvised notes, as if to gain a slight listening advantage, or to provide a counterbalance to an unexpected bend in pitch, or perhaps only to better shape their bodies to conform to the manipulated shapes of the music that flows from the horns. This was good jazz.

"That's A Plenty" begins with a verse and then a chorus, followed by a fanfare section that leads back into the chorus section. It is a driving piece played at a tempo of 160 beats per minute or even faster. Rex's mere ability to move his fingers from one functioning position into the next position at such a high speed was a physical feat of exact precision — no partially closed or uncoordinated closings — that most people and even many trumpeters would find impossible. But he was not just putting his fingers into any one of the seven necessary positions. His fingers always moved to the next note that seemed to perfectly complement the note before it or lead to the note after it, each note a specific and necessary link in a unified fabric being masterfully woven.

For every note a trumpeter plays he must determine a duration, a pitch, the proper volume of the note, whether that volume will change during the duration of the note, if the beginning and ending of the note will be abrupt or smooth, and whether to try to "bend" the pitch of the note to vary it slightly. At a meter of 160 beats per minutes a single beat passes in 0.375 seconds, but if that beat is comprised of a series of the rapid sixteenth notes — so named because one note comprises only 1/16th of a four beat measure — then the notes are played at a rate of up to 640 notes per minute, more than ten per second, and each note survives for less than one-tenth of a second before it is replaced by the next note which but for an instant represents all that the performer is. In the course of playing these hundreds of notes requiring thousands of reflexes it is often the exception, not the rule, by which a player is judged. One wrong note is heard as being much louder than the hundred correct ones that surround it, sensed like a single grain of sand on a sheet of satin, irritating and distracting. It is the sand that will be felt and remembered longer than the satin — the defining flaw that characterizes an entire performance and exposes the artist's limitations.

David heard no such errors from Rex today. The other guys were playing well, but professionals could have done better. The way Rex was playing, professionals could sit and take notes. His playing was "studio worthy". In a recording studio no second take would have been necessary.

They started into the third chorus, Rex playing a solo with the three trombones backing him up. They merely created a musical dance floor on which he could perform, and how his notes did dance! In his solo were fragments of many different songs. He first played, in order, a lick from most of the songs the trombonists had played thus far today, starting with the last phrase of "Happy Birthday" with a nod to David. He interconnected the phrases of these songs with a roaring stream of notes, as if the songs played thus far had established a resonating echo that could only be stilled by his resolutions. He then continued dancing around the chords of the melody, occasionally throwing in notes which created new chords which would not have otherwise been there. He continued tossing in these song fragments until he knowingly eyed Dr. Tew while playing a lick from "Angry" — *"I didn't think he'd hear that through the fire door,"* thought Dr. Tew — then followed this immediately with a playful line from "Stumblin' All Around" — *"Vicki told him about running into Dr. Tew,"* thought David smiling — as Rex raised his eyebrows to Dr. Tew. Jerry asked what was funny, but David silenced him with a wave of his hand. He didn't want Jerry's conversation to interrupt his enjoyment of this unexpected and apparently spontaneous birthday pleasure.

At one point Rex sounded out an awkward note pattern, smoothly and obviously intentionally played, which puzzled David. "Shostakovich!" said Jerry breathlessly with hands clasped chest high recognizing an obscure passage by the Soviet composer he had been required to learn for his music history class. Rex nodded toward Jerry as he continued to play as if to say "Well done, young grasshopper." It was Jerry's proudest moment of the week.

After several choruses, Rex took a step back while nodding at Doc, his signal for Doc to take a ride with a solo. Doc would later say he wasn't sure there would be any notes left after Rex had played them all, but Doc played a nice solo chorus and then bowed to Dr. Tew. Dr. Tew, who had seemed to crank it up a notch on the coattails of the improved sound provided by Rex played an inspired two choruses. He ended his solo with a four measure turn around phrase as he bowed back to Rex for another solo. Hearing the four measure phrase Dr. Tew had played in his closing, Rex started his next solo with same phrase. He then built on this phrase, embellished it, refined it, improved it, not in an attempt to show up Dr. Tew but because it was a good creative idea that he wanted to explore. As he reached the end of his solo, Dr. Tew rejoined him and they played an intertwined duet of rhythm and harmonies based on variations of Dr. Tew's original four measure phrase and built upon the chord sequence of "That's A

Plenty" which Pops continued to lay down.

During the trombone solos Rex had walked over to his gig bag and pulled out the rubber end of a toilet plunger and laid it on his desk. For the next verse he placed the plunger over the bell with his left hand, using it in an open and close fashion to create muted, muffled, or "wha, wha" sounds, squawks, and tongue-rolled growls, all at breakneck speed. After a verse he cast the plunger on his bed and all continued to the next verse at a wide open volume and tempo.

After a verse going wide open, Rex hunched his body just a bit to indicate he was taking the volume way down and the other three immediately followed. The contrast that resulted was a beautiful fast, tight, almost delicate verse which proved to be Dr. Tew's best verse of the day as he played an innovative counterpoint and stayed entirely within his abilities. This verse only served to make the next verse all the bigger. Any louder on the next verse and it might have been painful, but they kept it reigned in enough to be full and loud without going overboard.

The tight confines of the room did make it sound louder than it would have in a concert hall, but soon after the show had started the door opened and Hans Phillips stuck his head in, liked what he heard, and stayed. In a few more seconds Leland Jenkins pushed the door open against Hans, so they held the door open to provide more space, resulting in the sound spilling out of the room and into the six-story sound chamber that was the stairwell. After a few minutes students who would otherwise be moving out of the dorm, going to breakfast, or going about their day were backed up in the stairs enjoying the impromptu jam. The fire doors into the second floor hallway were also pressed open by the small crowd gathering, so the sound carried well down the hall. The performance was an electromagnet that attracted people and held them in place and not until it was over would it release its hold at which time they could then disperse in all directions.

As the sound and intensity built in what surely was drawing to the conclusion of the piece, Pops devilishly decided to give Rex a little more of the workout, so he subtly but ever so steadily began to increase the tempo, cranking the speed up even faster. Since he was the bass line, all the others instinctively followed his pace.

The room was crowded, heating up and loud. Rex was still mercilessly driving his trumpet, still dressed only in his jeans, a fine perspiration forming across his brow and back as the result of the early morning Georgia humidity and his recent shower. He did not give any thought to altering his relentless pursuit of speed and technique despite Pops' toying with the tempo, and as the group drew to what all those listening anticipated was the magnificent end, having done all they could do, he gave his trumpet a roll and pointed up, signaling that he wanted them all to continue on for another verse, but to segue a step higher into the key of

"C".

David had played "That's A Plenty" with Rex at Six Flags on many occasions. But they had never played it in the key of "C". Rex was now playing it faster, longer, higher, and better than David had ever heard him before. The last verse ended much too soon and was greeted with roars of cheers at its end. There were pats on the back all around. Pops was very impressed by Rex.

"You're pretty good" said Pops in understated praise, extending his hand to shake Rex's.

"You rush," replied Rex bluntly, aware that Pops had allowed the tempo to accelerate. He was a little irritated about that, not because he couldn't play it that fast or faster, but he felt the original tempo was musically better. Couldn't Pops see that?

Rex started to store his trumpet back into the gig bag, having quieted the musical demons that would have otherwise tormented his soul until he dispelled the inner need to play what he had heard. His spirits and ego were buoyed by the adulation from those around who praised his talents and cried out for more. Try though they may, however, the crowd could not talk Rex into an encore. He was now content to move on with his day.

The good natured crowd at the door and beyond quickly disbanded to go about their day, as two distant voices at the bottom of the stairs, unaware of the standard Dixieland jazz repertoire, called for "Free Bird".

As Hans Phillips was leaving the room the phone rang and since he was closest to it he picked it up and said, "Start talking!". The rest of the room continued the post-performance euphoric discussions.

As he listened he covered the phone's mouthpiece and shouted an urgent announcement to the room, "It's the University Police — someone is complaining about 'some weird trumpet noise'!"

"Let me have that," huffed Dr. Tew, while Hans headed out the door, just in case.

The others quieted to listen and heard him say, "Hello...um, yes... Buzz Off!" then hang up.

"Was that the police?" asked a concerned Jerry.

In a reply that got a good laugh from all within earshot he explained, "No... that Indian chanting in the background gave him away."

Chapter 9
The Mirror

Jerry peppered David with a redundant set of questions and instructions as both waited to interrupt the conversation now going on between the four stars, a post-performance debriefing of sorts. David hoped to finish with him and usher him on out the door as soon as Jerry had a time of brief congratulations of the players. This plan was interrupted by a bellowing call from the stairway:

"Gerald Perkins Barstow, it's time!"

"Oh my gosh," exclaimed Jerry, "I've left her sitting in the car all this time!"

In his fear and without otherwise thinking he grabbed David around the right bicep and pulled him toward the door with him. "Tell her something so she won't be mad all the way home!" Jerry pleaded.

In a pull, push and a shove David was halfway out the door and into the stairway. He managed to keep a foot propped against the door as it closed to create the impression of other more pressing commitments. He didn't want to appear rude, but a social interaction with an adult, especially Mrs. Barstow, could turn into a black hole of time and space, and he didn't want to miss out on whatever was still going on with Rex and the birthday guests.

He could see Jerry's mother one flight down. She looked like Jerry in a yellow muumuu and a disheveled bun plus seventy pounds, her face reddened by acne rosacea and every bit as untreated as his teenage acne. She refused to take another step on her already tired feet if her voice could yield the same result. She did so without regard for any consideration of how she would impact any relationships Jerry might be trying to cultivate.

"Hello Mrs. Barstow," he called to the woman he had met after a couple of football games last fall. "Thanks for letting Jerry come up for my birthday surprise!"

"Well Happy Birthday, son," obviously not remembering his name. "Jerry?!" she called up, leaving unasked the question that she thought, *"Is cake being served?"*

"Yeah, Ma!" Jerry cried, then turned to David and hurriedly ended his conversation with, "Thanks! Happy Birthday! Thanks for taking care of my horn! It was great! You've got a neat family!" as he ran down the stairs toward a summer of regression back into childhood.

With his foot in the door David had been able to monitor snippets of conversation that he was otherwise missing. Rex had turned down an offer for an encore and explained he had to be somewhere if he wanted to get something done this morning since he was already awake. It didn't quite make sense to David, but

Rex was dressing quickly. David was distracted by Mrs. Barstow so he tilted back toward the room as Jerry talked, to better be in on what Rex and the "boys", as he had heard Rex call them, were talking about. He heard Dr. Tew use the word "barnburner."

"That's the word Sandy Green would always use when talking to the crowd after Raz'Mataz played 'That's A Plenty' — 'that's a real barnburner,' he would say" thought David — was that a clue that Sandy was in on this? Distracted by this thought, Jerry's comment about that "You've got a neat family!" went unchallenged. With a slight time delay, David processed that comment but realized it would be futile at this point to drag out anything else with Jerry. He was now free to go back into the room, and he did so just as Rex went breezing out the door.

"By the way, David. Happy Birthday." In a manic series of brief sentences he called over his shoulder on the way out the room, "Thanks for the warm-up. I'll kiss you later. You've got some good trombonists in your family. Enjoy your date with Kay. Give her my best!"

"She deserves better than that!" quipped David through the closing door.

Rex's un-witty retort, likely better unheard, was unintelligible, lost in the slam of the door closing on itself.

The room was momentarily quiet as everyone digested all that had just transpired. David was in awe of what he had heard. He was also aware that he was hungry. Now that Dr. Tew et al had pulled off the birthday surprise of the century, David supposed it was time for them to go. The men were packing up the trombones and returning them to their places. David looked at his watch and saw the time was 9:03. He had only 27 minutes before breakfast hours ended at Bolton. He needed to wrap things up. He did not want to have to pay for breakfast somewhere else.

"Well that was great!" he said, still lacking for additional helpful superlatives. "Y'all are so nice to have done this. I'll remember this birthday for the rest of my life. I do wish you would explain to me how all this came about, but I understand," he said and continued, together with Dr. Tew as they both repeated, "Trade Secret."

"Yeah, right," David continued. "Well can I give you guys a ride somewhere?"

"Oh, I figured we'd walk to Bolton. It's only ten minutes — we should be able to get there before it closes," said Dr. Tew.

"You mean you really are going to breakfast with me? I thought that was just a ruse to get you back here for the trombone jam. You mean there's more?"

"We need to get on to breakfast," reminded Doc, who didn't look like he had missed many breakfasts himself.

"OK, let me get my keys," said David as he moved toward the door, adding,

"Did you notice that Jerry and Rex both assumed y'all were part of my family? I guess they assumed you were here to help me move."

"No, I'll leave the heavy lifting to Rex," laughed Dr. Tew. "But there is a bit of a resemblance. Come here," he called David back, standing in front of the closet door mirror.

David stood beside Dr. Tew, and Dr. Tew pulled him closer so both faces could be seen in the mirror. Even David was struck by the similarity he had not previously noticed. He looked into Dr. Tew's eyes in the mirror. He noted a thousand points of similarities as he scanned the face, the eyes, the chin, the nose, the forehead, looking for evidence that would refute Dr. Tew's observation. There was none. On the things that mattered most, tan, hair, wrinkles, David had him beat. But the similarities in the background landmarks were undeniable — practically identical. A cold chill removed any heat from the room as his skin contracted and his hairs stood in alert.

And with that Dr. Tew, Doc and Pops all energetically streamed out of the room, back down the stairs, heading toward the exit and then Bolton Hall. "Come on," urged Doc, "we're going to be late."

David stood in stunned silence alone in the room as the door slammed shut. "Whoa...," he said out loud, still standing in front of the mirror, alone.

He rapidly replayed the events of the day through his spinning mind which seemed almost in a free-fall, unable to grasp anything since having been presented this new and shocking puzzle. This was certainly all a part of the birthday surprise, but this was now bigger than anything he could conceive. This was bigger than anyone could conceive.

"Are these guys long lost relatives that my parents have been holding back? Where did they come from? Who are they? Who knows about this? This is getting pretty freaky!"

He was at least reassured that they seem to possess a good nature about them. Dr. Tew was definitely the darkest of the three personalities, but even he had a good natured side and he was able to laugh at himself and others. But what did all this mean?

If David looked like Dr. Tew, then he also shared the features of Doc and Pops. While Dr. Tew hadn't expounded on the question and David hadn't belabored the point, Dr. Tew had confirmed at the track that he was related to Doc and Pops. David hadn't given it much more thought with all of the other distractions of the morning, but Dr. Tew didn't really treat Doc like his father, and why would he call his own father "Doc"? Maybe Doc was Dr. Tew's uncle. And their interaction with Pops was hard to read also. Was he father to one and grandfather to another? By that age it was always hard to tell. Old people always seemed pretty much alike to David.

But if he looked like them so much, and was so obviously related to them, why hadn't he been told this sooner? His parents just weren't the type to hold back a secret like this — three long-lost or never known relatives who knew so much about everything else in David's life and shared so many similarities with his family suddenly appear and so Mama and Daddy decide that it would be a nice present to introduce them to him on his 20th birthday, but the parents don't bother to show up for introductions? No, that just wouldn't fit.

Maybe there was even more to the story. If David shared the genetic make-up of these guys, maybe he didn't arise from the gene pool he had assumed all his life. Maybe he was adopted and these guys waited until his 20th birthday to tell the full story so he could be raised by his adoptive parents without interference. But that was too hard to believe. He had two older sisters and a younger sister and two younger brothers. He remembered the birth of his youngest brother when he was five years old. Definitely not adopted. And he had seen pictures of his mother pregnant with him and it just seemed like an awful lot of deception for such a common thing as adoption. While David felt he could be objective enough to at least consider adoption as an explanation, he also felt he could rule it out as an option. Still, there was that strong resemblance...What if...

He felt guilty and dirty even considering it, but he had to. What if he was the product of infidelity. Certainly he resembled his mother to a degree, but what if...No! He refused to go further with that line of thinking. He was disappointed in himself for even considering that. His mother was simply not that kind of girl. There had to be a better explanation.

He suddenly had an epiphany where it all came together.

Last Christmas break he had read a book, or a condensed book. His father subscribed to and collected, but never read, the Reader's Digest Condensed books. Several times each year a new book arrived in the mail at the house that was a collection of four or five recent popular books, in condensed form. The past two summers David had enjoyed taking one to work with him and read many different books that way during breaks or rained out shows. And while he was home at Christmas he had read a selection called *The Boys From Brazil*. The plot centered around Nazi scientists who attempt to clone Hitler back to life. Multiple copies of clones were made and the infants placed for adoption in settings that replicated the social environment in which Hitler was raised. Was it possible that he was a cloning project? And now, on his twentieth birthday, he was being adopted into the brotherhood? He was going to meet his destiny?

He thought about how many times in his life he had been told by someone else that they knew someone from his hometown who looked just like him. A friend had once kidded that they should have a "David Patson Look-alike Contest". Sure, there's the old saying about "everybody has a twin," but maybe there were hundreds of him walking around out there as some strange cloning experiment was taking place.

"Nah. You're crazy," he reassured himself out loud. *"There's got to be an explanation."* So puzzled and curious, but without reservation or thought of the perils that are now documented nightly on the cable news broadcasts, he headed off to catch up with the strangers.

Chapter 10
Bolton Hall

David ran down the stairs and heard the heavy outside door slam shut as the men left the building ahead of him. Cloning was a crazy. These guys were all older than him. *"In a cloning experiment all the clones should be about the same age...unless somehow space travel was being used to accelerate their age... but wait, travel at almost the speed of light would cause them to age more slowly, not more rapidly. Given Pops' age, he would have had to have been cloned around the turn of the century,"* David thought. *"No way, unless, of course, aliens were involved. No, discard that idea."*

As he caught up with the group outside the three were discussing being on the campus.

"It certainly looks different now, doesn't it?" he heard Dr. Tew say to Doc and Pops, and they agreed, noting various objects or buildings along the way. David didn't want to change the subject, unspoken though it was, so he remained silent as they talked. It gave him time to think. *"Who are these guys?"* he wondered, again. This morning's events had been so amazing, so bizarre, so unbelievable... *"It must be something Mad-man arranged. He's the greatest joker in the crowd and would go to any length to pull off a complicated prank, if it was worth it. He's the only one who would go to such great lengths. But why would he go to such trouble? And what else does he have planned? He couldn't have coordinated the music by himself. Will Rice would have to have a role in such a great trombone surprise."*

To save time they took the shortcut that would take them down the long cement stairs, into the large parking lot of Sanford stadium and past the large old band room and gymnasium at Stegman Hall. At the top of the stairs Pops looked toward the rail along the right side of the steps and even leaned against it, but decided finally against sliding down the rail to the bottom, although many students would do so every day. Since David was behind the group by a step, he opted not to slide either, lest he bump one or more of them as he slid.

When they were all at the bottom of the stairs and started across the parking lot he could be silent no more.

"Dr. Tew, with all due respect, I really would like to know what's going on," he said respectfully.

Pops responded, "Patience my young Padawan," with a smile, which Doc mirrored, eliciting no response from Dr. Tew. "You will understand it all in due time. But we want to make sure to pull this off the way it was planned."

"Can't you tell me anything?" pleaded David, uncharacteristically. He was trying to be a good sport, but this was beyond anything he had ever experienced.

"Oh we could tell you lots, but it really wouldn't matter," replied Pops.

Doc interrupted with a comment to Dr. Tew about Stegman Hall, "there off to the right", and their conversation returned to reminiscences.

Alone in his thoughts, David concluded that there must be yet another surprise. If it was half as fun or as good as the trombone playing, it would well be worth being patient. He wasn't quite sure what Pops meant by "It wouldn't matter," but Pops didn't seem threatening, so he had no reason to interpret it as such. But still...

Whatever the source, he was increasingly certain that somehow Will Rice was in on this. He really did care deeply for David, and would have been willing to go to great lengths to surprise David on his birthday even if, or perhaps because, he couldn't be here. The trombone impromptu could have only been coordinated by a true aficionado like Will. Will would have known the details of the specific solos and trombone licks and had the contacts to find these players. Rex might have had similar resources, but was not the type to go to anywhere near the amount of trouble that would have been necessary to coordinate such an event.

David fished for information. "Do you guys know a guy named Will Rice?"

"Yes, I used to," admitted Dr. Tew, pausing as if not wanting to give away any unnecessary hints.

"Bingo!" thought David victoriously, now a little more patient to let the mystery unfurl.

"What are your favorite birthday memories?" asked Dr. Tew, steering the topic. His memory primed by this morning's recollections while running, David easily recounted his birthdays to them. They were a good audience, asking questions often enough to keep the information flowing, and they laughed easily at his stories, stroking his ego as only laughter for a well-delivered line can. Almost before he realized it they had crossed Lumpkin Street, walked the sidewalk past Tanyard Creek, ascended the stairs along Legion pool, crossed the curving Cloverhurst Avenue and arrived at Bolton Hall. They entered into the "cow pens" as Will Rice had called it, because at mealtime students were often packed into this large, low-ceiling room like cattle as they queued up to file into the cafeteria past the cashier. Students on the meal plan entered through the turnstile after electronically verifying their meal card, while all others paid a flat rate for the buffet now being served.

This morning found the cow pens almost empty. A trio of guys and a hand-holding couple were all heading toward the rear exit which led to the high-rise dorms further up the hill on Baxter Street.

There was no wait to go into the cafeteria. Doc bowed at the waist and motioned with a sweep of his outstretched right arm that the birthday prince should proceed on through the turnstile. Doc then produced a crisp new twenty dollar bill and generously treated his two companions to breakfast with David's earnings.

The main floor of Bolton Hall had a very open feeling with a twenty-five foot high ceiling. Today Bolton seemed cavernous, much bigger than necessary. Most days, however, it was packed with students enjoying food of whatever quality. The dining tables for groups of eight spread out to the right and then beyond in a split level area that afforded additional seating up or down a half flight of steps. The entrance to the second dining area across the room and on the same level had already been blocked off for the remainder of the morning as the cleaning crew — more correctly the one student employed as the cleaning crew — slowly mopped the floor, cleaning up in preparation for the lunch hour. The late morning hour and thinning campus population resulted in a sparsely scattered collection of students. Some were rushing through a breakfast timed to occur just before Bolton closed after a long night of cramming for a final exam. Others were there for a less hurried breakfast before activities culminating in their departure from Athens later in the day. The sounds of conversation were few and quiet, and most of the noise in the dining hall could be accounted for by the activities required by food preparation and clean up. The clinking of glass and silverware bouncing on trays on their way to noisy dishwashers seemed amplified by the size and emptiness of the large dining area.

David led his guests toward the serving line to the left. He took his tray, silverware and napkins and first selected the safest bet, a small glass of apple juice from among the choices of juice already poured. As usual, there were also orange, grapefruit, and cranberry juices to choose from, but at this late hour there was a great risk that any of those three choices would be bitter from standing out too long. He then pushed his tray on and by-passed the limited fruit selection, having already decided that for his birthday he would have pancakes and scrambled eggs. As his plate was being served he looked back to his left at Pops and Doc. They had both selected a glass of grapefruit juice and were standing facing each other, glasses in hands raised as if to toast. Pops said, "GO!" and they both chugged the glass of certainly bitter juice as quickly as possible, Pops slamming his empty glass back onto the tray just before Doc did. Dr. Tew seemed to act as the silent judge, peering over to make certain Pops' glass was adequately empty for him to be declared the winner. Pops and Doc both followed their feat with a wide-open mouthed "haaa", as if that would more rapidly clear their contorted faces and tearing eyes.

David might have laughed at their antics, or even challenged either to a rematch with cranberry juice, had he not been so disturbed by his thoughts. This "grapefruit chugging" was something he and Rex had invented. They had been in line together one morning and for some reason had been making jokes about students who went off to the great University of Georgia and couldn't handle the freedom and responsibilities, deciding rather to measure their accomplishments in life by whether or not they could do the truly important things in life such as chug beer. David had challenged Rex to a chugging contest with grapefruit juice that morning, and they had done so right there in line. Now whenever they ate breakfast together more often than not they would both grab a grapefruit juice and without further discussion have a face off, silently raising their glasses in a toast before one or the other announced "go" and then they completed their duel in the finest of 18th Century traditions. David knew well that the colder and fresher the juice was the less bitter it would be, but even on a good day, eyes would water and nose run as salivary glands attempted to repair whatever damage occurred during their purge. In two years of eating almost every meal at Bolton he had never seen anyone else chugging. Were these guys trying to parody David? Were they there to make fun of him?

He began to feel vulnerable, like the butt of a joke, where everyone else knew the routine and he was going to be laughed at. He did not like the feeling which replaced any joy he had felt only moments before. He took his plate and dispensed milk into a glass, then headed for a table downstairs, lest anyone else in the cafeteria see whatever else these clowns had up their sleeves. The other three were soon to follow. They set down their trays at the table with him, the only four people on the lower dinning level. David sat motionless and slump shouldered, starring at his food. Dr. Tew sat beside him, and Pops and Doc chose their places on the opposite side of the table.

"Why the long face?" asked Dr. Tew, in a question that struck David to the core. Was this some type of joke trying to link David's looks to theirs again? How long would they taunt him and not let him in on this trick that was bringing them such collective pleasure at his expense?

"Are you guys trying to imitate me? Are you trying to make fun of me?" he asked, voice shaking as he tried to hold back the tears that exposed just how confused and scared he was becoming, not caring at this point if he was about to sabotage some long planned and well-coordinated effort by Will Rice.

"Oh, no...no, not at all," replied Dr. Tew, his face now expressing a true concern that was also reflected in the appearance of Doc, while Pops had a knowing look that seemed to indicate a confidence that everything was going to be OK, enjoying the advantage that emanates from possessing facts that another does not.

In a mixed script of television shows from a by-gone era, Pops slid back in his chair and started in with a more affected baritone voice, trying his best to sound like a booth announcer as he proclaimed:

"Well, David, I guess it's time for us to flip all the cards and find out who our mystery guests are. Contestant Number One, what is your name, please?"

On cue, Dr. Tew pushed back his chair, stood with his hands by his side, and answered, "My name is... David Patson... and today I'm forty years old."

Chapter 11
Augusta

At one time in its history, the entire country of Canada could be defined in terms of two towns and a river — Quebec and Montreal connected by the St. Lawrence River. The same could be said of the colony of Georgia in its infancy when the cities of Savannah and Augusta were birthed, connected by the Savannah River.

On June 9, 1732, the same year George Washington was born in Virginia, King George II of England signed the charter granting a group of trustees led by General James Edward Oglethorpe permission to establish the thirteenth British colony, thusly named in honor of the king. In addition to enhancing the ego of the king, Georgia would afford an opportunity for the poor in England who wished to attempt a better lot in life. The new region would enhance the defense of Carolina against the Spaniards to the south, and further augment the developing trade and maritime defense activities along the eastern coast. The land deeded was that below the Carolina border as defined by a river, and north of the Spanish territory of Florida, extending west to the Mississippi River.

On February 12, 1733, Gen. Oglethorpe and 114 colonists arrived at Yamacraw Bluff, which would be renamed Savannah, located at the mouth of the Savannah River on the Atlantic coast of the new colony. A settlement was established and Oglethorpe set about the task of organizing and fortifying his colony.

In colonial America the location of cities was often determined by the natural resources and geography which the arriving colonists found, and Georgia was no exception. Exploration of the Savannah River revealed a navigable waterway unimpeded by rapids or falls for over 100 miles inland, at which the Appalachian plateau abuts with the costal piedmont, creating a series of shoals and a rock ledge in a several mile stretch of the river. This natural disruption of the river served as a crossing point for Native Americans and early settlers. In 1735 Oglethorpe ordered an outpost created at this point in the river to facilitate defense and trade with American Indians. Oglethorpe named the town in the honor of Princess Augusta of Wales and drew up a plan for the layout of the second city in Georgia.

Augusta grew and prospered with the increase in fur and tobacco trade from the colony. During the American Revolution the state capital city of Savannah was captured by the British and for a period of time Augusta was the war-time capital city, and then again was the capital from 1785-1795. Two signers of the Declaration of Independence are buried there.

Augusta continued to develop into the 19th Century. In 1828 Georgia's first medical school was granted a formal charter by the state general assembly. Located in Augusta, the Medical Academy of Georgia would become the Medical College of Georgia.

A series of canals was built mid-century to service the water needs of cotton mills and by the end of the 19th Century Augusta was second only to Memphis as an inland cotton market.

Augusta proudly boasts of being the boyhood home of President Woodrow Wilson, hosting the Master's Golf Tournament every spring, being the birthplace of the Southern Baptist Convention, and being home of the South's oldest newspaper.

Despite her long pedigree and antebellum charm, she could not compete with the city that started in the middle of nowhere and wound up the center of everything — a small development at the southern end of the Western and Atlantic Rail lines, named "Terminus", renamed "Marthasville", and finally named "Atlanta" in her first eight years. Despite having to rebuild after the Civil War, or perhaps because of this forced opportunity, Atlanta's growth, development, and importance to the region continually increased. With less loss from the war, Augusta had less reason to change, and some critics would suggest that this has been her greatest fault. Others praise Augusta as a marvelous self-contained community, three hours from everything: three hours from Atlanta, three hours from Savannah beach, and three hours from the Appalachian mountains.

Being three hours from "everything" allowed Will Rice to study without distraction when he cloistered himself in his student cubicle on the second floor of the Carl Sanders Research and Education building on the campus of the Medical College of Georgia. He, like David, was deep into finals week, the last week of his first year of medical school at MCG.

The very presence of Will at MCG continued to shock and stun those from his high school class who lost track of him and then casually met up with him again after a few years. In high school Will could have been voted as the student most likely *not* to go to medical school — or to college, or even to technical school. Yet now he was closing in on the end of his first and very successful year at medical school.

For reasons that will be left to the psychologists to argue, Will had been a very poor student in elementary school and high school. Perhaps it was his father's military career that resulted in frequent moves and new schools; perhaps it was due to the importance he placed upon music and the false impression that music could carry him as far as he wanted to go in life, regardless of his education; perhaps it was that he didn't feel he could compete academically and so to save face, he never entered the competition. Or maybe he was just saving himself for the part that mattered.

In high school he showed no academic ambition, no discipline, and was a distraction to others at times with his devaluing of the educational process. More than once he warned David not to get "burned out", as if studying in preparation for college would result in David's inability to perform once he got to college. There was no hint at an aptitude for the sciences — he made a "D" in high school biology. The only hint of any future success was that he had mastered auto mechanics and music. He could handle any challenge his old Volkswagen Beetle threw his way, which it often did. His musical ability was recognized by his selection into the Georgia All-State Band and the McDonald's All-America Band.

Unfortunately for him, the SAT only tested his ability in English and math. His college entrance scores and high school transcript were inadequate for most colleges, and so it was almost too late when he decided that he wanted to go on and major in music in college. Fortunately for him, a local college apparently had admission standards commiserate with his performance to that point, and he was accepted into their school of music.

While a student at the school of music, Will's outlook on life changed. In high school he had enjoyed hanging out with successful and ambitious students. At one point he even lived with David's family when Will's parents moved to retire to their family farm in Alabama but Will desired to finish up his high school education in Georgia, as if that would matter.

Living with David, Will had the opportunity to witness firsthand the work ethic and value that was placed on study and self-discipline, starting from the top with both of David's parents. The Drs. Patson were both good examples of what hard work could accomplish in life. David's dad was raised by a widowed mother, and David's mom was the first person in her family to graduate from college. David's older sisters also fascinated Will at several levels, including their pursuit of knowledge.

Once in college, Will looked for that same academic discipline in those he encountered, but came away disappointed. His passion was music, but at this second-rate school of music no one else demonstrated the sudden desire for excellence that had been awakened in Will. Fortunately for him, music was not the only course he was required to take. His first quarter he was enrolled in a basic science course as part of his core curriculum. To his surprise, he was able to do well in this class. Rejecting additional education in music, but encouraged by his science grade, he decided to change his major to agronomy in preparation for a career alongside his father on the family farm.

Surprisingly, more classes in science begat greater confidence, and by the end of his first year the student who had made a "D" in high school biology now wanted to study medicine. He applied to the University of Georgia and was accepted into the School of Arts and Sciences with a proposed major in chemistry that would prepare him for application to medical school.

His college years in Athens had been difficult because his preparation had been so minimal. Subjects that did not interest him — English, Literature, History, Social Science — only served to drag down his grade point average, but he sloshed through them with overall better than predicted results. Subjects that did interest him — Biology, Chemistry, Calculus, Physics, German — were now objects of intense devotion and he demonstrated a mastery and retention of subject matter that amazed his fellow students and professors.

While a freshman David was quite challenged when asked for help by a student one quarter behind him in calculus. David was trying to remember all those formulas he had already cleared out of his mind to make room for new information, but Will interrupted and was able to clearly and concisely explain to the struggling freshman how to approach the problem, although he had done no calculus for two years. It was humbling at times for David to have to admit what a great student Will had become, but he did so readily. Will worked hard, played hard — real hard — and tried to be the best student he knew how. Will deserved all the praise he received, and more, for the turnaround he did in school.

His application to medical school was somewhat anxiety producing. For the first time, David could actually see a lack of confidence in Will, who realized the quality of students he was competing against for the limited number of positions available to the large pool of applicants. During a moment of Will's negativism, David coaxed Will into a bet — Will was so certain he wouldn't get accepted into med school that he would shave his head if he got in. David was glad to see how much Will cared, and he, along with many others, rooted for Will to get in. Finally, during final exam week that previous May, Will had been accepted into medical school at the Medical College of Georgia in Augusta, Georgia, the Garden City. A trip to the barbershop was accomplished on the same day with a large cadre of friends in tow, the results of which were still quite obvious when Will sat for his freshman class picture for the MCG year book three months later.

And now Will sat in his MCG cubicle, the first year of medical school almost completed. He was wiped out and had a long day of study still ahead of him. His histology final yesterday had gone fairly well, but had thrown him off his sleep-wake cycle, so he had already studied three hours today and it was only 9:30 in the morning. The anatomy exam tomorrow would be his last of the year, and he wanted to ace it. He knew he could; he had been doing well in anatomy all year. For the most part he had already learned the material two or three times for previous tests, but with only 24 hours to go, he didn't want to be over confident. He would burn today studying, with a nap after lunch as a reward, and an appropriate night's sleep before the big test tomorrow. Then a great summer of time with his sweetie, his parents, and a couple of weeks up in Officer Training

School at Rhode Island to fulfill the requirements of his navy scholarship. His time in Newport would be a small price to pay for the full coverage of all the costs of medical school, plus a monthly stipend, that was allowing him to acquire the lifelong security and satisfaction which a career in medicine had to offer.

His mind burned with all the details of the anatomy of the human back, where his anatomy course had started so many months ago, and then of the chest, and of arm and hand. The arm and hand was the section he found easiest to review, it was all so straightforward and mechanical — just a series of bones pulled by strings like a marionette. Simple, but fascinating, a miracle. He loved that about anatomy, and almost everything else in medicine. Medicine was the science of explaining everything about the unexplainable. He had reviewed his class notes in these three areas, and now would check for any margin notes in his Grant's Anatomy text before moving on to the next section, abdomen and pelvis, followed by the more challenging head and neck.

As he stretched for a moment his mind thought back to the night before the first day of medical school. He had purchased his books and picked up the course syllabus in Anatomy. Since Anatomy was the "huge" course of the first year he was all geared up to get started. He glanced over the introduction and the text of the syllabus that evening before going to bed. "If 'all the world's a stage', you are now being given a front row seat," he recalled from the introduction. How true that had been. He had been a little nervous about how he might react going into the anatomy lab that first day. He had purchased his white lab jacket and dissecting kit, so he was ready to start, but to enter a room of multiple tables, each containing the preserved and fully complete body of a recently alive person... he had hoped he wouldn't do anything to embarrass himself. That night he had a dream, influenced by a Clint Eastwood movie he had seen. In *The Outlaw Josie Wells*, the title character played by Eastwood is a western settler who at one point in the film tracks across a sacred Indian burial ground. It is winter, and the corpses are at rest on high platforms built of sticks, the bodies collecting snow as if to further emphasize the cold and bleak finality of death. Will had dreamed of an anatomy lab with similar platforms. He feared walking into such hallowed grounds.

To his relief, the first weeks of anatomy were spent studying the structures of the back. To facilitate this, all cadavers were already in position face down on their tables, in body bags which also contained the preserving fluids necessary to maintain the remains at room temperature. The bags were unzipped only as needed during those first weeks to reveal the base of the skull to the small of the back, making the deceased seem much less human. For this Will, and probably many of his classmates had been thankful. By the time it was necessary to turn the cadaver over, the dissection process was much more routine and depersonalized. Not that he could ever forget that he was dissecting actual human flesh. His professors would not have allowed that if Will had wanted to try. He was always impressed by the great respect the professors demanded for the specimens being used. It was evident from the opening lecture that no horseplay or gallows humor was appropriate in the anatomy lab. Any tissue removed from the body, no matter how small, went back into the body bag. At the end of the course all the bodies and bits of tissue were cremated. A ceremony was held toward the end of spring quarter to pay final respects and tribute to the memory of those who had donated their bodies for such a selfless but enduring purpose. The ceremony had been optional for students to attend, but Will went, partly out of appreciation, and partly out of curiosity. He was impressed by words of praise and spoken by both his chief anatomy professor, and his class president. They spoke the language of faith and healing, and the two seemed closely intertwined. The ceremony was also attended by some of the family members of those being remembered and their loss was still evident in their faces. He would be eternally grateful to the man who had allowed Will to know him, and thus the miracle that is anatomy, so intimately.

Realizing his mind was starting to wander, he decided he needed an ever so brief break to get himself back on track. He wouldn't blow his last day by sitting in his cubicle and not studying. He was studying at his cubicle rather than at his apartment so there would be fewer distractions. No phone, no refrigerator, no TV, no music, no bed. The biggest distraction he would face there was other students.

By unspoken agreement the cubicle areas themselves were an hermitage reserved for study. Sixteen students per study area had space for a desk and a closet to store their books and supplies on campus. Some students rarely if ever used their cubicle spaces, choosing to study at home. Others studied exclusively at school, unable or unwilling to have their study intrude into their home environment. Most students found it necessary to study at both places.

The disadvantage of cubicle study was that when taking a break, even if only to walk to the bathroom or get a drink of water, but all the more so if going to the concession area, it was almost impossible not to strike up a conversation with another student whose study demands also left him starved for human interaction. The choice between getting back to study versus having a meaningful conversation about how unfair the grading was in Community Medicine or why it was necessary to memorize so many useless names in microbiology was an easy one. Before long, a precious hour of study (or sleep) time was squandered. So he applied previously learned knowledge.

In order to have spending money that his family could not supply, Will had always had a job since the age of 14. He had worked at a roller-skating rink before he was old enough to drive, bumming rides with friends, riding a bike, or even walking to work. At the skating rink he had the opportunity to learn to skate, and he learned quickly. When he was sixteen he applied for a job, any job, at Six Flags Over Georgia. He would eventually audition for a musical position in the park, but initially the job offered was in "grounds" which meant sweeping up trash. Will gladly took the job. It hardly seemed like work compared to summers he spent working on his grandparent's dirt farm in central Alabama, where pay was never even an option, but eating was.

At Six Flags he tried to make sweeping trash with his short broom and bin-on-a-stick interesting, but eventually time dragged. Then one day it struck him that at work there were acres of smooth asphalt all around him. *"What a great place this would be to skate,"* he thought as he swept yet another piece of trash off the ground. *"Perhaps one night they should have an employee party and let us all skate around from ride to ride."* Continuing this line of thought as he worked, he then had a more realistic thought. *"If I wore skates while I swept I could cover a lot more ground and have a lot more fun."* He approached his supervisor with the idea, and before long had approval from the park manager to try out the novel idea. By the end of the summer several other sweepers were doing the same thing, and it impressed the bosses and enchanted the customers.

Will rose from his desk, and as was now his new custom, skated once around the outer hall of the second floor of the Research and Education building. The waxed tile floor was perfect for the skates, and their smooth rubber wheels were quiet and not at all damaging to the floor. Skating provided a relaxing release, and prevented him from stopping to talk and socialize. Not that he was against socializing. That was the problem — he was too social. He had to schedule his time tightly and now was not the time to use his time for anything but studying.

He made a quick stop at the restroom and water fountain, and was on his way again, breezing past fellow students in the hall with a quick hello as he passed. In less than three minutes he was back at his desk, skates still on his feet, where they would remain as long as he was studying in the cubicle. The skates were just one more point of evidence of his unique, innovative, carefree approach to tackling life and anything it sent his way.

As he opened his anatomy notebook, he noticed what he had not seen earlier in the day, and suddenly a disappointment and regret filled his heart. There was the birthday card he had picked up at the bookstore two weeks ago. "Shoot!" he muttered, or something approximating that. He had meant to send it to David on Monday, and now here it was, Wednesday, David's birthday — and he hadn't even addressed it yet. He had totally forgotten about David's birthday, and he felt miserable. He hadn't done a single thing for his best friend's twentieth birthday! He really prided himself on not letting school get in the way of important things, things important to him. He had messed up. So he set the card aside. He would mail it at lunch, to David's home address since now he wasn't sure where David would be when the card was delivered.

Back to anatomy.

In college Will's life had turned golden. Although he could not fully know it at the time, the future held many even more wonderful things for him. He had already graduated from UGA, enrolled at MCG, and met a wonderful young nurse who shared his enthusiasm for life. In school his tension-breaking antics and friendly unpretentious nature made him one of the most beloved members of his class. He would marry the woman even more wonderful to him than he could imagine hoping for. He fathered a son who was his very connection with all that was joy in life. From the time of his graduation at UGA he would reap the rewards of a bountiful, unlimited nonstop seven year harvest of biblical proportions in a warm and sunny time of youth, of love, of laughter, of life. Then there would come a cruel, hard, dark, cold, unending winter.

Chapter 12
Breakfast Epiphanies

"My name is... David Patson... and today I'm forty years old."

David sat frozen in his chair as he tried to absorb this new claim. His mouth was half-opened with a faint, uncertain smile, his eyes half-closed as his brain rushed for an explanation for what he had just heard. Pops continued,

"Contestant Number Two, what is your name, please?"

With this, Doc pushed back his chair, stood with his hands by his side, and answered,

"My name is... David Patson... and today I'm sixty years old."

David let out a little combination sigh/cough/chuckle as he tried to comprehend what he was hearing. If this was a joke — *"What else could it be?"* he thought — it was a very good prank. The kind that could wind up in the newspaper. *"Oh, man, I'd better stay cool. I don't want anyone to think I fell for this. I almost lost it just a minute ago. Just stay calm, man. Everything will come out in just a minute — it's got to!"* he thought, trying to reassure himself. Whoever had set this up had gone to an awful lot of planning, effort and detail. He was not going to give them the pleasure of making him look like a fool in his recently sleep-deprived state. He could take a joke, so he'd wait this one out and find out the ending. He had to admit, this was good. He couldn't deny the goose bumps he was feeling all over his body.

"Contestant Number Three, what is your name, please? My name is David Patson and today I'm eighty years old," asked and answered Pops while standing.

David sat back in his chair, his eggs and pancakes cooling before him, and folded his arms across his chest, trying to appear to be in control of his response. He looked up at Pops and Doc across from him, then over a Dr. Tew beside him. They stood silently, offering no further expectation, awaiting David's reaction.

"Well then, shall we?" he said, lifting a fork of eggs to his mouth.

"Perhaps the grace first," reminded Pops, who immediately offered a brief but functional blessing as heads bowed, followed by a chorus of "Amen" all around.

David returned the fork-load of uneaten eggs to his plate.

"Well, this certainly is a nice birthday surprise," he said, trying to sound nonplused. "Y'all are good."

"You obviously don't believe us," said Dr. Tew as the three sat back down and started to eat.

"What's not to believe?" replied David. "Sounds like your ordinary run-of-the-mill birthday party guest list to me."

"A predictable response," observed Doc, "Why don't you give us a test?"

"Yeah, right," replied David, sarcastically. Just how gullible did these guys think he was? "What do you do for an encore — go fly around the room?"

"Oh, no," Doc responded. "We don't have any more supernatural powers than you do, because we're you. Come on, give us a test!"

Thinking this must be the next part of the morning show, David decided to play along with this new line of requests.

"OK, what is my dog's name?"

"Poogie," responded Doc who then added, "you named her that at the suggestion of Buffie who knew a stable owner by that name."

"OK, easy question," thought David, but it was true that ten years ago for his birthday he had gotten a dog from the pound and his sister had come up with the name that stuck.

"What did I have for breakfast yesterday?" he asked next.

"Not a good question," said Dr. Tew. "Why should I remember what I had for breakfast 20 years ago? But I do wish you'd go a little easier and lay off the cholesterol. I want to stay healthy."

"What are my sister's middle names?"

"Trick question," replied Dr. Tew. "There's Jane and Kathryn. Then, let's see... This is 1977 so Tricia is married now, so her middle name is Patson, but she didn't receive a middle name at birth, and then she had one legally added-"

"OK," interrupted David, almost rudely, "That's easy enough. All a matter of public record," he said, trying to sound confident, realizing the trivia about Poogie wasn't actually public record, but maybe Buffie was in on this trick too.

"How many steps went to the basement in the Atlanta house where I grew up?"

"Good trivia," said Dr. Tew, "but I couldn't go up or down them without counting them all. There were 14, and the top four curved to create a 90 degree turn."

Pretty good — but that house was still there. It was possible they had gone there to research. "Where was my secret place to hide stuff there?"

Doc fielded this one. "The top wall of your closet."

"*Spooky*," David thought. Growing up he had shared a large room in the basement with his two younger brothers. His grandfather had built out the addition, but never installed a ceiling. In his closet there was a flat plank created by a 2x4 at the top of the wall board, near the rafters of the floor above. He had to get on a stool to reach the spot. He couldn't recall ever hiding anything there that had actual importance or value, and its fascination with him had lessened as he got older. As a result, he had forgotten to check that spot for any treasures before his family moved out. He sometimes wondered what he left behind.

"A good guess," he thought. Maybe his mother had seen him climbing up there at some point.

He decided to dig deeper. "Who did I have a crush on in the sixth grade?" This was something he had never discussed with anyone, not even Rex or Will. He had never admitted to anyone just how beautiful Connie Lewis was. But she was in the seventh grade and at that age one year's difference is a social chasm too great for any love to bridge.

"Connie Lewis. To this day, the most beautiful girl you'll never know," said Dr. Tew, smiling from the memory.

Using his fork full of eggs as a prop as if to make his acting confident more believable, David sat speechless, searching for an explanation as he pretended to need to pause to take a bite. But breakfast was the last thing on his mind. After the eggs, he lifted his glass of apple juice to his lips and feigned a swallow, actually only wetting his lips as his brain raced futilely for logic. He had never confessed his interest in Connie to anyone. On the other hand, how hard would it be for one of his sixth grade classmates to guess the answer. After all, she was the most beautiful girl in the school.

"They could have an auditorium full of people who've known me during my life. There's a hidden microphone so they can hear my questions. Then they send the answers into a tiny earphone in these guy's ears," he thought, realizing that explanation was about as plausible as the one Pops had offered.

"Still not convinced, are you?" asked Dr. Tew.

"Come on," said David. "This is a very impressive trick, but there's got to be an explanation."

"You lied about Vicki Post," said Dr. Tew. "You went out with her and then you kicked yourself for not being able to find her more...'interesting', because you find her so 'interesting'."

"Another lucky guess," thought David.

"You did great on your biochemistry final and that's an academic victory you'll remember the rest of your life," added Pops.

"I'm not falling for this," thought David.

"Your best one mile time ever was 6:12 at the end of winter quarter," continued Dr. Tew.

David had never told anybody that. He didn't have to report his time to the coach for the grade in the class, and it had never really come up in conversation. He had even told Kay his time had been "OK", but they hadn't discussed it beyond that. He was certain no one could know that exact number, unless they had been there filming the run that day.

He said nothing as Doc piled on, "Your instant banker card PIN number is '1975', the year you graduated from high school."

Now David felt violated. No one should know that number. He had never shared it with anyone. It must certainly be illegal for a bank employee to reveal such information. Why would they do that?

"The first time you kissed Kay, you had no idea what you were doing. You botched it and almost bailed out, and to this day she thinks it was the sweetest, most romantic, most tender kiss you could have given her," sighed Pops.

David felt even more violated. Kay and he had never even discussed their first kiss. How could they guess this stuff? What business was it of theirs?

"Still not convinced?" said Dr. Tew, "take a look at my hand." He placed his right hand flat on the table, palm down, fingers spread.

The mole jumped out at David immediately. He had an identical mole squarely in the middle of the back of his hand — the exact same location. David reached his right hand across his body and put it beside Dr. Tew's. He felt a little sorry for Dr. Tew at the comparison. The skin on the back of David's hand already had the nice tan he had been cultivating since spring break. Dr. Tew's hand was visibly older, not at all tan but heterogeneous in its skin tones from sun damaged splotching, and early wrinkles and creases where David's hand was smooth. He also had a ring on his fourth finger that had an onyx stone with a golden snake on a staff in the center which David recognized as a medical symbol. The ring showed enough wear to make it evident that it wasn't a new ring. On the top border of the ring were the words "Medical College" which were continued on the bottom border, "Of Georgia". The right side of the ring had the block letters "MD". Without invitation David rolled the ring on Dr. Tew's finger to reveal the other side of the ring, the number "83" — the year David hoped to graduate from medical school. His goose bumps once again appeared.

Seeing David's interest in the ring, Doc and Pops reached their hands out onto the table to reveal identical hands, moles, and rings, the only difference being apparent aging. Without speaking David leaned forward and gently scratched at the mole on Doc's hand. It didn't come off.

Needlessly, he checked the dates on both rings, finding an "83" in each case.

"So how'd you do this?" he asked softly. Pride was no longer at stake. This gag had gone way beyond anything he could imagine. Who would go to all the effort to set this up? Just to get three rings like that could cost fifty dollars or more. Who would spend that much money just to pay for three rings, much less everything else required to make this happen? If he was to be hoodwinked, so be it. If these guys were lying, he would let them have their joke. But if they were telling the truth...

"No!" he shouted inside his head. This was the craziest thing he had ever heard of, and he wasn't going to be taken in. He needed more information. A better explanation would come.

"So why are you here?" asked David softer still.

"It just seemed like a good day to come for a visit," said Dr. Tew. It's not every day a boy, er, a man turns twenty. This is one of the big days in your life and we wanted to re-live it, so here we are."

David still hadn't started eating although the others were now well into their meals. "Go ahead and eat. You'll see we're telling the truth," said Pops.

With nothing else to do, David started to eat.

"How did you get here?" he challenged them again between bites.

"Oh, that's not important," said Pops.

"How long will you stay?" asked David, trying again to get some kind of hint about what was actually going on.

"We're just here for today," came Doc's reply.

"Who's elected President in the next election?" asked David, quickly, as if the speed of his question would catch them off guard and leave them floundering, as he realized he didn't know the answer either, so theirs might not matter.

"1980...Ronald Reagan," said Doc.

"Stupid question," thought David. But then he couldn't resist bragging about his single Ronald Reagan contact. "You know, my jazz band was hired to play for him when his campaign came to Atlanta just before the Georgia Republican Primary last spring. We were in this giant ball room and he was headed next to Texas for the primary there, and as he finished his speech he said, '... and as I leave Georgia, I hope to find the eyes of Texas are upon me,' and then he started to walk off the stage, right past the platform we were set up on. We were supposed to play as soon as he finished, so I shouted out 'Railroad' to Rex and Sandy — Rex didn't know the song as anything but 'I've Been Working On The Railroad'. So right cue, as if rehearsed, we play 'The Eyes Of Texas Are Upon You'. The crowd went wild. Reagan walked past us with his hands clasped together raising them over his shoulders like this," he said, as he demonstrated the well-known sign of victory and heroics, "smiling at us and loving the crowd. It was a great moment. He seemed like a good guy." He ended his story, unable but to feel a little excited about his brush with greatness and the ability to add something interesting to the conversation which was otherwise too wacky for his comfort zone.

"I know," said Dr. Tew, as if bored by the story, "You forget, I was there."

"Where was it then?" asked David, a little embarrassed by the reception his story received.

"The old downtown Atlanta Marriott," said Dr. Tew. While David didn't consider the Marriott to be that old, Dr. Tew was right. David tried to recover and go in a different direction of questioning.

"Well then, do you have any insider tips for making money? Can you tell me any Kentucky Derby winners?" he asked, remembering hearing about how much had been bet and won in the recently run race.

"You know I really don't know much about horse racing. The only thing I know about the Kentucky Derby is sometime around now a horse named

Secretariat will win, although that won't really help you", said Dr. Tew.

"Smooth, but not as good as the rest of your performance today", thought David, feeling a little more in control. He instead said, "Nope, that's no good, he won a few years ago. How about a hot stock tip?"

"Well, over the next few years you could try the Magellan Fund, or Microsoft, but that's not really going to help you much either," said Doc. "But you know, I don't really keep up with the market that much. I'm sure there were lots of great opportunities missed."

"Micro-soft? Sounds like my brain in a German final," David couldn't help joking to himself. Why wasn't this going to matter? Were these guys going to take him away? That would sort of be incongruous with their story line that he was going to be around until he was 80 years old. Were they going to dope him with something so he wouldn't remember today? He decided to try to remember that Micro-soft name, just in case.

"Alright, then, maybe you know something about sports in Atlanta. Anything big to report?" asked David, realizing there was no way to verify this, but maybe their story would expose something else.

Dr. Tew replied, "Well, the Olympics were held in Atlanta in 1996."

"Whoa..." thought David, caught up in the fantasy being spun, *"that would be cool."* He didn't know much about the Olympics himself, so he decided to refine his question. "Do the Braves ever win the World Series?" he quizzed.

With this the eyes of the other three all became a little more animated and almost as if they were trying to hold something back. Dr. Tew nodded a short affirmation.

"When?"

"1995."

"1995!?" asked an exasperated David. He had hoped that if these guys were going to make up a story, they could come up with something really fantastic, something really unbelievable, something more immediate. "By then I'll be ...38 years old! Do you realize how old that is?"

"Tell me," said Dr. Tew smugly, trying not to feel offended by the youthful perspective of his breakfast companion.

"And that's just the first time," said Doc, knowingly, smiling at Dr. Tew, who now seemed to be as interested as David in what Doc might reveal next. "The Braves won more consecutive division championships during that run than any team, in any sport, ever! It was a great era in Atlanta sports.

"Bingo!" thought David, knowing it was just a matter of time until the truly unbelievable would be uttered and expose the charade. "Wow!" he said laughingly, a little disappointed to face the reality that such a thing could never actually happen in his lifetime. Nevertheless, he decided to play along.

"I'm sure I must go to the game — maybe they even let me play?" he said, trying to make a joke to show he was still in control of his senses.

"No," said Doc, "you spend that Saturday night at home with a three-year-old princess named Rebekah and one-year-old prince named Lloyd and your wife in her second trimester of pregnancy with your third child. None of them nearly as impressed by the fact that the Atlanta Braves, the team you have died for since they came to Atlanta, are about to win the greatest, most suspenseful baseball game ever played in Atlanta. But do you know what? At that point in time, you like being a husband and dad so much, that's the way you want it. So you hear some of it on the radio, see some of it on TV, and in the end they win it — a score of 1-0, *a one-hitter* — without your help."

"Whoa... what an imagination," David thought. David was searching for clues or errors in what they said, lacking the apparent advantage that the prescient others claimed to hold. The names of his "children" were simple enough to make up, both family names. But what about his wife? "You didn't mention my wife's name," said David.

"Oh, she's 'Kitty'", said Doc.

"Oh no!" thought David. *"What happened to Kay? Can't she at least be a part of this fantasy?"* The only 'Kitty' he had known had been the short, squatty little old lady with gray hair in a bun who had been his great-aunt when he was a boy. Repulsed by the thought of the future life they were painting for him with some squatty woman named Kitty, he avoided the urge to make further humor with the comment he thought nonetheless, *"Hey, I'm trying to eat my breakfast here!"* and he chose instead to redirect the interview.

"So what's it like to live in the future?" asked David, facetiously. He was immediately surprised by the solemn tone in Pops' voice.

"The future is certainly an incredible place, but the important things, or the things that should be important, don't really change. I can remember the biggest pleasures in my grandparent's lives, in my parents' lives, weren't the things they could own or buy. They were so much more focused on their families."

"The people you see every day and who may seem important in your life right now will, for the most part, move on after college. Enjoy them now for a season and invest yourself in a few, but don't do so at the expense of your family. In 30 years you won't be in contact with most of these people but you'll still have five brothers and sisters who care for you very much, your wife, her family, your parents, your kids. You need to stay plugged-in to their lives along the way, and with any spare time that's remaining you can create your second circle of friends. Family will always be first, don't treat them like inferiors. It pains me to see people who would rather spend their weekends, vacations, even holidays with other people than their families. What kind of message does that send?"

"I didn't really expect a sermonette for breakfast," thought David, his appetite now awakened by the pancakes he ate as he listened to Pops' mulling. He

had gotten along so much better with his sisters now that he rarely saw them that he wasn't sure about all this family stuff. There would be time for that when he was old. For now he politely nodded his head in agreement and kept listening.

"I thought I'd be wiser at this point in my life, I thought I'd know more," admitted Pops. "It seems like every day I think or do something stupid, something regretful, something hurtful. When do we learn?"

There was silence which revealed only the distant clinking of utensils in the kitchen. Dr. Tew and Doc seemed to be equally interested in hearing what Pops had to say, perhaps even more so than David. *"They certainly know how to act sincere,"* thought the still dubious David.

Doc now weighed in with his thoughts, "You are right, of course. The other big difference for me is to realize how much I've changed. I was walking along the street the other day and looked across in a big window. There was an old man looking back. I more expected to see a 20-year-old student, but the characteristic gait and posture of advancing age was there for me, and all the world, to see. I can't believe that old man is me. What must I look like to a young girl like Vicki Post? Yet I can still have very youthful urges in the presence of such a fair miss. Thoughts she might think shocking from me, but accept as natural from Rex or you. Still, I am you. I close my eyes and I feel 20 years old — or 80 on the days when my arthritis flares," he said with a wink to Pops.

David, not wanting his secret thoughts dragged into this conversation, felt a little uncomfortable with this turn in the discussion, and having nothing to say, said nothing. Dr. Tew expounded upon Doc's thoughts.

"Believe me, those young girls wouldn't give you a second thought when you're forty either. For them, forty and sixty are about the same. Here I am at the prime of my life and they don't even realize it."

In unison a chorus of three pairs of eyebrows responded in disbelief, the right dipping as the left raised. Doc had to respond, and did so heatedly.

"Why don't you grow up? I saw you looking at Vicki like you were God's answer to single-handedly solve the world's under-population problem."

Pops looked at David and pursed his lips to contain the laugh that might have otherwise escaped with this poor analogy. If Doc noticed, he didn't slow down.

"You've got a wonderful wife. One perfect woman in your lifetime should be enough. Why even think about entertaining anyone else at all, an inferior one at that!"

"You're being a little hard on yourself," Pops interjected straight-faced, but enjoying the uniqueness of the situation and hoping to lighten the mood. He had not come here to fight.

David was curious to hear more about his supposed wife, and the tempers that were working up between Doc and Dr. Tew. *"Their little birthday trick seems to be taking a detour,"* thought David. *"A cat fight might be just what this group needs to open up the conversation. Maybe they'll tip their hands and I'll understand what's actually going on here."*

"Well, I'm embarrassed to think how unappreciative he can be to such a wonderful woman. The day he decides to treat her right will be the turning point in his marriage, and in his life."

"I treat her just fine," spat back Dr. Tew.

"'Just fine' isn't good enough. She deserves to be treated like a woman who has stood behind you all the way for...thirteen years," said Doc, doing some quick math in his head. "At this point in your life she's given you three great kids, and two more will follow," which had David and Dr. Tew both open their eyes a little wider. "When was the last time you looked at her like you looked at Vicki Post this morning at the stairwell?"

"She doesn't look like Vicki Post," countered Dr. Tew.

"She shouldn't have to. In your mind, she should look even better. She is your life's mate." Continuing with a pointed finger directed at Dr. Tew, Doc said slowly and emphatically, "Don't you ever forget it. Don't criticize her for the way she looks, for the way she cooks, or for the way she does the thousands of other things that represent her acts of love toward you on a daily basis."

"I don't criticize her," spewed Dr. Tew.

"Oh, not so it would show on paper,' replied Doc, "but she is the butt of your lame jokes, which should never be the case, in private or in public."

"Come on, it's just a little biting or sarcastic, but cutting-edge humor — it's funny," pleaded Dr. Tew, sounding a little defensive now. "If she can't take a joke—"

Doc interrupted his sentence. "It's not funny if it's mean. Sarcasm is cloaked sadism. You have to enjoy hurting other people. The fact of the matter is she would be justified in setting you straight. Unfortunately, for you and her you won't get it right for a few more years. Instead, you just get worse, more egocentric, more impressed with yourself — before you finally realize how good your life is right now."

"This is getting good," thought David.

"I give her all she needs and more," said Dr. Tew.

"She doesn't 'need' you, she 'wants' you," said Pops, softly, not trying to be funny.

"Then in the end, you both wind up with more money than you need, probably as much as if you had gotten in on Microsoft earlier, and not because of what you do, but because of what she does," added Pops.

"Now this I've got to hear," said Dr. Tew.

"No." he said, spreading his hands on the table. "I've already said we're not here today to play a prospective 'This is Your Life' or see how we can sensory overload David with incredible information about the future. There is no need to spoil that for David. We've already said more than we need to," said Pops.

There was a pause in which no one said anything. David waited to see where the script would lead.

"But since you've been so high-minded and uppity all day, you need to hear this," began Pops.

"No, I'll tell it," said Doc. "It's my story."

Pops shrugged and nodded to Doc as he said, "OK".

"After I turned fifty I became increasingly dissatisfied with the practice of medicine, or should I say I became dissatisfied with the interference with the practice of medicine. It seemed like the tail was wagging the dog. The insurance companies and the government were increasingly telling patients and doctors what to do, when to do it and how to do it. More and more requirements were being placed on doctors, adding expensive layers of cost that had nothing to do with providing good care. How many different computer codes do I really need to be able to record an accurate diagnoses? But every year the government seemed to redefine the codes and require I use them, and then I'd have to replace all my paper billing sheets, and reprogram all my computerized electronic billing, all at considerable cost and inconvenience, but for what?! I still get mad just thinking about it. But let me get off my soap box and continue."

"I decided to get involved in the politics of medicine, so over the years I ultimately became a delegate to the American Medical Association," at which an impressed Dr. Tew widened his eyes and nodded his head in tribute to such an accomplishment, in doing so easing some of the tension that had just been generated. "It was at the annual meeting in Chicago in the year 2015, and the US presidential election was already starting to heat up. Senator Couric, one of the candidates for president that year, was there to address the delegates. In the question and answer session I was selected for a question, and had a question all prepared that was about three levels deep into the problems of medicine. But the senator addressed most of my concerns in the question just before mine. I didn't want to listen to another version of the same pabulum, so I changed my question, right there at the microphone, with all the national press cameras spinning and flashing."

"Now I should preface this by telling you that in 2008 we remodeled the house, and Kitty and I wanted to put in some good toilets, toilets you don't have to flush three times to get the job done. Ever since 1992, when the Congress passed legislation prohibiting the use of normal toilets and showerheads, all residential-type toilets manufactured in the U.S. could use no more than 1.6 gallons per flush. Shower heads are limited to 2.5 gpm, I mean gallons of water per minute — believe me, I am now an expert in the stimulating history of plumbing legislation. But I digress. The short end to the remodeling story is that it couldn't be done, we had to buy geriatric toilets because they flush better with their taller and deeper bowls, and we had a friend buy us a shower massager in Thailand — it's great."

"Anyway, I'm standing there in front of Senator Couric, wondering if the senator from the great state of New York had already flushed three times today and suffered the lower water flow of a showerhead that is reminiscent of a gnat with an enlarged prostate, or if senators were spared such inconveniences in their world. So, in about that many words, I pointed out that since the flooding of 2009 and 2015 it seemed that with all the extra water around what this country needed was a good toilet, and if elected president, what would she do about it. At first there was stunned silence, then laughter, then applause, then a standing ovation. Apparently, I had struck a raw nerve with the American public. In an otherwise slow news day, the press was all over this like white on rice. Every major network and cable news show had my question to her as their lead story for the next twenty four hours, and her stammering reply. One columnist said 'she suffered from constipation of ideas' at that instant. In a campaign that to that point had been nothing but a beauty contest, toilets became a hot button issue. Every candidate jockeyed for a position that would prove favorable to the "Pee-Party", as the issue was labeled, while all the polls showed that the number one litmus test for a presidential voter that year would be proposed toilet and showerhead legislation. I was on all the talk shows and gave interviews to who knows how many journalists. Fortunately, the AMA helped handle the nightmare of scheduling and details and provided me a press agent. I was on the cover of Newsweek and some lesser magazines, and all the journalists started calling me 'Doc', which has stuck."

"Until you have grandkids, and then you'll be 'Pops'," inserted Pops.

"Can't wait," replied Doc as an aside. "But anyway, they like to interview me because at that point, what do I have to lose? I became a bit of an anti-establishment folk hero. A couple of plumbing manufacturers offered me good money to endorse their products, but of course even their products were suboptimal, and I said so, but they paid me anyway — a lot! I was a hot ticket item."

"The issue eventually got put on the back burner, but not before it derailed the Supreme Court nomination of Judge Lipscomb when it was leaked that she had an illegal high-volume toilet in her recently built home. So I had my fifteen minutes of fame, but still no good toilet legislation."

"So I get rich off of inadequate plumbing?" asked Dr. Tew.

"Well I told you all of that so I could tell you this," continued Doc, with a mild air of superiority. "During this time a woman reporter decided to do a story on 'the woman behind the man' to find out more about Kitty and what she was like, and to see what she had to say about what it was like being married to a firebrand like me. Kitty was, of course, her usual calm, reserved, pleasant self, and really didn't say anything the reporter could use. As the interview was wrapping up the reporter asked her if Doc was a funny person, and she responded, 'he thinks he is,' not meaning anything at all by it. The reporter asked her what she meant by that and she explained how the whole time I've known her that whenever I've cracked a joke to her, whether she laughs or not, I tell her, 'you ought to be writing this down'. Well son of a gun, unbeknownst to me, she was writing them down, *all of them*, sometimes once a week, sometimes five a day, but she had a couple of notebooks-worth of things I'd said. The reporter asked her if she could look at the notebooks sometime, and Kitty said sure, there was nothing to hide — Kitty even made copies for her because she didn't want to inconvenience her and didn't want to risk losing the books. She considered the jokes a love letter of sort, spoken in my love language of flirting and humor, regardless the topic. Oftentimes she had jotted a note along with the joke to better put it in context of the events of that day, or she wrote her own thoughts and response, verbalized or not, in the margin. If she didn't understand the joke she'd write that down. If she thought she did understand it, even though as it turned out sometimes she didn't, she'd write about that, too."

"So this woman reporter takes these notes, and thinks they are a hoot. Sometimes she laughs at what I said, but more often, she laughs at what Kitty thought, correctly or otherwise about the joke. Some of the funniest things Kitty writes are about jokes that totally went over her head, but the women readers seemed to like how she used the jokes to comment on being married to me and what it meant to her, and her warmth and wisdom in marriage are obvious. You see, this lady reporter, Jean Jennings is her name, showed the notes to her editor. They both decide there's a lot more there than a story, there's a book. So she writes the book as a ghostwriter for Kitty, and they make a 70-30 split. The book is a roaring success, blows away the other non-fiction for the New York Times, sells over seven million in hard back alone, and all this money pouring in with a book written by Kitty that she didn't write. She did a little editing and clarification, but this Jean Jennings is really a good writer, and writes exactly like Kitty thinks, it's scary how good she is. Now there is a great wave of attention for Kitty and this book, called "Survival Guide for the Wife of a Wit". Kitty did a lot of book signings and media events that year, and she was just a natural for connecting with men and women across the country. She made it look so easy, but she knew exactly what she was doing. She's really good at it — a lot smarter and funnier than I could ever hope to be."

"The book made me take a look at the things I said, and why I said them. Up to that point in my life I didn't much care if I said something that hurt someone's feelings as long as I could claim I had just been trying to be funny. I had never given it much thought up to that point — maybe it was a power grab on my part. But whatever it was, it wasn't considerate. I'm sure my siblings would have had a more pleasant childhood if I had learned my lesson much sooner. You see, as I read Kitty's book, I was ashamed about some parts of the book because the humor did have a cynical and sarcastic bite at times. To most readers it was just that, cynical humor, but I realized how often I had said something that could have been hurtful to her and to others I was supposed to love. I have explained it to Kitty, that I shouldn't have been so sarcastic towards her. Sure, most of the rest, OK, all of the rest of what I said *was* funny," he said vainly.

"She, of course, was very gracious, insisting I was just trying to be funny. See — even there she got to zing me without realizing she was doing it! She said I was just *trying* to be funny, not that I *was* funny. But she was right."

"The book changed me, and more for what I read than for the millions of dollars it earned us. You see, the merchandising, which included an incredibly popular line of greeting cards, earned more than the book, and Kitty had to do almost nothing for her cut of that. Jean wanted her to write another book, but Kitty didn't want to have to try to write something else, and had nothing left to say."

Pops then picked up the story, as now Doc joined David and Dr. Tew listening to the future unfold. "But even more happens that you don't yet know. Jean convinced Kitty to let Jean write a sequel, not based on anything Kitty says, but just in keeping with the theme — stuff Jean makes up. So they reached a licensing agreement and Kitty still gets a percentage on the sequels she 'writes', even though Jean does all the work on this now and Kitty just does a final read and edit on the follow-up books — there were more — and we made more money after I turned sixty than all the years in medicine before. But that is a burden within itself. I feel a great responsibility now deciding what to do with all this money I will leave behind," Pops said with less energy.

His energy returned as he added quickly, "So, be careful what you say about toilets." Ending his soliloquy this way earned him a laugh from the crowd, especially David, who continued to try to put this all together. He was still very perplexed by this whole thing — the instant banker number, the personal trivia. There was, of course, the undeniable physical resemblance that seemed very real. Somehow, however, he felt more comforted, less alarmed by the easy manner of storytelling that had unfolded during breakfast, and he was able to enjoy the entertainment as he tried to figure out what it meant.

David looked around the cafeteria and realized that by now everything was likely closed down and being prepared for lunch, but he was in no particular hurry to leave, his breakfast club seemed in no desire to leave, and the student-employee mopping the floor, now on their level, didn't appear to have any concerns that they were lingering, so David listened to a half-hearted attempt by Dr. Tew to once again justify his humor. David knew that he personally would never treat a woman like that. Sure, he tried to make jokes, and sometimes they were at other people's expense, but wasn't that what humor was all about, twisting the reality of a situation? Perhaps part of the birthday present was to create a sort of "This Is Your Life" in reverse. These guys were supposed to tell stories that put David into the future, for some reason — comedic entertainment, to teach a moral, whatever. It was an interesting idea, so David decided to test it further, and maybe learn more about them in the process.

"So you are telling me that the things that have happened to you are the things that will happen to me?" asked David, trying to allow them to think he understood what was going on.

"Well, yes, I guess you could phrase it that way," said Doc.

David remembered Dr. Tew's story about playing in a band for gerbils. "You mean all that fuss over two gerbils, it really does happen? To me, in a gerbil band?

"Next year," said Dr. Tew. "Mad-man didn't get into med school that year — he did the next year but by that time was having such a good time in graduate school that he turned them down — so he returned to UGA to work on his master's degree in chemistry. He elected to continue to live in Reed Hall rather than the more stuffy graduate student housing. He arrived with two gerbils in the fall. For some reason he was really into gerbils for a while. He would sit in study hall doodling pictures of gerbils, and he created a panel of graffiti in the second floor bathroom stall that was an ongoing saga about "The Adventures of Harry the Gerbil". He took his gerbils very seriously. The other students found out about them and wanted to keep them for Mad-man when he was gone for the weekend. It got to the point where the students would sign up for a night to keep the gerbils, whether Mad-man was gone or not. Since the gerbils were especially popular with the girls, Mad-man loved all the attention, and the rest is history."

"The students even erected a memorial statue to the gerbils in the Reed Quad and Mad-man was asked to draw up a design for the statue of a gerbil. The statue was created by some of the sculpture students and it looked really good. Mad-man was *proud* of that statue. He said it was the highlight of his life. The Gerbil Jam Jazz Band was put back together to play for the dedication of the statue. I couldn't tell you about that initially because you'd think it should be there now — but it's still there."

"Well, not exactly," corrected Doc. When they remodeled Reed Hall the gerbil statue disappeared just before the rededication of the building in 1998. Mad-man told me about it when I was there for a football game the following fall. He was still really viscerally angry at the administration for removing his statue. I don't think I've ever seen him that mad about anything."

"You see Mad-man in Athens in 1998? What was he doing there?" asked David, temporarily allowing for a willful suspension of his disbelief.

"He was a full professor in the Department of Chemistry by that time."

"Whoa," chuckled David slowly as Doc nodded in confirmation.

"He had written a letter to the *Red and Black*, in Rex Lee's name, of course, criticizing the students as a bunch of wimps for not protesting to the administration the removal of an icon that embodied the spirit of student power and autonomy. Nobody took the bait, and nothing further happened, except some offended student — or professor — found Rex Lee's house near Atlanta and had the yard covered in toilet paper and a big 'WIMP' spray-painted onto his driveway the next weekend. Mad-man took me by his lab that weekend and while we were there he showed me a copy of the crime report that had been printed in Rex's hometown paper and reprinted in *The Red and Black*."

During that revelation Dr. Tew and David had erupted in laughter which now continued.

"So somebody got mad at Rex for calling them wimps, but nothing became of the gerbil?" asked David when he stopped laughing.

"Well, not exactly," Pops started. "I've already told you I'm not here to give a prospective history lesson — that's not the purpose of today. But I've *got* to tell you this. When Mad-man became President of the University —"

His speech was now inaudible, completely drowned out by the absolute gut-splitting howls of laughter that convulsed from the bodies of the other three as they slapped the table, their thighs, or one anothers' backs as they heard this news. Mad-man Madison had become President of the University of Georgia?!

He started again, "In 2019 when Mad-man became President of the University one of the many positive contributions he made during his administration was to spearhead a vast and ambitious campus beautification project. An incredible amount of funding was raised, individual sectors of the campus were almost entirely razed and replanted, large trees were relocated as avenues and walkways were re-routed into more curving, wandering byways. Fountains and reflecting pools were installed. Magnolias, azalea, dogwood, forsythia — you name it — if it grows well in Georgia it was planted in great, profuse display. The federal government took note of the project and poured in even more money to encourage other universities to preserve and emphasize their heritage with indigenous plants and pollution-free walkways. Dr. Madison was very involved in almost every aspect of planning and integrating the various stages as they were developed, working hand-in-hand with the well-respected dean of the School of Landscape Architecture, Dean Smith, who brought into reality all the suggestions that Dr. Madison had to give. Mad-man received an enormous amount of national attention for his undying devotion to the project. The Vice President of the United States even came to Athens for the final dedication and ribbon cutting ceremony. During the dedication ceremony Senator Hudson praised Dr. Madison for the maturity, vitality and vision he was bringing to the office. This was a cloaked reference to the initial concerns that he was too old for the job when he was first inaugurated as president."

"Once the massive beautification project was completed, there was always a large satellite photo of the entire campus on the wall behind Mad-man's desk in the office of the president, the desk he always sat at to have his official photos made or to hold television interviews, with that picture always in the background. Now you may think it is just a coincidence, and Mad-man would deny it to his grave, but if you're looking for it, when viewed from the satellite the outline of the campus and its streets and plantings seems to resemble an abstract of two gerbils... 'cavorting'."

With this ending the laughter and pounding on the table returned, even louder than before. Doc's face reddened from the brief inhalations that could not gasp enough air to compensate for the volumes of racking, uncontrolled gales of asphyxiating laughter that flowed. Dr. Tew's face was a contortion of sheer pleasure despite tears streaming down both cheeks. Even David laughed like the good audience he was, caught up in this fantasy — what a good storyteller that Pops was, his animated eyes and hands building the story as he developed it.

When the laughter died down they looked around and noted their level of the cafeteria was deserted. The mopping was done and its pusher had returned to the upper level. The background kitchen sounds were quieter now, and breakfast was over.

"Well," said David, "that was a fun meal. I don't know how you guys pulled this off, and I don't know who writes your material, but this has been a breakfast I'll never forget. I don't know how to thank-you."

"Oh, there's no need to thank us," said Pops. "Just make sure we get invited over to the birthday party with Kay today."

Chapter 13
Walking Back

David sat silently in his chair as he looked across at Doc and Dr. Tew and tried to process what Pops had just proposed. To this point the morning had been fun — weird but fun. Very spontaneous, unplanned, improvised — just like good jazz. But he knew women. When it came to showing off their domestic skills and hosting visitors, they preferred to proceed as if performing a well-rehearsed symphony. Everything would be written out and choreographed to work perfectly for the desired effect. Kay would want this afternoon to follow a scripted plan that she had already drawn out in her mind. She had probably already set the table for two — with silverware and a table cloth, probably even candles, despite the daylight hour. She had likely made a centerpiece from the late blooming azaleas or perhaps some of the pansies still in bloom in the community plantings bordering her apartment complex's parking lot. The menu was planned, background music selected, the meal half cooked, her ideas for ways to surprise him already etched in stone. Now Pops wanted him to call her and tell her there would be a slight last-minute change in the guest list?

Not to mention the fact that, while these guys were fun and definitely interesting, he didn't want to share what limited time he had with Kay today with them.

"I don't think that's a good idea," said David, unable to think of a way to say it more tactfully.

"Oh now, come on, David, we're your own flesh and blood —"

"Literally —" offered Doc.

Pops continued, "I don't think she'd mind. She's a great hostess, and you know it. Just call her and see what she says."

"Have you met her? How do you know her to say she's a great hostess...how do you even know I have a lunch date with her?"

"David, you've just got to trust us and believe us. If we can prove without a doubt that we're out to do no harm, can you trust us? Why don't you believe us?"

"How am I supposed to explain to her who you are?" asked David, playing through the possible scenarios that would develop if they started trying to convince her of the story they had told him.

"Just tell her we're your uncles, or uncle, great-uncle and great-great uncle," said Doc.

"Well, I'm not sure that would be all that believable... With all due respect, I don't think that Pops looks anything close to being 20 years older than you, Doc. And Kay works at a nursing home, she knows what old people look like," he said, completing his thought before thinking it through.

"Thanks a lot!" snapped Doc, more for theatrical intent and simply to make certain David measured his words better in the future. Meanwhile Pops slumped over against Doc's shoulder, consoling him while laughing.

"So my three uncles just show up out of the blue on the last day I'm in town?"

"Exactly," said Dr. Tew. "Tell her we're here to help you pack."

"Hah! What have I got to pack but a trombone and a duffle bag. Kay would know that was a lie."

"Alright then," continued Dr. Tew, "tell her we're in town for a medical meeting... we're staying at the Holiday Inn."

David threw up another objection: "But she's only cooking a meal for two."

"Since you're going to meet her at 2:00, we can tell her we've already eaten at the Holiday Inn'" said Dr. Tew, who was apparently more thoroughly practiced in the art of deception .

Their discussion was temporarily interrupted by the dining hall manager who had been patiently standing near the table for the last few minutes, unnoticed by any of them. "Are you gentlemen about finished? We need to collect your dishes and clean your table before we open for lunch at eleven o'clock," he said.

Embarrassed a little to have inconvenienced anyone by such a blatant disregard for the time, all four men rose and headed for the upper level as they thanked the manager and apologized for the delayed exit. They took their trays to the drop-off counter and headed outside for the walk back to Reed Hall.

The foursome looked to be in no particular hurry as they sauntered along the broad tree-line walks of the nation's first state chartered institution of higher learning, the conversation more lively than their progress. As they approached the huge oaks which marked the sidewalk of Baxter Street, David attempted to summarize what the other three, with Pops taking the role as the point-man, had continued to argue that David should do. He was starting to feel more than a little nervous about this whole proposition, but these guys weren't backing down. He almost feared how they might sabotage his afternoon with Kay, well-intentioned though they might be, if he didn't somehow gain control of the situation. As they arrived back in the room, he realized he had made no headway in the debate, Pops was so emphatic, but perhaps they had one good point. She was an adult. Let her decide for herself. At least ask her if they could come, and if she said "no," so be it. The confidence with which Pops negotiated that point made David wonder if perhaps he didn't already know the outcome. Could he possibly be in cahoots with Kay? Had she been the one behind all of this? At this point he didn't see how she could have done this. He didn't see how anyone could have done this. Now they were asking him to lie to Kay. But that would certainly be better than trying to explain the truth. Nevertheless, he had a hunch now that Kay was somehow in on this, so he would try to make it easy on her and go along with whatever plan she had developed.

"So you're OK with that?...You're sure...Um, OK...Yeah, Great! We'll see you soon. Bye!"
Dr. Tew and Doc were sitting on David's bed with their backs against the wall, smiling as they listened, while Pops was standing eagerly beside David with his arms folded in anticipation across his chest, eyebrows raised. As soon as the phone was in the hook Pops asked, "So what did she say?"
"Well, she was glad to hear how well the Organic Chemistry final went — Oh, man!" He interrupted himself, "I forgot to ask how her Qualitative Chemistry final went! Oh, well, I'll ask her at lunch."
"No," said Pops, patiently, "What did she say about lunch?"
"Oh yeah, that," he teased in reply. "She believed all the stuff about you being my uncles, that you're not coming to eat, and that you'll be no trouble at all. She didn't seem disappointed or put out at all. So I guess you're invited."
"Was that all?" asked Pops as the others listened in on their afternoon plans.
"Well...she said we should come on over now," said David.
"Yes!" cheered Pops.
"But first," said David, "I'm taking a little trip to the bathroom to powder my nose." With that he opened the top drawer of his dresser, opened the bottle of British Sterling, patted a little cologne on either side of his neck, closed the bottle and then the drawer, and headed out of the room. Pops headed to David's desk, sat down, considerately folded David's discarded shirt from the day before, and began to examine the desktop's contents with no particular intent.
After a minute Dr. Tew got up from his place on the bed, stretched to relieve a stiffness that was not there, casually went over to the dresser, opened the top drawer, splashed on a bit of British Sterling, then saying nothing, headed toward the bathroom.
Another 30 seconds of silence later Doc, smiling, said to Pops, "I'm in!" rose and went to the dresser where he also dabbed on a bit of the British Sterling. Without looking at Pops he simply said, "I'll be back," as he headed out the door, knowing Pops would figure out where he was going.
Alone in the room, Pops stood and walked over to the dresser. He located the well-used bottle of British Sterling and applied an appropriate amount to each side of his neck below his beard line, then an extra measure on his shirt across his chest. He returned the British Sterling to the drawer and located David's hairbrush, and then moved over to the mirror where he brushed his hair, then his beard with great attention to detail, finally gently smoothing hair and beard with his fingertips when he was done, to transfer whatever fragrance remained on his

hands.

David returned to the room just after Pops had returned the brush to its rightful place and returned to his seat at the desk. "Don't you want to take advantage of the bathroom before we leave?" asked David.

Pops stood and answered David as he headed toward the door, "I'm on my way. I just didn't think we could all use that urinal at the same time."

The walk to Riverside apartments was a brief one, made briefer by the now brisk strides that Pops took as he led the way to Kay's. Dr. Tew and David kept up with Pops' pace, and Doc followed a little slower from behind. As they walked the conversation turned to birthday presents.

"What do you think she's going to give you for your birthday present?" asked Doc, his question punctuated with an involuntary huff for added measure.

"I hadn't really thought about it," said David back over his shoulder, continuing Pops' tempo. "I think this may be the first birthday that I haven't asked anyone, even my parents, for anything for my birthday. All she mentioned was cooking lunch for me, so that's really all I'm expecting."

"You don't think she'll give you a gift?" asked Dr. Tew. "Women care about things like that. She'll give you a gift," he pontificated, knowingly.

"What makes you so sure?" asked David, to which Dr. Tew rolled his eyes, as David answered his own question, "OK, I know, I know, I'm supposed to believe that you are me, I am you, you've been here before."

"So do you want to know what it is?" asked Dr. Tew, with a bit of an attitude.

"Of course not," replied David, but then to continue testing this day-long trick which was being played so successfully on him, he said, "Well, OK then, tell me what color it is."

"Beige," stated Dr. Tew, "in a white box."

"But if you and Kay are in this together, you could easily know that information...beige, huh?"

The group was now approaching the Riverside parking lot, and David could see Kay's sparkling aqua 1976 Vega parked in its usual spot. It had been a high school graduation gift from her grandmother, actually her step-grandmother, and she treated it in a way that showed just how much she appreciated the very generous gift.

Dr. Tew and Doc paused briefly at her car to admire it. Doc asked, "Is this her car?" as Pops forged on ahead, calling back to the other three, "Come on you guys, let's go meet Kay!"

They ascended the single flight of stairs that led up to the second floor exterior walkway which led to Kay's apartment. Pops stopped first, just past the door with "2113" on it and waited as first David, then Dr. Tew and finally Doc arrived. David knocked three times, and almost instantly Kay's voice shouted, "Coming!" and she opened the door.

Chapter 14
Kay

Kay Powell was born in West Palm Beach, Florida on November 13, 1958 as her parents were completing yet another stop in the nomadic career of a U.S. Air Force pilot. The eldest of four children, she rapidly developed the finest traits of responsibility, leadership, honesty, efficiency and adaptability that might be impressed upon a child in her position. Her great intellect was wrapped in a warm and engaging personality that lifted those around her, and balanced by extraordinary musical talent, first on the piano and later the clarinet. As if that were not enough, exercise, elegance and estrogen commingled perfectly into a finished creation of outstanding physical beauty.

Colonel Powell's precipitous retirement from the Air Force, a characteristically unselfish decision by her parents to avoid further overseas assignment at a stage in life when their children were entering the critical time of high school and college, had found the Powells retiring to Peachtree City, Georgia. That spring Kay graduated from her Illinois high school as valedictorian of the Class of '76, then immediately moved to Georgia.

This sudden change in family plans also required that Kay redirect her expectations for college. In-state tuition rates and geographic convenience logically narrowed her choices to but a few, and the University of Georgia became her selection. She had to scramble to meet admission deadlines, but she was easily accepted. Not so easy, however, was finding an open dormitory with such a late start. She considered herself lucky that she had been able to find an opening in Riverside Apartments, immediately adjacent to the eastern boundary of the campus. Her roommate was Jenny Montgomery, a junior year education major, who already held the lease to the apartment but suddenly needed a roommate when her previous roommate decided to leave UGA for reasons of matrimony.

The year at UGA had gone well for Kay, extremely well. She had maintained a stellar academic record in the Honors program while she breezed through the core classes that were required to earn her degree. The Honors program had been great for her for a number of reasons. The best part about the program, she would claim, was meeting David in their Honors English 105 class winter quarter. David would always say it was the only English class he ever looked forward to attending on a daily basis, and that Providence must have been working overtime when he had been unable to schedule English during his freshman year and thus waited to take it as a sophomore with a class that was primarily freshmen.

Honors English 105 was a small class of twelve students who sat around a large wooden table with the professor, Dr. Harris, at the head. The first day in class David had sat on the right side of the table on the corner farthest away from Dr. Harris. Kay had arrived earlier and taken the seat beside Dr. Harris, also on the right. As a result, David's view of Kay was screened for the first several minutes of the class.

David estimated that Dr. Harris was about 60 years old. He had a shiny bald head and trim body which were complemented by his brown woolen blazer, white dress shirt and dark brown knitted tie. Nothing about his appearance conflicted with his profession.

Dr. Harris had each student stand and give a brief introduction. David was awestruck by the final student who introduced herself as "Kay Powell". She was composed, confident, and comfortable speaking before the group. She was beautiful! He suddenly wished he knew more about the Air Force, Illinois, and English that her mother taught in middle school. His mind raced digesting this information so thoroughly that he almost missed the part about "Peachtree City", but when he heard that he knew he had an ice-breaker! Peachtree City was in Fayette County; all the kids went to Fayette County High School, as did anybody else who lived in the county. Unless she had gone to a private school, she would have gone there too. Why hadn't he known her in high school? They must know some of the same people. He could ask her about that after class. Maybe not today, since he did not want to seem too aggressive. He had all quarter. He wanted to make a good first impression, not rush things. He was chicken.

In such a small class, participation in discussions of literature was mandatory, a significant part of the grade. With Dr. Harris' direction, such discussion and debate flowed easily from the students in attendance beginning that first day. Even amongst a class of honors students, Kay stood out as the most well read, the best prepared, the most interested, and the most articulate. More than once her insight inspired Dr. Harris to praise her intellect to the rest of those gathered. "You will make a fine English educator, Miss Powell, just like your mother, I'm sure," he had said. David was happy for Kay to receive such praise, and glad to have one more piece of information about her. An English major... well, it could be worse.

Stimulating conversations were to be had in Dr. Harris' class — so stimulating that David usually felt compelled to seek additional intellectual fulfillment even after the class had officially ended by striking up a conversation with Kay as she walked down the hall out of the building, or even before they left the classroom. Anything to prolong the time spent with her, trying to make certain she knew he was a serious student, not just another Georgia boy trying to move in for the kill. If he ever hoped to date her, he sensed he first had to impress her that he was a serious student. He was committed to doing everything right this time.

His first opportunity to interact one-on-one with her in order to better expose his inward genius came as class ended that first day. She had remained and chatted briefly but politely with Dr. Harris. David had intentionally stayed at the table, busying himself with his book, backpack, pen and papers, seemingly engrossed in the complex decision-making process of where to put what when packing his backpack for the long five minute journey back to Reed Hall.

"Looks like we're in for an interesting quarter," he observed as she walked past, with a comment that would have earned a "C-" for creativity from Dr. Harris.

She kept walking as she nodded, smiled with pursed lips and said, "Indeed," then disappeared out the door.

Over time these conversations developed to a single sentence or two with an actual and identifiable topic. These initial discussions were always and only about a class subject. He did not want to seem too pushy. She might pause with him in the hall or they would walk toward the outside door together. Between class times David could spend hours at a time thinking about how to position himself by the door before class, where to sit at the table during class, what to say in the discussions after class, all to make certain to optimize the opportunity to make a good impression. He was chagrinned to realize how inept he felt in her presence. He had not been this nervous around a girl since his early high school days. After all his years of effort with nothing to show for it, he was committed to treating this lady right. He was not going to blow this chance. He would take things nice and easy. If he had known how immediately taken with him she was, he might have breathed a little easier.

After the second week or so he casually mentioned that he thought he heard her say she lived in Peachtree City, and that he was from Fayette County, too. He could probably give her a ride home if she ever needed one and he was headed that direction. She explained her connection to Peachtree City — she had lived there so briefly she did not really even know what county it was in. When he said they might have been at the same high school if she had moved into the county earlier, he thought he saw her eyes brighten. Or maybe not. She had not really responded to the offer for a ride, but then he had so nervously pushed the conversation on to high school that he had not given her the chance to say. Now if he brought it up again, he might look too assertive.

He came to cherish the time spent in his daily conversations with Kay, but he could not figure her out. She was so articulate, so energetic, so friendly, how would any guy ever know if she just wanted to be "friends"? At this point, if he asked her out on a date, he might blow the whole relationship he had been crafting over the past few weeks. What if she said, "No"? Then where did he go from there? She might get all paranoid about being around him discussing literature while he stood there making her feel as if he was stalking her.

As the days quickly flew by, he tormented himself wondering how to make their daily rendezvous mean more to her. She already seemed so refined, so complete, so content in her life, what could he possibly offer her? How could he smoothly slip into their conversation something about the fact that she was the most beautiful woman he had ever met, she was the most fascinating person on the entire campus at the University of Georgia, or that he knew he was going to marry her? There was never time to say much. She had to hurry off to her next class, French, which started only 15 minutes after English ended. Then one day as class was ending Dr. Harris helped out in a way that made David eternally grateful.

"Class, I am not inclined to give my students many opportunities for extra credit — I think you are given a fair opportunity to demonstrate your abilities in my class and on my tests. Extra credit can serve either of two functions. It may simply inflate the grade, or it can induce a student to seek independently a greater understanding of the topic studied. Frankly, no one in this class seems to need either. For that I must congratulate you. None of you plans to pursue a career in the study of English and yet I can truthfully say..."

David's mind went off task momentarily as he puzzled over Dr. Harris' praise. Wasn't Kay an English major? "*Listen!*" he reminded his wandering mind.

"...I cannot recall a recent class where I have been so challenged in my leadership role to stay ahead of my students. My profession would be enhanced were some of you to pursue further studies in this building," he continued. Was he giving a subtle nod toward Kay with that last remark?

"But I digress. This Saturday evening the on-campus film will be the Zeffirelli version of *Romeo and Juliet*. I believe you will find this to be one of the finest performances you will ever see — on stage or film — of this work. I would encourage each of you to see it, if you have not already. Given that this film was first released almost ten years ago, if you saw it then, you will probably appreciate it in a different light by seeing it again. We will have a brief discussion of the film at the beginning of class the next Monday, which is also our last day of class before the final exam Thursday, so we'll spend the rest of that day as a review and overview day. Those contributing to the discussion on *Romeo and Juliet* will receive an extra half point on their final course grade. I'm sorry to have held you a little long today. Class is dismissed."

David's head spun with thoughts as he tried to construct his next conversation with Kay. He wanted to find out what her major was, if not English. If she were this good in English class, she must really blow them out of the water in her major studies classes. That conversation would have to wait. Somehow he needed to find out if she planned to go to the movie.

"Do you plan to go to the movie?" he asked her. Realizing this might sound like an unwanted invitation, he casually added, "A half point is not really all that much extra credit."

"Well, I'd really like to see *Romeo and Juliet*," she countered, "regardless of the extra credit. I've always heard my mother say what a fine version that was. I just don't know. My parents don't like me out on the campus alone after dark but my roommate, who usually likes to do things with me on the weekend, is going home this weekend."

She looked at her watch as he held the door leading outside open for her. A brisk March wind chilled them both as they exited the building. David was shivering, not certain if it was the cold or the situation. "Ooo, I'd better get on to French," she said, with a voice that almost sounded regretful as she turned to go toward north campus.

David always went south to Reed Hall while she headed north to French, but today he was emboldened. Winter quarter would soon be over and he was an adult. What did he have to lose? He could always claim he was just trying to keep her safe.

"Well, let me walk with you to your French class," he offered. "You know, this campus can be kind of scary during daylight hours, too." "*Dumb thing to say!*" he immediately thought.

She giggled. He had never heard her do that before. It sounded sweet, gentle. *Wow!*

"Thanks for your gallantry," she said playfully, maintaining a quick walk toward French.

He bought himself a little time to build his courage while he talked about the sonnet they had just read in Dr. Harris' class. Finally, he emboldened himself with a deep breath and said, "So, umm, about *Romeo and Juliet*. I'd hate for you to miss it just because your roommate was out of town." "*Another dumb thing to say,*" he winced internally.

"Well, maybe they'll be showing it again some year," she said remorsefully, then gently bit her lower lip, realizing time was running short before her French class. Why was he dragging this out?!

"*She has such beautiful lips*," thought David.

"Well maybe I could help you out some way," "*Dumber thing to say!*" he immediately thought to himself. He panicked to realize how quickly they had arrived at the Foreign Languages building.

"Oh no, you shouldn't," she protested, pausing, tipping her head slightly to the right, bowing her head slightly, looking over at him, waiting, trying not to look at her watch.

"*Oh, no! What did she mean by that? Was this the brush-off he had been trying to avoid all quarter?*"

"OK," he said.

Then, in a flash of brilliance at the last possible second, he blurted out, "Well then, why don't you give me your phone number just in case I come up with something?"

"*Dumbest thing yet!*" he critiqued, yet she quickly flipped open the spiral notebook she was carrying, jotted her number and name, standing on her toes briefly as she wrote. She tore out the sheet and gave it to him, all the while quickly apologizing, "I'm so sorry, but I've just got to go. We have a test today. I look forward to hearing your plan." With that, she hurriedly disappeared into the building.

"Good luck on your test!" he called to the closing door.

"*You smooth dawg...*" he thought, proud of his accomplishment.

David unwrapped the paper again, studied the phone number again. Yes, it had seven digits. So far, so good. He had contemplated just what to do all afternoon and while he ate dinner that night at Bolton Hall with Rex.

"What's that paper?" Rex asked.

"Just some notes for my English class," David replied with the incomplete truth.

"Why do you keep looking at it? You don't usually try to study during supper."

"Just some important stuff I learned today that I wanted to review so I don't forget," he responded, all he said again being technically true.

David hid the note deeper in his pocket. He wanted to talk with Rex about it, but this all seemed so personal. He did not want any coarse jokes or suggestions from Rex. He could handle this alone.

He walked back toward the room with Rex, still not sure what he would do, but sure he would do it.

"What are y'all doing in English?" asked Rex as David yet again returned the paper to his pocket, not even opening it this time, not wanting to risk Rex seeing its contents.

"Same old stuff," answered David dispassionately. "And now Dr. Harris wants us to go see a stupid old movie for class credit."

"What movie?"

"*Romeo and Juliet* is playing at South PJ Saturday night. What a way to waste an evening!"

"Well what else were you going to do? Is this the British version?"

"I don't know. I thought they were all the British version. But come to think of it, he did say it was the Zipperelli version or something Italian like that."

"Yeah, I've heard of that version," said Rex. "I read that they originally offered the part of Romeo to Paul McCartney."

Rex certainly knew his musical trivia. David continued his feigned disinterest.

"Well, sounds like a waste of a good Saturday night."

"I tell you what," said the sympathetic Rex. "Why don't I go with you? It's only a buck for a ticket. We studied 'R and J' last spring when I took English. Maybe it makes more sense as a movie."

"Nah," said David. "I think a group from the class might go and you'd just be bored with a bunch of literature geeks."

"Good point," said Rex, glad to be off the hook.

They were soon back in their room. As per their evening routine, Rex grabbed his trumpet and headed off to the music building practice rooms, knowing David would be heading off to study in the study hall, late into the night. Tonight, however, David lagged behind, sitting at his desk, studying his treasured parchment. As soon as he was sure Rex was well on his way to practice he walked over to the phone, took a deep breath, swallowed, cleared his throat, tested his voice with a practice "Hello" and dialed the number.

A female voice answered on the fourth ring. "Hello, this is Kay Powell speaking."

"Um, hello Kay. This is David, David Patson from English class..."

"Oh yes, Mr. Patson. So you have a first name, do you 'Mr. Patson'," she said confidently. "I've only heard Dr. Harris call you 'Mr. Patson'. How are you, David?"

"*Is she kidding around with me,*" he asked himself nervously.

"I'm fine, thanks, and you?" he said, trying not to heave from anxiety.

"Well, I'm fine thank you," came the polite reply.

There was a painfully long silence. He started to sweat. Profusely. His mouth felt dry. "*Why didn't I drink more for supper?*"

"Uh, how did your French test go today?"

"Well it's very kind of you to call to ask. *Très bien, merci.* It was a pretty straight-forward test."

"Good...very good...," he said, wishing his phone cord was long enough to reach over to his desk chair or bed so he could sit down. He began to pace a small figure-eight pattern, constrained by the length of the phone cord.

More painful silence. David couldn't understand why his room had to be so hot. Then they both spoke something at the same time so the other couldn't hear. "Go ahead," he said, glad to yield the floor.

"No you go ahead," she replied.

"Ladies first," he said.

"No, I was just going to say that it was a pretty routine test and I hope I did well on it."

"Tell me," said David, relaxing ever so slightly. "did you realize that no one in our English class is an English major? I was kind of surprised. In fact, I kind of assumed that you were an English major, you do so well in there."

"Oh, no," she laughed, *that* laugh. "I don't think I could ever be an English major. I'm not cut out for that."

"So...what is your major?"

"Biology," she said, softer.

"Ha!" David exclaimed. "You don't seem like a Biology major!"

"Good," she said. "You know how most people view Biology majors — geeky, nerds, study-dogs...fairly boring and one-dimensional. I prefer to be more well-rounded." *"You got me there,"* he thought to himself. He couldn't help thinking about her well-roundedness.

"I find that I seem to enjoy hanging out with non-science folks more often than not," she added, her words making him cringe.

This was not going well.

"What is your major?" she asked.

"What do you guess?" he stalled, hoping for an enlightened answer he could not synthesize.

"Well, I had just assumed you were a Classics major or something like that until Dr. Harris made that remark about none of us being headed in that direction. You really seem to have a passion for the subject."

Now he had to laugh! "No, I have a passion for making an 'A' in that class. I have to come clean and admit that I'm a Biology major, too." Now the silence came from her end of the line.

He spoke. "Glad I don't strike you as a nerdy bio-geek!" And with that they headed down a wonderful 45 minute long path discussing biology, pre-meds, the advisory program, getting into medical school, and many other related items which would likely be boring to anyone but a Biology major, and are thus not recorded here. To his credit, David never once mentioned the Kreb's Cycle.

They emerged with a fuller knowledge of each other. "This is really amazing!" concluded David as they reached a pause.

"Why look at the time!" she noted. "David, I had better tell you to hang up. You've got finals coming up in Organic Chemistry and you certainly need to be studying for that. I keep hearing how hard that course is."

Shocked back into reality by the mention of Organic Chem, David knew she was right, and that she, too, had a demanding schedule. He prepared to hang up.

"Well, I guess you are right," he said. "We should probably both get to studying."

"Well thank you again for calling to check about how I did on my French test..."

"Oh shoot," thought David, *"that's not why I called!"*

He felt nervous again. His bladder felt very full. *"Why did I drink so much at dinner?"*

He blundered forward. "Oh, by the way, before I go," he started, trying to sound casual. "I've been thinking about that extra credit assignment. Why don't I just take you there? I could get you back home safely, and your parents wouldn't have to worry about you being out alone after dark." *"Smooth, doesn't even sound like a date..."* He held his breath, eyes closed tightly, phone receiver cradled between his left shoulder and ear, arms crossed across his chest, his hands tightly grasping his ribcage as he heard his heart racing, pounding in his ears.

"Oh, David, that would be so kind. Are you sure that wouldn't be too much of an imposition?"

"Oh, not at all!" he said, exhaling, trying not to sound exhilarated. *"Not as long as you don't mind riding around in a beat up old Maverick..."* "Where do you live?"

"I live in Riverside apartments, just across the tracks from East Campus road. It's not that far from here to PJ Auditorium. You could just park here if you'd like and we could walk from here," she said. She elected not to tell him that the reason she had a car on campus was that her parents did not want her riding with any other students they had not pre-approved. This plan would avoid that hassle.

"We're practically neighbors! I live in Reed Hall," he replied. This proximity allowed him to rationalize next, "It will be easier for me to just walk over than risk losing my parking space here." *"At least the Maverick won't be a part of that first impression."*

"OK," agreed Kay. "Now, it's getting late. You better go now and study really hard to make up for the time I've used tonight. Call me again tomorrow night and we'll iron out the details. I can't bear the thought of making you waste a minute more tonight."

"Well, OK, if you think that's best, then I'll call back tomorrow night."

Despite the incredible feeling of walking in the clouds, he studied better that night than he could recall ever studying before. His life, his plan for his life, all seemed to have more order, more definition, more purpose. Kay had told him to study really hard, and he would. For her, for them. He wanted to do everything right.

He looked forward to English class the next day with a mixture of dread and anticipation. The pessimist in him said that he was reading too much into this — that she only needed an escort to get her to and from the movie safely. He could only go down from here. Anything more that he did would blow his cover, expose his ruse, and she would back away from him forever. The optimist said this was just the first day of a new direction in their relationship. She had talked with him on the phone for a long time last night. She did not have to do that. Or maybe she felt she did, in order to get him to walk her to the movie. In either case, it had been a great phone call!

Nothing seemed different that day at English class. He arrived there with only a moment to spare after hoofing it from his Organic Chem class, and they exchanged a few pleasantries, he said, "Hello, Kay," and she said, "Hello, David." *"That's good, she remembered my name,"* he thought, not wanting to appear too changed in the eyes of his classmates or Dr. Harris. David had been too nervous to look at Kay when Dr. Harris again mentioned *Romeo and Juliet*. *"What if she didn't realize we have a date? What if she came up with a simpler way to go to the movie?"* he worried. The pessimist in him worked overtime without reason.

Things proceeded fairly normally after class as he walked her toward the door out the building, listening as she gave her thoughts on a final point that Dr. Harris had been making when he ended the class. She didn't seem to think it odd that he turned headed north with her to walk on with her to her French class. He made a few remarks about their English discussion, enjoying the luxury the longer walk allowed. He concluded as they arrived at the Foreign Languages building. Neither had said anything about their conversation of the night before.

"Have fun in French," he said, thinking, *"What a stupid thing to say!"*

"Thanks," she said, rolling her eyes as if French were an unbearable chore.

"Well, um, I'll call you tonight, then," he continued in a non sequitur.

"I'll look forward to it," she smiled, disappearing into the building.

David repeated the same pre-phone call ritual that evening after Rex had left the room. Nerves thus steadied, he dialed the number he had so instantly memorized. Kay picked up on the fourth ring with an identical, "Hello, this is Kay Powell speaking," as the evening before.

"Hello Kay. This is David, David Patson," he said.

"How nice of you to call," she said, genuinely.

Hoping to seem more casual, more spontaneous, David had taken the liberty of jotting a few notes to himself about things he and Kay could talk about over the phone before he got to the details of the movie Saturday night. He led her down a convoluted conversational path where they discussed Fayette County (he loved feeling like an expert and knowing more about her new neighborhood than she did), music (he was not surprised to arrive at his own conclusion that she excelled in this, also), and growing up in the Air Force (she effortlessly rattled off the names of cities he had never even heard of before, with no idea what countries they were located in). Finally, he felt confident enough to make more complete plans for Saturday night.

"Um, now, with regards to our extra credit assignment — you still want me to walk you over to PJ?" *"Dummy, don't give her an opportunity to change her mind! What are you thinking!"* he scolded himself.

"If you don't mind," she answered.

"Oh, no, not at all."

Silence. *"How do I say this?"* he asked himself.

"I guess you need to know my apartment number. It is on the second floor of the first building you'll see as you cross the tracks, number 2113," she volunteered.

"OK, 2113," he echoed, thinking, *"How do I ask her?"*

Silence.

"What time should I be looking for you?" she asked.

"Well, um, yes, that's what I wanted to check with you. The movie plays at 7:30 and 10:30, so I figure we're better off going to the 7:30 showing. PJ seldom sells out at 7:30," he said, hoping he sounded informed but not overly expert regarding Saturday nights on campus. He didn't want her to think she was just another Saturday night for him.

He continued, "But, um, I've read studies about how important good nutrition is for the learning process and I think that for an assignment like this we should be certain that we are appropriately prepared." He was trying to sound intellectual and authoritative. This was with her best interests at heart, obviously.

She stifled a giggle. *"I love her laugh,"* he thought, realizing she was seeing right through this. But he loved making her laugh; it made him feel wonderfully alive.

She composed herself and said with a serious tone, "Yes, I've heard that."

"Well what you may not know is that the best brain food in Athens is just up North Campus on Broad Street at the Blimpie sub sandwich shop. I think we stand a much better chance of understanding the zeal that Dr. Harris feels for this movie if we first eat there. What do you think?"

"I'm sure Dr. Harris would think that was the wise thing to do," she said, again sounding quite serious.

David continued, "OK then, allowing for walking time — it is still OK if we walk isn't it?"

"I wouldn't want it any other way," she said agreeably.

He felt more confident and began to loosen up. "Well, allowing for walking time, I think I should pick you up at number 2113 at 5:30, just in case service is slow, or there is a wait, or you need a lot of time to decide what type of sandwich to have."

His efforts at humor were again rewarded with that lovely laugh. *"Hey, she thinks I'm funny. I should be writing these down!"* he thought, impressed with his self-perceived comic genius.

Almost before he knew it Saturday arrived. With it arrived a wet cold-front that produced a steady drizzle of rain when David awoke just before 11:00 a.m. Since final exams were next week, he was committed to studying all day for his newfound inspiration. Finals would be tough, especially Organic

Chemistry, but he would be ready.

To optimize his time and money, his brunch consisted of a carton of milk and a PayDay candy bar from the vending machines on the dorm's first floor. He would shower later, just before his date. In what was as close to a study ritual as he had, he put on a pair of gym shorts and a long-sleeved denim shirt and went barefoot down to the study. He submerged himself in Organic Chemistry reviewing hundreds of his own questions and creating more. He did not emerge from the study until it was time to prepare for his date.

He shaved, giving up on his failed experiment to grow what only he would recognize to be sideburns, removing three weeks of scant scraggly growth. He then showered, brushed his teeth, put in his contact lenses, and returned to the room where he dried his hair. He was not disappointed to have the room to himself this afternoon. Rex was playing in the Pep Band at a basketball game, and wouldn't be back until later.

After drying his hair he turned on the radio to listen for the last few minutes of the basketball game just in case the Dawgs had gotten lucky. They had not, so he dialed over to a rock station and set about selecting his wardrobe. He started with the shirt, a long-sleeved Bulldog-red cotton dress shirt, opened at the button-down collar. This had been a Christmas gift from his parents three months ago, worn only once before. *"Don't want to look too casual,"* he thought. Next came a pair of everyday jeans. *"Don't want to look too formal,"* he reasoned. Not much choice for the shoes — his Adidas would look fine.

He dabbed some British Sterling around his Adam's apple, thankful that this three-year-old gift had lasted so long, since it was currently out of his price range, or at least had not been very high on his list of priorities — until tonight.

His navy blue hooded windbreaker would keep him from getting wet, just as it had been doing anytime it had rained over the past two years while walking to and from classes all over the campus regardless of the weather. He took another look at his watch, then killed two minutes admiring himself in the mirror until his watch indicated it was 5:20. He headed out the door and down the stairs.

As he opened the door leading to the outside, he suddenly realized that with the continuing light drizzle he needed an umbrella if he would be asking Kay to go walking up the campus to Blimpie's, down to PJ and then back to her apartment. For a moment he considered driving, but with parking as difficult as it could be in Athens, they might wind up walking about as far whether he drove or not. Instead, he stopped by his Maverick, thankful that he could save the Maverick introduction for another night — hoping there would be another night — and grabbed the seldom used collapsible umbrella that he kept in the trunk of his car. It had been a high school graduation present from his uncle, but not very practical to this point in his life. Now he felt suave carrying it alongside him in the light mist, not bothering to open it up yet.

He walked through the Reed Hall parking lot, crossed East Campus Road, walked across the gravel railroad right of way and tracks, and was standing in the Riverside Apartments parking lot with two minutes to spare. He recognized the building he thought to be Kay's from her description, and headed up the stairs to the second floor. He turned left, the only option, and headed down the concrete walkway. The walkway had a brown waist-high iron railing to the left, looking out over the parking lot, and was bordered on the right by a long wall punctuated by doors. Each door had a single narrow glass pane in the wall alongside it. The windows beside each door contained white venetian blinds which were, for the most part, closed. He proceeded, checking the door numbers attached to each black door, until he found the one labeled 2113. He took a deep breath, and knocked three times.

Almost immediately the door opened and there stood someone who wasn't Kay. She was shorter than Kay, heavier than Kay (probably heavier than David and about his age), with mousey straight shoulder-length brown hair. She wore oversized gray sweatpants, a plum colored sweatshirt without a logo on it, and fuzzy aqua bedroom slippers. Whatever she lacked, she seemed to compensate readily with a warm and engaging smile.

"Hello, does Kay Powell live here?"

"You must be David," she greeted him, "come right in. Kay is almost ready. I'm Jennifer."

David stepped in holding his still unopened umbrella by each end as if it were a nightstick. Uncertain as to whether one shook hands with a girl one was meeting for the first time in such circumstances, he was glad for the responsibility of holding onto the umbrella which thus prevented further formalities.

"Looks kind of messy out there," she said, buying time for Kay.

"Always seems to wait for the weekend to rain," said David, feeling like one of the old guys back home at church who always had something to say about the weather.

He scanned around the apartment briefly, impressed by the difference between this place and the quarters he occupied with Rex. The walls were clean and white, the carpet was a tan shag. He stood at the entrance to the living room and opposite him was a comfortable peach colored sofa that served as a divider with the kitchen-dining area that was the far side of the room. A hallway opened out from the middle of the right side of the room, collinear with the sofa, and from this hall emerged Kay. He would study the rest of the apartment another time.

Kay's coal-black hair was as always, parted in the middle, fashionably short with bangs in front and blown back along the sides, consistent with her physique in creating the appearance of an ice-skater or gymnast. Tonight her hair seemed a little more fluffed than usual, softer, more styled. Her complexion was perfect, not made-up, just radiant. She reminded David of one of the Breck girls he'd see in his mother's *McCall's* magazines. She had a long sleeved white turtleneck sweater with light brown slacks and dark brown deck shoes that looked fashionable yet right for a night spent walking in the March wetness.

"Hi David," she said. "I see you've met Jennifer. Let me get my coat and we can go."

She put on a bright yellow waist length raincoat with the hood tossed back. "OK, I'm ready," she announced.

"Well then, let's go," he answered. "Nice to have met you, Jennifer."

The walk to supper was about as pleasant as he could have hoped for. The rain had let up to the point of being less than fine mist. He offered the umbrella, but she said her hood would be fine. *"Not one of those women who is afraid to muss her hair,"* observed David, thankfully.

The most remarkable thing about the walk to supper was how unremarkable it was. David could not believe how comfortable he felt walking through North Campus as Kay and he talked. Not that the conversation itself was so rich in its depth or topics. To an impartial observer their exchange might have seemed even mundane, though it was not that at all. Simply put, a normal guy was having a normal discussion about normal things with a girl who was anything but normal. That was part of what David was enjoying. There was nothing contrived about how they interacted. The busy rush of the weekday school schedule was replaced with a relaxed tempo of gait and of speech.

The imposing buildings where they had classes Monday through Friday seemed like harmless sleeping giants as David and Kay walked past. He tried to portray to her just how beautiful this area of campus would be during the peak of spring when the dogwood and azalea took center stage. She was a good listener, and every bit as interesting, intelligent and enthusiastic about the issues covered as she was when the topic had been limited to English literature. Now she was talking about things that seemed more logical for a discussion between two college-enrolled teenagers on a Saturday afternoon.

"This is how life was meant to be, this is how a relationship with a woman should be!" he thought as he listened to Kay and realized that never before had he felt so genuine with a girl. He did not feel apprehensive about what he was going to say, he did not feel worried about what she was going to think. He certainly cared about these things, but somehow he trusted her, he trusted the situation, and was just having too much fun to let any pessimistic thoughts ruin the moment. Having such a relaxed approach made him more able to communicate his own thoughts, he was not afraid to speak around her, he didn't feel tongue-tied around her. He could joke, he could be himself. He almost felt guilty to realize how he had failed himself, how he had failed other girls, in not cultivating a relationship like this before. He had just been spinning his wheels,

wasting his time, wasting their time, while he tried to mature enough to be worthy of a situation like this. This was a new experience for him. Was this love?

"Too busy having a good time to think about that right now," he told himself. Not that he hadn't been thinking about love — a lot, recently and for a long time.

Chapter 15
Love?

In kindergarten David had to dance a reel holding hands with Rhoda French. He fell instantly in love. Later that year he kissed her in the backseat of carpool on the way home from school. He had a 104 degrees fever the next day, but he believed she was worth it. She was the first girl he ever kissed. She would not be the last.

Rhoda was his girlfriend most of the time during elementary school, although he was never quite sure when she was and when she was not. By the time they reached the sixth grade she played the clarinet, wore glasses, had braces and got the seven-year itch. They were broken up for three weeks before he finally found out through Cindy Reeves that Rhoda and he were no longer a couple.

During elementary school he usually had at least two or three other girls he called his girlfriends, all at the same time. At that age alliances seemed more important than monogamy. Nevertheless, even at a young age he realized there was something special about a relationship with a woman, with more involved than just the aspired to physical act of someday holding hands. There should be emotional commitment.

In the fourth grade he had a dream one night. The teacher lined up all the boys and girls on the playground and made each boy choose one girl to kiss. She then asked each boy why he chose that particular girl. Without fail, each boy indicated his kiss was because his girl was beautiful. David woke up in a somber mood with the dream fresh in his mind. He dreamed he had kissed his current girlfriend, Kate Harden, a cute wavy-haired brunette saxophonist in his elementary school band. He had told the teacher the kiss was not just because he thought she was beautiful, but because he loved her.

By the seventh grade he had settled into calling just one girl his girlfriend. Nicki Ray was a petite dark-haired clarinetist with a pixie-cut hair style. They would hold hands after band class, taking periodic breaks to wipe their hands dry. She was the first girl to make his palms sweat. She would not be the last.

In the eighth grade he became enamored with Mindy Black. He met her at church. David admired everything about her. She played piano and organ so well that her dad bought one of each for her house. She had great hair — long straight flowing walnut-brown hair that enhanced her tall and slender appearance. She was articulate and refined. David looked up to Mindy, figuratively and literally. The first Sunday after school started he found the nerve to ask her what was the best thing about being in high school, since she was now attending a Grade 8-12 school. She replied, "Being around boys that are taller than I am."

Not deterred, realizing his growth spurt had to come sooner or later, he would look over across the church at her every Sunday. He knew if he looked her way long enough she would look over to him and return a brief smile. Eventually he worked up to three or four shared smiles per twenty minute sermon. Their long-distance romance improved one night at a Bible study where she remarked how cold the November air had become. Wishing to impress her with his self-imagined profound intellect, he demonstrated the principle of friction by rubbing his hands together then holding one of hers with his. She did not protest, so they held hands the rest of the evening, and anytime they could for the next month. Then she apparently became impatient and started holding hands with a much taller tenth grader.

In the ninth grade while on a band bus trip on the way back from a high school football game, some friends paired him up with a French horn player from the marching band. Mary Scott was a cute slender girl with short hair who had dimples that could make him smile. Alas, his family moved to Fayette County after his ninth grade year, so he was left to wonder what might have been. The truth be known, he was left to wonder because she had left to wander, with a trumpet player, even before he had moved to Fayette County.

As he began the tenth grade in a new school, he was glad to be in the marching band with an instant social group. Now that he was fifteen years old he could double date and some new friends set him up on a triple date with the very popular Linda Day, who was also fifteen. She was undisputedly the most stunning clarinetist in the school's marching band. With long thick wavy blond hair, Linda had won the county-wide high school beauty pageant at the age of fourteen. Nature had already smiled on her in ways that had made it an unfair contest.

Linda also had a very sharp and clever wit. She was fun to be around. ~~It was that sharp and clever wit that had first caught David's attention and was the primary motivating force in why he asked her to go out.~~ (**NOTE FROM AUTHOR TO EDITOR**: *William: Please strike the prior sentence from the galley proof before sending this manuscript for final printing. In the unwritten contract between author and reader, good fiction should possess a component of believability and abide by the fundamental laws of the universe. The reader who remembers the effect Linda Day had on any heterosexual adolescent male would instantly recognize such a ridiculous misrepresentation of reality on my part, potentially jeopardizing the plausibility of this entire novel.— DLA*)

Unfortunately for David, and even more so for Linda, he had a wart on the palm of his left hand which had been treated by the dermatologist two days before their date. By the time the night of his date arrived he believed that his hand had healed well enough to try holding hands during the last part of *The Candidate*. She didn't seem to mind either, until after the movie as they were all six walking back to the car. He casually mentioned that his hand was feeling much better, at which time she asked if there was a problem. That was when she got her first view of the raised red-blue-purple swollen blister on his hand, the same palm she had been pressing hers against for the past 30 minutes. Her make-up suddenly seemed insufficient to provide necessary color to her face. They became much better friends once she decided she would never ever date him again.

Next there was Beth Byrd, slim with long straight blond hair. They were able to date alone as soon as David turned 16. She went to a different school than he did, but she attended the same church as David. Like him she would also be the valedictorian of her high school class. She was the most intelligent girl he knew, which he only later learned is a trait which should be high on the list of things a gentleman admires in a lady.

David likely would have learned many refinements from Beth had he only realized that dating was an opportunity for a caring couple to create and improve a relationship by discovering more about each other. He insecurely, but probably accurately, feared the more she discovered about him the less there would be to like, so he spent a lot of time taking her to movies. The benefit of going to a movie was that a couple could spend a lot of time together without actually having to say anything to each other. He became very gifted in the art of non-communication, which he only later learned is not a trait high on the list of things a lady admires in a gentleman.

Despite an absence of effective communication, they still managed to learn valuable lessons by dating each other. She learned that a 16-year-old is more boy than man.

His learning was more diverse and his need for training more evident. Unfortunately, this education usually came through trial and error. She subtly taught him that spontaneity is not considered romantic if it means waiting until Thursday night to call a girl with a request for a Friday night date — she was inexplicably unavailable. When properly motivated, he was a fast learner.

He still wore glasses in the 10th Grade. Once, in a darkened theatre, he leaned over toward her to whisper a comment during a Paul Newman movie. He discovered, at her expense, that the corner of one's glasses can inflict quite a painful injury into the temple of the head of one's date. She was the first to complement him on his new contact lenses when he started to wear them at the beginning of his senior year.

With her he also refined the art of making a woman feel warm, safe and protected while in the already warm, not particularly unsafe, Old National Twin Theatre. The first time he decided to put his arm around her during a movie he smoothly (so not to seem amateurish) and quickly (so not to be noticed or rebuffed) swung his left arm up and over to rest on the back of her seat. Unlike her, he had not yet completed his growth spurt. Underestimating the depth of his cushioned seat, he miscalculated her height and forcefully drove his bony elbow squarely into her unsuspecting forehead. She assured him the two inch contusion in the center of her forehead was not painful and did not require the ice he offered from his cup of Coke. He couldn't recall noticing before, but she insisted that she always cried at Robert Redford movies.

At Easter he had an Easter corsage delivered to her at home addressed to her cute nickname, signed with his cute nickname, nicknames which they had never before actually used on each other. He was surprised to see her mother wearing the corsage in church on Easter Sunday, and even more surprised to later hear that her father silently accepted the adulations that came his way for sending such a beautiful flower.

Sadly for Beth, she also learned from David that 17-year-olds are more boys than men, and also 18-year-olds are more boys than men. Amazingly patient, having finally completed her exhaustive study of boys, she seemed to have no difficulty graduating to more mature individuals when David went off to college.

She was the first girl to make him cry. She would not be the last. Nonetheless, one benefit of dating Beth so consistently throughout most of high school was that he managed to botch only one dating relationship, rather than to blunder through a succession of disappointed girls in high school. This worked in his favor. Beth went to another high school, and at his school he made no secret of the fact that he considered her the only woman in his life. As a result, plenty of girls in his high school thought of him as a brother more so than as dating material. What few skills he developed in communicating with attractive women, or simply being himself around charming ladies, he acquired primarily from being "just friends" with his platonic harem of hometown girls.

As his failed relationships mounted, his confidence grew. Working as a musician and performer at Six Flags put him constantly before an admiring public. His ego thrived on the praise provided by his audiences and the predictable gaggle of girls that would hang around after the last show many evenings. As accommodating hosts, he and the other guys in the band felt obligated to honor their requests to ride the Great American Scream Machine or other such thrill rides after dark. Yet, when he was honest with himself, he had to admit how shallow these girls must be — he realized they were admiring the position he occupied rather than the person he was. He was a real person, wasn't he? Was there not something unique about him that would set him apart for that special woman someday, more than just being another stud in the meat market? Through it all, however, he adhered to his standards. Shallow girls at least had to be pretty.

The autumn after he graduated from high school, he started at UGA with optimism that perhaps there he would meet 'Miss Right'. Pursuing the likes of Vicki Post turned out to be a waste of time and bored even his not yet matured mind. In his worst dreams he could imagine what it would be like to capture the heart of a Vicki Post and then being married to that mindless body, watching it age a little more every day.

Rex soon introduced David to a Redcoat Marching Band member he thought he should know. Rex was right. In fact, David often teased Rex that if Rex could have done as good a job selecting women for himself he could have saved himself a lot of trouble. Helen Henderson was predictably trim, with great hair, and excelled at flute. She had a good sense of humor and looked great in a sweater — wet or dry. She and David hit it off almost immediately, but what was there not to like? She was quickly received into the circle of roommates of Suite 270, and David sometimes felt like maybe she was dating all four of them, as Will, Rex, and even Mad-man were very fond of her, and she of them.

Having the other guys involved in their relationship sometimes made it easier for them to spend a lot of time with each other without having a lot of time to have more serious discussions, the kinds of discussions that girls seem to like, and that David, as a well-seasoned non-communicator, had not yet mastered. She was a great listener. The self-absorbed David could monopolize fifteen minutes on the phone excitedly telling her the things he was learning. He would practice reciting the entire Kreb's Cycle and other equally mundane biochemical pathways he learned in Biology as he prepared for his next test. She listened attentively (or perhaps she was just balancing her checkbook) while he droned on.

He realized there was something very special about how he felt toward Helen, but his mouth was incongruent with his heart. He hoped he could talk with her about how he really felt toward her. He thought he had plenty of time. What was the rush?

He loved to make her laugh. She was humored when he would talk like a duck. She was not humored when he would duck any talk about commitment. Flustered by his foolishness, marching band notwithstanding, she gave him his marching orders. True to her standards, she had ultimately realized she deserved more than he was delivering, and she told him so. She was right.

And so David entered his Blue Period. Not that he was depressed, but he was far from contented. He spent a good bit of time listening to Karen Carpenter and the likes singing about unobtainable bliss. *"The hardest thing I've ever done is keep believing, there's someone in this crazy world for me..."* he would sing with Karen, not really knowing what he wanted or expected from love. He thought about love, what it meant, where it came from. He realized he wasn't an overly verbal person. Love in his family had seldom been voiced with, "I Love You", but was far more often demonstrated by acts of love. He had certainly liked some of these girls a lot, maybe even loved one or two of them, but he had intentionally never voiced it. He reasoned he owed it to himself, and to them, to know what he was talking about before he confused them, too. He respected love, and when he told a girl he loved her, he planned for it to stick. Whatever his feelings had been so far, he had not been able to make them stick.

He realized how "unstuck" he had become about the same time he decided to stop bringing girls by to meet his parents. One evening after introducing a girl to his father, Daddy responded by asking her, "Now which one are you?" David decided he would keep things simple and not bring another girl by the house until she demanded it. Assuming, of course, there would ever be another girl.

Just how confused he was about what he expected from women struck him during his Christmas break of his sophomore year at UGA. He had a streak of five dates with five different girls on five consecutive nights when he returned home that December, but then there he sat on Christmas Eve, alone. He was a Prince to many, a King to none.

A pensive period that week after Christmas had him looking back, analyzing his life, looking forward, pondering the future. He had to admit to the glaring fact that the only common factor in all his failed romances was him. He felt like the Thomas Edison of dating — he now knew a thousand ways not to make a long-term relationship work. Maybe he should just stop dating girls. He quickly rejected that banishment — he had a decided preference for their company. He could not recall a time in his life when he had not. Drastic for an improvement in himself, his confidence in his own abilities was now zero.

He attempted to use the scientific methods he had so successfully learned in school, applying logic and reasoning to assess his situation. This even led him to produce introspective drivel which only he could appreciate as poetry, which ended with the observation:

> *At times I'm aware*
> *of a long-standing pain,*
> *that no logic can cure,*
> *'cause my heart's not my brain.*[1]

Not blaming any of the girls who had helped him see so many of his own imperfections, he was appreciative of what they had each contributed to his acquired education, often at their own expense. He prayed that when he did meet the right woman he would be ready.

---

[1] *Editor's note: Drivel notwithstanding, David continued to dabble in creative poetry and song at times throughout his life. He finally met with minor critical acclaim with a song he wrote for his wife's 44th birthday, "An Audience of One". See a copy of this song on our website at www.AndersUSA.com/Extras.*

Chapter 16
Dinner and a Movie

As Kay and David entered the otherwise empty sandwich shop the young woman wearing a green apron looked up from the thick textbook she was reading and greeted them from behind the counter, then returned to her reading.

David and Kay remained a few steps away from the counter while he asked her what she thought she would want to eat. Kay admitted she had never eaten a Blimpie before.

"You go ahead and order if you know what you want while I read over the menu," she said, looking up at the menu board hanging over the back wall behind the counter. "She can only make one sandwich at a time, so that will give me a minute to decide."

He had seen girls order like this before — wait for your date to order first so you can see how big his budget is, then get the same thing. Not wanting to have her think she had to scrimp on the size of her meal, he decided to order large, hoping not to seem rude by not taking her order first, but it did seem reasonable to go ahead and place the order for one of them.

He was hungry from having eaten so little thus far in the day and was ready to celebrate with a feast. Since Blimpie's didn't offer his favorite food — steak — he would have the closest thing offered to steak. He would also go all out and get the best thing in the shop, those light crunchy sweet Sparky's Vanilla Creams, specialty cookies shipped from who knows where that he could find only at Blimpie's. He deserved an extra reward after a long hard study session, and what better way to celebrate this eventful night than with such a delectable dessert. His mouth watered at the thought of the treat ahead.

"I'll have a 12-inch roast beef, all the way, with a bag of chips, a large Coke, and a pack of Vanilla Creams, please," he said after the waitress saw him step forward to the counter. He pulled the chips and cookies off their racks as he spoke.

The waitress repeated his sandwich order and looked almost thankful to have a reason not to be studying as she began preparing his meal. Kay stepped up beside David. "Is the turkey good?" she asked him, apparently ready to order.

"I've had it before and it was good. I was just in a roast beef mood today."

"Then I'll have a small turkey sandwich with everything except cheese, mayonnaise, mustard and onions. *"Yikes! I forgot about the onions! Who eats onions on a date?"* he blasted himself.

"Do you think they would give me extra pickles?" she said to him. He thought it odd she didn't just tell the waitress, but maybe that's how things were done in classy restaurants. He'd ask Will Rice about that someday. *"Will would be impressed to meet Kay*," he thought, proudly.

"Anything else? Chips? Dessert?" asked David.

"No, that's fine, thank you," replied Kay.

Speaking louder and to the waitress who was now wrapping his sandwich in paper, he said, "And she will have a six-inch turkey with everything, hold the cheese, mayonnaise, mustard and onions, with extra pickles."

"And to drink?" asked the waitress.

"And to drink?" asked David.

"Water," said Kay to David.

"Water," said David to the waitress.

"*Cheap date*," thought David, uncritically. "*And a very healthy eater at that.*"

David selected the table furthest from the counter activity, which in such a small shop really was not that far from the table closest to the counter activity. He placed their tray on the table and set out their food as Kay took her place at the chair in front of the shorter of the two wrapped sandwiches. David sat down and unwrapped his sandwich then opened it to inspect its contents, nonchalantly removing the onions. He flashed a glance up at Kay to see if she noticed, but her head was bowed with her eyes closed. A twinge of guilt pricked his conscience for not being thankful for such obvious blessings, but he simultaneously felt even greater elation at being with Kay and realizing what a special person she must be. "*Not afraid to be who she is,*" he observed.

He busied himself with his sandwich, waited until he sensed she had again opened her eyes, then acting unaware of what had just transpired looked up from his sandwich and said, "Let's be thankful for this food." He bowed his head and prayed, "God, thank you for this good food and the time to enjoy together. Amen," thinking "*I hope that was non-denominational enough, yet adequate.*" Somehow he and Kay had not gotten around to religion yet in their discussions. He was a Baptist. Suppose she was Jewish? Or what else? He had just assumed she was similar to him. At least she said the blessing over her food. He would need to explore that further, obviously.

He bit into his sandwich, enjoying the rich beefy flavor, the fresh bread, the texture of the lettuce, (and the equally flavorless tomato), and the way the mustard blended with the oil. As he chewed he began to also taste the onions he obviously had not entirely removed. "*Too late to take the sandwich back apart now. I'll look like a picky eater, or a fool who didn't know what 'all-the-way' means when ordering. Just remember not to breathe in her face now!*"

"My mother called me this afternoon," began Kay as they started their meals. "She was so excited that I was going to be able to see *Romeo and Juliet*," she continued, not revealing the true source of her mother's excitement. "I had mailed her a letter when I found out I'd be able to see the Zeffirelli version. She was so thrilled she immediately called me as soon as she received it today. She told me a lot about plot, structure, you know, all the things that Dr. Harris would hone in on. She's an English teacher and loves to teach Shakespeare. She thinks we'll really enjoy this version. She particularly likes the age of the actors used in the film. Olivia Hussey was only 17 when she filmed the movie, much closer to Juliet's age than most actresses, much more realistic to Shakespeare's intention of the portrayal. She thinks Dr. Harris must have a special group of students if they will spend a Saturday night earning extra credit watching classic theatre."

"Always good to impress a girl's mother with your academic pursuits," he reminded himself, wondering if he would ever have the pleasure of meeting Kay's family. David had finished the first six inches of his sandwich before she stopped talking. Not that he minded her soliloquy. He enjoyed listening to her speak.

He picked up the conversation so she would have time to eat her sandwich, and they enjoyed the leisure of the time he had built into their schedule. Since they had sat down, three girls had come into the shop together, but with only one other group eating in the shop he felt no rush to hurry through their dinner.

When his sandwich and chips were gone he started to open his pack of Vanilla Creams and wondered if he should offer Kay some. She had already turned down any of his chips. He laughed inwardly, joking with himself that he was unsure he could bear the rejection if she also declined a Vanilla Cream. She appeared to select a healthy diet, and he didn't want to seem disrespectful of her choices.

"Vanilla Creams?" he offered as he peeled away the plastic cellophane revealing six round two-inch cookies. "Take two, they're small." She took two and said, "Thanks! I've never heard of these before."

"I need some more Coke. Can I get you some water?" he asked, rising from his seat.

"Please," was her muffled reply as she tried to be polite with an immediate response, affected though it was by a mouthful of her first bite of the light crunchy sweet treat. He took her cup. She smiled as she dipped her chin a bit, swallowing the dry cookie without the benefit of any water to wash it down. "That's delicious!" she reported.

He refilled their drinks and returned to the table. He could not help but notice there were now only three Vanilla Creams.

"Those are really good cookies," she said, so he offered, and she accepted, another one as she drank more water. "What are they called again?" she asked, placing her cup back on the table.

"Vanilla Creams," he replied. "They don't seem to sell them anywhere else I know of except here. Want another?"

"If you don't mind...OK you talked me into it," she said playfully and the fifth cookie was soon gone. He received such pleasure just knowing he had found something she enjoyed that he almost did not mind that there was now only one Vanilla Cream left. Being her provider was a good feeling.

He sat back in his chair and their conversation veered off in yet another direction as they learned each other's favorite Bee Gees song. After a few more minutes David looked at his watch. They both eyed the last Vanilla Cream sitting untouched on the cellophane wrapper in front of David. In perhaps the most selfless act yet of his young life, David concluded, "We'd better think about going soon. Why don't you finish that last Vanilla Cream and then we'll leave."

Without protest, she honored his request with a smile.

Nighttime had descended while they ate. The rain had stopped but everything around them remained wet. Wind blew in gusts at times, noticeably colder than before they had gone inside for supper. They made good use of the outer pockets of their jackets, although David now felt like a bit of a nerd for having to keep up with his unused umbrella. Since Kay walked to his right, he tucked the umbrella under his left armpit, mostly hidden from her view, allowing him to keep his hands warm.

They retraced their steps through the North Campus past the Honors Program building, the Law School, the Library, enjoying the lighted tree-lined walks of the oldest portion of the campus which were beautiful even before the arrival of spring. After several minutes they were ascending the stairs to the PJ plaza, too soon for David's tastes. He was loving this evening, but it was going by too fast, and now they were going to have to sit quietly for two hours and watch some stuffy Brits in a 350 year old play. He would have preferred to have continued to just talk for another four or five hours at Blimpie's while eating Vanilla Creams.

The Psychology-Journalism complex of buildings on the University of Georgia campus included two large auditoria at opposite ends of an open two level plaza. David had never been in the North Psychology-Journalism auditorium, but he was very familiar with South PJ, as it was called by most students. From the PJ Plaza he could look southward across Hooper Street at the Reed Quad. The close proximity to Reed Hall made it convenient to take advantage of the dollar movies shown on weekends and some combination of the foursome of Will, Mad-man, Rex and David plus or minus other guys would often spend Saturday night catching up on the offered movie, which was never a first run.

He paid for their tickets feeling like the last of the big spenders, fending off her offer to pay for her own ticket. They entered into the 300 seat auditorium from the rear and descended its steep stairs. With ten minutes remaining before show time, most of the seats remained empty. David led them to two seats in the center, two-thirds of the way up, which he knew offered the best viewing and audio experience.

Kay excused herself and went back up the stairs. Upon further reflection this sounded like a good idea to David. A few seconds after she exited, he left his umbrella on the fold-up half-desktop writing surface which was attached to the right side of his chair, just like every other chair in this large classroom.

He returned descending down the left aisle as she was descending the right. As if choreographed, their return to the center seats mirrored each other as the crossed the otherwise empty row and met in the middle at their seats indicated by David's umbrella. He gallantly stood while she sat first, as he folded the desktop back to its rightful position along the right of his chair.

The cold air outside had left the building inside fairly cool, so neither took off his/her jacket. David felt a little awkward sitting right beside Kay in the large auditorium that was, he surmised, only 20% full. He would always leave an empty seat between him and Will or Rex in such a situation. That was just another rule in the Unwritten Code by which they all abided. Now here he was wedged into the seat right beside Kay with plenty of open seats all around them. If she thought this was odd, however, she said nothing, as she resumed their conversation.

"I'm surprised there aren't more people here," she observed softly, as if speaking in a library.

"Well there are still five minutes left. I'll bet more folks will show up soon," he said, as the aisles were starting to become busier.

"I don't see anyone else from our class, do you?" she asked.

He looked around and analyzed the crowd. Mostly singles, couples, and a few groups of three. Some singles had already lifted their desktops upright and placed a spiral notebook or notepad on the desk, apparently here for a class assignment also. The audience contained more older students, probably graduate students or even faculty, than he would see at a midnight showing.

He amused himself recalling one night the men of Room 272 had come here for a midnight movie. Periodically PJ would offer a third screening time on a Friday or Saturday night, showing a second movie, different from the feature movie shown around 7:30 and 10. The midnight movie was usually an offbeat classic comedy or science fiction story, frequently somewhat unknown or esoteric.

One night Will suggested they go see a horror movie showing at midnight. No one was familiar with the particular film, but no one had a better idea, so they all headed off to South PJ. In 1976 no one had ever heard of *The Rocky Horror Picture Show*, and certainly no one had yet started treating it like the cult classic it would become with such wild interactive audience participation. During the movie that night, the crowd was otherwise like that for any other screening. When Will let out a loud "Whoop!" after the now famous line, "Come up to the lab, and see what's on the slab," he was immediately reminded by the projectionist that further disruption could serve as cause for ejection without refund. The evolution of audience participation in future years would confirm that Will lived on the cutting edge of societal evolution.

As reserved as that midnight audience had been, this group seemed even more so. Not certain with just how much of his roommates' antics he wanted to expose her to so early in their relationship, he opted not to introduce this as a new topic so, not seeing anyone from his class, he simply responded, "No."

He sat back in his seat and stared forward at the large empty screen in front of them.

She, too, looked forward. "Well it's unfortunate if they don't have a better turn out because they should show more films like this," she said, as if Dr. Harris were listening.

The Rocky Horror Picture show had been packed, David could remember.

"I think I would rather be watching Clint Eastwood," David admitted.

"I'll bet you just wish you didn't feel manipulated by Dr. Harris into seeing this movie. But just give it a chance. I'll bet you enjoy it. You like literature. What's not to like about Shakespeare?"

"Not enough .44 Magnums," panned David, looking straight ahead.

She laughed, loud enough to draw the concerned glance of more than one of the other movie goers. *"I could listen to that laugh all night,"* he smiled, glad he could elicit the response.

"David, you say the funniest things," she said, still laughing, but more controlled, a little self-conscious about her outburst.

Wanting to continue to mine this humorous vein, inspired by the note takers around him he added, "You should be writing these down."

She playfully punched his left arm and the lights went down.

David had to admit to himself he was sorry the movie was over. Now he could start talking to Kay again, that was good. But during the entire movie, over two hours, he had sat right beside her, the most perfect spot in the universe. She had deferred the use of their shared armrest to him. The closely arranged auditorium seating meant his left arm had been lightly pressed against her right arm. Even through the layers of shirt, coats, and sweater that separated them, that contact felt wonderful.

They made their way up the steps of the aisle out to the lobby. The clustered bodies at the glass double doors on either side of the lobby implied something was slowing the exit from the building. They both narrowed their gaze to see into the dark outside through the lobby's glass walls, and the change in the weather was obvious. The rain was coming down hard now.

"I thought the rain had passed," said David.

"Good thing we're waterproof," she added.

"Glad I decided to bring this umbrella after all," he admitted.

"You thought of everything!" she replied. Her praise made him feel ten feet tall.

They buttoned their jackets and put on their hoods then queued up to go outside. The air temperature seemed suddenly surprisingly cold, made all the more so by periodic stout gusts of wind. She put her hands in her coat pockets. David pushed the handle button that extended the umbrella shaft as he led the way out a door, holding the door open behind him for her with his left hand while he manipulated the umbrella open with his right. With precision timing he held the umbrella over her head the instant it opened and she exited. The umbrella was only about half as wide as he remembered it being.

He quickly summarized his situation and options. He could concede defeat, give her the umbrella and walk alongside her in the rain. *"Too weird,"* he decided. If he held the umbrella in his right hand, he'd have to almost wrap himself around her without touching her to get his right arm out in front of her, his left shoulder behind her, and his body under the umbrella. *"Too aggressive,"* he concluded. He could hold the umbrella in his left hand, walking along with her at his left side. Without contorting his body rightward, she would get soaked on her unsheltered left side. If he rotated his right shoulder backward and led with his left shoulder, he could hold the umbrella with his left hand extended back at the wrist. He would then have to crane his head back over his left shoulder all the way home any time he wanted to look at her, hoping he was holding the umbrella centrally enough over her to keep her from getting wet, since he wouldn't actually be able to see her very well.

Stepping out into rain he tried the left handed and over the shoulder approach. *"Still weird,"* was his assessment and he opted for a modified right hand approach. He grabbed the umbrella from his left hand with his right hand and let his left arm drop by his side alongside Kay. They walked across the plaza toward the stairs, but he realized that while his left arm was by no means bulky, it was taking up a lot of premium space between Kay and him, the driest part of their shared territory. Meanwhile, his right shoulder and leg were receiving a large amount of the downpour with this compromise. He was, however, keeping Kay dry.

They reached the stairs and started to descend down to ground level. David and Kay went slowly down the dark slippery first step together, but he felt like a circus tightrope walker holding the little umbrella a bit off balance on the changing surface. He realized he needed to keep Kay safe through this descent and with the purest of intentions moved his left arm from between them and securely cradled Kay's waist with his left hand. He felt a blend of two strong arguments in his mind: *"She's going to think I'm making a move on her,"* and

"Let her think what she wants. I'm going to protect her even if she doesn't think she needs it." His desire to protect her overrode any fear he had of rejection, so hugging her waist as they went down the stairs together he simply said, "Be careful."

If Kay had any objections to this new posturing, she voiced none. Before they had looked a bit like two elderly people hunched under the umbrella in an effort to fight the rain and the cold, moving awkwardly along. Now they descended the stairs smoothly as if rehearsed. He planned to let go of her waist once they safely reached the bottom of the thirty or more stairs, but he realized how much drier his right half was with this new position. She seemed to have been crafted to fit perfectly — his left armpit over the back of her right shoulder, his left forearm across her smooth back, his hand cupping her trim left waist. Now as he approached the last step he was having misgivings about letting go, ever. The rain was still falling hard, they had several more minutes to walk, he was quite comfortable now, and she didn't seem to mind. If anything, she seemed to be leaning into his one armed hug, not away from it. Her head was tipping toward his left shoulder. Was she just trying to avoid the rain, or was she putting her head on his shoulder? In his mind he could hear the Lettermen singing, "*Put your head on my shoulder...*"

Despite the heavy rain, or perhaps because of it, they did not pick up the pace of their walk as they headed east up Hooper Street. David was glad not to be walking too quickly. He realized this incredible night was headed to a conclusion, and he didn't want it to end. He wondered if she wanted to extend the date. It was already after 10:00.

"So what are you doing tomorrow?" he asked casually, as if oblivious to the fact that he was strolling along with the most perfect woman in the world.

In a relaxed voice that told him she wasn't too upset about the current circumstance, she said, "In the morning I'll play piano at the Presbyterian Center, then spend the rest of the day studying for finals."

"You play the piano for a church?"

She replied, "Yes, I figure if I'm going to be there anyway, I might as well help out however I can."

"I need to come hear you play some day."

"OK, but not tomorrow. I'd be too nervous. I'd need advanced warning so I could practice extra." He wasn't certain she wasn't pulling his leg about being nervous. If she could play in front of a hundred people, what difference would one more make. He decided not to push the issue. He would remain a Baptist for at least another week — so much for trying to keep her out too late.

Oddly, they did not say a word about the movie as they walked through the heavy rain. Perhaps that would seem too much like "talking business". Perhaps the topic of teens in love was too raw, too intimate for the moment. In any case, neither spoke for a while now as they walked back to her apartment, each silently processing the new world in which they were walking, or hoped they were walking. In the insecurities of youth, she was not quite sure he wasn't just being protective, and he was not quite sure she wasn't just trying to stay dry. But there was no denying the facts. This was not how Rex and he would have been sharing an umbrella.

They crossed East Campus Road and walked across the grassy shoulder, the saturated ground squishing under their feet with every step. The soggy grass gave way to the gravel railroad right of way. As they stepped up onto a railroad crosstie, her deck shoe slipped a bit against the oily smooth surface. He instantly stopped and tightened his grip at her waist, bracing her against his side and hip as she reflexively grabbed his right wrist with her right hand and clinched her left hand over his right hand holding the umbrella.

"You OK?" he asked quickly as they stayed still long enough to be certain both were stable.

"Thanks. These crossties get slippery when they're wet," she observed, maintaining her grip on his arm and hand. They more carefully, more slowly, proceeded across the length of parallel crossties, bracing each other as they stepped over each rail, gingerly making their way through the deluge.

They stepped back onto the gravel bed. She lightened her grip, but did not let go. He *really* liked the touch of her hand on his. That umbrella was getting heavy and he needed her to help carry it, he reasoned, teasing himself inwardly. He marveled quietly at his situation. There was a momentary silence which was not awkward, just a pause for them to breathe in the evening that they were both so glad had happened.

For reasons not clear to David, Kay stopped walking, halting their progress at the edge of the graveled area. They continued to look ahead where they could see the lights of Riverside apartments through the trees ahead. He tipped his head to the left so he could momentarily brush his cheek along her hood, then rested his cheek against the cold rubbery surface of her hood. He clinched his jaw slightly to prevent his teeth from chattering in the cold, although he didn't particularly feel cold.

"David..."

"Yes, Kay," he replied softly. He knew her hair was soft just under her hood, and she smelled good. He silently protruded his bottom lip and sent a small puff of his own breath up into his nostrils. He was very aware of the onions he had not been able to remove from his sandwich. He began to vent his breath subtly off to the right side through the corner of his mouth.

"David, Dr. Harris isn't the only person who manipulated you into going to the movie tonight." Her voice quivered slightly. "... I lied to you...Jenny didn't have plans to go home this weekend. I made that up."

She had waited five hours to report this obvious historical discrepancy? He was sure there was a good explanation. If not, he was honored to be the target of such premeditated deviancy.

"Oh, that's alright. I'm thankful you did," he said positively, trying to lighten things up.

She spun to her right so she could face him. He followed her lead so they were face to face under the tight confines of the protective umbrella. She had let go of his hand and his right forearm so she could use both hands to emphasize her speech. His left arm was no longer around her warm trim waist. This was not progress.

"No, it isn't alright!" she said emphatically. "Here it is, the first time you ask me to do something with you," *"the FIRST time...that means she realizes there are going to be more!"* he thought joyfully, trying not to look elated during her tirade.

"...and I start off by lying to you. That was wrong of me. I feel just terrible. I hope you can forgive me." She hung her head and dug her hands into her coat pockets.

There was silence. He hoped she wasn't going to impose a penalty on herself, a penalty on him. Would they have to stop dating before they ever got started?

"Oh, Kay, don't be silly," he said, trying to defuse the situation. Instantly realizing this seemed to trivialize her distress, he employed a mildly dramatic turn of his head downward and away to the right. Now able to vent away his onion breath, he said more softly, "If it makes you feel any better, you're forgiven." Then he waited. *"Now I'm being manipulative,"* he thought to himself ironically.

Her posture softened a little as he maintained his downward gaze, better able to vent away the onions from her otherwise close face. *"Dang onions!"* he thought.

He longed for what now seemed so long ago when he had strolled with his arm at her waist. Those simpler times seemed an eternity past. Not wanting to appear to be a ventriloquist for the rest of this discussion as he tried to avoid blowing onions in her direction, he slipped his arm back around her waist and nudged her back into their former, more comfortable position. She accepted this as a further token of forgiveness for her unforgivable deed, no matter how unworthy she was. What a wonderful, sensitive, caring man this David Patson must be. He heard her sniff. He again put his cheek against the side of her tilted head.

"But now I need to get something off my chest. I lied, too," he added, his voice slowing and becoming more earnest, more firm, more confident. Since he was no longer face to face with her the onions were less an issue.

"What?" she replied, now surprised.

"Yes," he declared boldly. "I said the best brain food in Athens was Blimpie. I was wrong. The best brain food in Athens is BoxCar Pizza."

"I love pizza. It's my favorite food!" she interrupted.

"Well then, we must put that on our 'to do' list once we get through finals," he offered, realizing that the schedule for their final exams next week meant one or both of them had a final every day next week. Each realized there would be no time to waste during such a critical week. But after finals week would come spring break. They would both be back in Fayette County for that week, but no mention of that had yet been made. Any such talk would have seemed premature only a few hours ago.

"Then here's what we should do. During spring break I'll take you to the best pizza place in all of the South Atlanta area."

She spun back again and faced him, slipping out of his grip again. *"Not progress,"* he thought again.

She enthusiastically grabbed him by his left bicep with both hands and squeezed as she exclaimed, "Oh David, that would be such fun!"

"The girl likes her pizza," he thought, not fully appreciating that pizza was not the only component of the offer that now had her so invigorated. He took a deep breath and turned his head toward her, now face to face, silent, eye to eye. After a fleeting second, he cast his head down and to the right again, exhaling onions as he said softly, "So you forgive me?"

She punched his appreciative left arm as she laughed, "You are so silly!" Now it was she who comfortably repositioned herself alongside him, snuggling quietly back to her rightful place as she resumed her hold onto his right forearm and wrapped her left hand over his right hand, helping him again to hold the umbrella. He put his arm around her waist.

They started walking again, even more slowly than before, her head on his shoulder, his cheek against her head. He held her a little tighter around the waist, only partly because they were walking down the brief pine straw covered slope that led to the Riverside parking lot. Almost regretfully he pondered what a great night this had been.

His heart quickened as he realized in only a few minutes he would have to decide whether to risk a goodnight kiss. Kay was too special to risk messing this up. A kiss on the first date was quite a statement. Maybe she had lied only because she really wanted that half point extra credit on her final grade. She hadn't said why she had lied, just that she had lied. But if he couldn't kiss her after such a fantastic evening, when could he? This was getting way too complicated, and for a brief instant he longed for a simpler time when he was content to speak to her after class.

Quietly climbing up the covered stairs now, he wondered what she was thinking. She felt so right beside him with her hand on his, helping to hold the now unnecessary umbrella. He was not about to change anything that would reduce hand to hand contact, so he continued to hold the umbrella over their heads as they walked down the walkway to her apartment. They stopped by her door, and turned to face it, side by side. Now standing still, she could rest her head even more firmly against his shoulder. She spoke first.

"Looks like Jen is still up studying," she deduced from the light behind the Venetian blind alongside door 2113. His heart raced. She had not reached for her key, so that must be her sign that a kiss was OK.

"Yep," he relied, unable to respond intelligently otherwise.

She replayed her hand. "David, I really do appreciate you offering to take me to the movie. I really had a wonderful time." She gazed up toward him.

He turned his face from the door to hers. His heart was pounding as if he had run the entire distance from PJ. The umbrella which had served such faithful duty as protector and prop now was an obstacle. He didn't want to appear too deliberate in taking the time to fold it up. That might give her time to change her mind. So he tossed it back over his right shoulder, only to see it fly over the second story railing out of the corner of his eye.

Refusing to be distracted, he did not break the eye to eye contact he now maintained with Kay. Her hand still held his right hand and forearm, but if he was going to kiss her, he was either going to have to tip her head up a little more to get under the overhang of her hood, or he was going to have to make a very ungraceful bending at his knees to accomplish the task. Taking a final breath of clean air that he hoped would cover the onion odor he could still taste, he lifted his hands toward either side of her face as she released his arm and hand. He tilted her head back just a little, his mind racing in the moment as he reminded himself that a quick closed-mouth kiss would not betray his onion breath. Now feeling more confident, he pushed her hood back off her head and started to close the distance between her face and his as he gently cupped her face in his hands. She closed her beautiful eyes.

His nervous stomach churned, and he was instantly aware of a backwash of gas and onion taste up the back of his throat that required him to tighten his lips to prevent the otherwise inevitable burp that would have terminated their relationship forever. Panicked, he bulged his cheeks slightly to dispel some of the pressure now welled-up in his throat. He was too near to her face to risk any emission at such close range. A kiss with such tightly puckered lips could be a real turn-off for her, worse than no kiss at all! But if he aborted the kiss at this last second, what message would that be sending?

There wasn't enough time to think. He bailed out, sort of. He redirected her face downward, slightly, and softly placed a kiss lasting only a second on her head just above her bangs, his lips electrified with the feel of her hair on his lips. He then nuzzled his left cheek against her hair as he quietly blew the silent burp harmlessly away over her shoulder. He felt her sigh and relax.

"I had a wonderful time, too," he said, also relieved. He held this wonderful position as she gently placed her hands on his waist.

He was prepared to remain exactly like this the rest of the night. Then he saw a ruffle of the venetian blinds and realized Jennifer had just that instant parted them briefly for whatever reason. Not wanting to cause Kay any embarrassment he said, "I think your housemother expects you home."

"Ah, yes," replied Kay, coming back to earth. "I should get my key. Do you want to borrow an umbrella?" she said, retrieving the key from her right outer coat pocket, smiling.

"No thanks, I obviously can't be trusted with one," he said, looking over the rail behind him. He took a step or two back as she placed her key and opened the door and then stepped in looking back over her shoulder. She paused, looked at him with the eyes he would remember forever, and said, "Thanks again for a beautiful evening."

"Goodnight, Kay," he said, and with that she went in and closed the door. He performed a pirouette then headed for the stairs, gliding down them as he touched his lips lightly with his right second and third fingers, as if to make certain they were still there. When he reached the bottom of the stairs he looked over to the bushes against the building where his umbrella might be. He walked in that direction and found his umbrella tangled in the hedge. He shook it and held it over his head as he set off across the parking lot. He heard a call from the second story walk above him. He turned and was surprised to see Kay had reappeared, standing at the railing of the walk turned balcony.

"Good-night, Romeo!" she waved.

"Good-night, Juliet!" he answered, and realized he was a lucky man.

David was a little surprised to find Rex awake, sitting at his desk. Usually at this time on a Saturday night Rex was either out or already asleep. But there he sat, working at his desk. David started the conversation as soon as he entered the room, beating him to the punch, if there was to be one. David still wasn't sure how to introduce Kay into their conversation. This was a new form of relationship for Rex and him to be discussing and he didn't want to put up with any joking, good natured or otherwise, at this point. Kay was too perfect to be the target of anyone's joke.

"What'cha doin'?" he asked Rex.

"Studying music theory. Why do they have to make it so confusing? This isn't how a real musician thinks. If you did all this stuff while you were playing, you'd be four measures behind before the introduction was done! How was the movie?"

"Very British," he said flatly, hoping to steer the conversation away from his evening.

He readied himself for bed as he asked, "Doesn't everyone have to take music theory?" hoping this would distract Rex long enough to allow him to change. Rex ranted a few minutes on the problems in the music department while David agreed, egging him on. David was ready to go down to the bathroom when Rex concluded, then asked, "Who'd you wind up going to the movie with?"

"Another pre-med student from the class — rained liked a flood out there," he said as he headed out the door, hoping the chauvinist in Rex would assume a guy went with him and let it drop.

When he got back to the room Rex had already gotten into bed and turned out the light. David quickly stowed his toiletries and followed suit.

"Good night, Patson."

"Good night, Rex," he responded in the dark.

David started to reflect on the perfect evening he had just spent. Thirty seconds into his thoughts Rex added, "Patson, you don't put on British Sterling for a pre-med student!"

"You do for this one, Rex," he said. "Now go to sleep. I need my rest for finals week!"

David floated in his bed, waiting for the sleep that he knew would aggressively fill the vacuum created by the adrenaline depletion he had experienced after a day of good studying followed by the long anticipated date. His lips still tingled from where he had kissed her. He touched them again just to be certain they were still there.

He went over every minute detail of his evening, chagrinned at how stressed he had felt in anticipation of the entire date. He contemplated the lesson he had learned this night — if he were a millionaire and spent thousands of dollars and hired a private jet to carry her around the world, he would not have had a better time. Yet he marveled that the things that stuck out most to him, the things that led to the evening being so perfect, were the things that he hadn't planned, or wouldn't have planned — the rain, the inadequate umbrella, the Vanilla Creams, the dangerous stairs, the slippery crosstie, the onions — everything had turned out so perfectly. The touch of her hand on his, the perfectly sculpted waist of this woman, the kiss on the head that would have to do for now, how special and perfect he felt with his arm around her. He reflected on the Genesis story of creation, how God had created woman out of man's side. Perhaps this explained why she seemed such a perfect fit. He began his evening prayer thanking God for creating woman, a woman named Kay, as sleep flooded over him.

The following Monday in English class David sat beside Kay at the table for the final day of class. They dutifully discussed *Romeo and* Juliet, although

David found it almost blasphemous to attempt to reduce such an event to simple words. The class discussion in no way reflected the reverence he now felt for this movie which had played such an integral role in such a key evening in his life. Hearing Kay's discussion of the movie, with her emphasis on the universal romantic appeal of the characters, almost made him a little nervous. He was disappointed in his own contributions to the discussion, which sounded dispassionate to him, contrasted with his actual feelings that he dared not put into words.

Afterwards, he walked her to French, making certain to get her phone number in Peachtree City so they could plan their pizza date once the pace of the world slowed after final exams. They made a tentative agreement that the date would be Saturday night, each realizing that parental obligations might override their plans at the last minute, since neither was aware of what responsibilities awaited them at home.

Finals week came, and with it the flurry of hard work and sleep deprivation that is typical on college campuses. He phoned her about ten o'clock Tuesday evening. Jen answered the phone and reported Kay was already in bed for the night. He was immediately concerned that she must be ill to be retiring so early, but Jen reassured him that she was a great believer in adequate sleep, especially where final exams were concerned.

He called her earlier on Wednesday, about 7:30 that evening, and wished her good luck on the upcoming English exam. They talked only five or ten minutes since he knew she needed to be studying for her three finals. With great self-discipline he truncated their talk at ten minutes (just after she said she was really getting nervous about the coming finals — was that a hint to hang up?) He encouraged her and then hung up.

David's first two finals were on Tuesday and Wednesday, while Kay's first final was David's last, the English final. When Thursday came, they both utilized the full two hours given to complete their exam, a writing assignment. They walked out of the class together, with David downplaying his own performance and predicting Kay's success; she likewise assured him how well he must have done and how much better she would have done with his grasp of the subject.

They quickly moved onto more pleasant topics as they slowly headed toward the Foreign Languages building where Kay's next final exam would begin in 90 minutes. This pattern of avoiding a discussion of things related to the class — they had not talked about the movie on the way home, now they did not talk about the specifics of the English test immediately after the test — seemed a bit odd for a relationship that for so many weeks had been limited to discussions of literature. Perhaps, having been so tied and restricted by the initial conversation boundaries needlessly established by David and respected by Kay they now delighted in their newfound freedom. Or perhaps they did not wish to become academic competitors.

Pre-med students can be a fairly competitive lot, not cut-throat toward fellow students, but rather too hard on themselves. They do not glory in the academic demise of a known classmate who performs poorly, realizing this does not elevate their own chances in the small pool of admissions available to medical school. With a limited number of positions offered by medical schools, the seemingly limitless number of desirous applicants rapidly replaces any weakened aspiring doctor. Thus, it may be difficult for even an excellent pre-med student to be happy with his own performance if he is aware of another grade better than his. Insecurity may set in as the student questions why he only earned a 95 final grade while another earned a 97. Will that 95 keep him from making the cut into the next level?

For this reason another Unwritten Code has developed among such students, that they will not compare grades too closely. Based on their own reactions during the quarter, David and Kay were each confident that the other would receive an 'A' for the class, and they confirmed that much with each other when grades were mailed. They never did compare final test scores or numerical averages from Dr. Harris's class more closely. David had been so proud of his writing on the final English exam — his use of strong verbs, his insightful analogies, the way he threw in the casual yet clever reference to Mercutio while writing about Donne's "An Anatomy of the World" — that he was confident of a strong final performance for Dr. Harris. David tried to imagine how much pleasure Dr. Harris would experience as he enjoyed the brilliant writing submitted containing insight that even Dr. Harris himself would benefit from reading.

David protectively elected not to discuss grade specifics with Kay. He did not want to do anything that might cause her to question her own academic abilities. While David had great confidence in Kay's ability, she was a just freshman, with a more fragile, female psyche. He was more experienced in academic competition, a seasoned upperclassman. Theirs was not a level playing field, so it would be unfair to compare his grade to hers.

He needn't have worried. Kay demonstrated similar wisdom in not discussing her grade with David, or the letter she subsequently received from Dr. Harris which stated, in part,

> "As is my custom, I am pleased to write this letter to congratulate you for being the top scoring student in Honors English 105 for Winter Quarter, 1977...If you ever find yourself in need of a letter of recommendation supporting your subsequent academic pursuits I would be honored to provide an endorsement of your qualifications."

They sat on the bench outside the entrance to the Foreign Languages building. David felt guilty for feeling so relaxed now that he was through with finals and thus had no school responsibilities for ten days, even as Kay had two challenging exams remaining. David had to leave town before Kay's French exam would be over. He hated to leave her, but several weeks ago he had agreed to give Luke Noble a ride to the Atlanta airport if Luke would pay for the gas to get the Maverick to Atlanta. David knew Kay would like the opportunity to cram the last minutes before her test, so he regretfully bid her "Au revoir" and scampered up to Blimpie's, where he purchased a pack of Vanilla Creams. He made a bee-line for her apartment and left the cookies in a Blimpie's bag on her doorknob. He included a note which read, *"Good luck preparing for your final final! See you Saturday — Romeo"*.

Spring break week was, predictably, far too short and far too long. David and Kay did go for their pizza date on Saturday night. That was her first introduction to the Maverick, and his first introduction to her mother. He was relieved to see how warm and engaging her mother was, but not surprised. Kay had modeled her skills well.

The majority of David's week was spent doing yard work for his dad, who paid him $2 per hour for any extra work he did in the yard beyond the normal duties expected of him. He actually enjoyed the physically taxing but otherwise mindless work of maintaining his family's 5 acre lot. He burned dead tree limbs, cut the lawn's first growth of spring, and dug up the plot for the family vegetable garden. The University of Georgia seemed a million miles away, almost. He could not help but think about the analogy he could write for Dr. Harris as he contemplated the soil that was his life's story while he rototilled his father's garden. To this point he had failed in his harvest of love by having his rows planted too close together, his roots too shallow. Now he was working to get things right. He had cultivated the soil all winter quarter, he had only one plant in his entire plot of land, and the roots there would be properly nurtured with appropriate nutrients to allow them to grow deeply while he vigilantly guarded against allowing any competing weeds to spring up. Dr. Harris would be impressed.

He had plenty of time while he worked alone to process the events of the past quarter. He realized how fortunate he considered himself to know Kay. It would not have taken a clairvoyant to predict what he would have listed in a personal want ad, if he had been so inclined to place one, in describing his ideal woman. Based on the high points of his choices in women thus far, she would be slim, with great hair, a sense of humor, and a beautiful appearance. She'd also likely be musical (probably a woodwind player, with keyboard a definite plus), a good communicator, and highly intelligent. He calculated it to be statistically improbable that he could find all those qualities in one person. But to find all those qualities in a woman whose only apparent flaw was an isolated failure in discernment that allowed her to feel the same way about him seemed an impossibility, until now. Yet Kay was all that and more. She was everything he felt he was not. He had seen she was mature, poised, comfortable in social situations, always knowing the right thing to say or do. And indeed, she possessed all of the best qualities taken from all of the girls he had pursued to this point. She was musically talented, not just on a wind instrument, but also on the piano. She was beautiful — she had great hair, she was easy on the eyes and she took good care of herself. She was very intelligent, and she liked to laugh at David's jokes. She was comfortable in her faith. David hoped he was worthy of such a lady, or, he teased himself, that at least that he could keep her fooled until he actually was worthy.

That week David and Rex also played a Raz'Mataz Dixieland job with Sandy which Sandy had booked for the last Saturday night of spring break. The job meant no date when Kay returned to town — she was gone all week on a trip to the North Georgia mountains which her parents had arranged as a surprise getaway. Still, he welcomed the opportunity to pick up another $35 and sock away all the cash he could. He planned to be taking Kay on as many dates as he could afford when they returned to Athens. Spring quarter would be starting in just two more days!

Chapter 17
At Kay's

The group was now approaching the Riverside parking lot, and David could see Kay's sparkling aqua 1976 Vega parked in its usual spot. It had been a high school graduation gift from her grandmother, and she treated it in a way that demonstrated just how much she appreciated the very generous gift.

Dr. Tew and Doc paused briefly at her car to admire it, Doc asking, "Is this her car?" Pops forged on ahead, calling back to the other three, "Come on you guys, let's go meet Kay!"

They ascended the single flight of stairs that led up to the second floor exterior walkway that allowed access to Kay's apartment. Pops stopped first, just past the door with "2113" on it and waited as first David, then Dr. Tew and finally Doc arrived. David knocked rhythmically three times, and almost instantly Kay's voice from the other side of the door sang out, "Coming!" and she opened the door.

She was wearing a powder blue terry cloth sleeveless shirt and dark navy satin shorts with white anklets and white Keds shoes. While her dress was by no means immodest, the smooth curves of her toned arms and runner's legs were impossible not to admire. She had already honed her skin tone to perfection with a springtime tan that seemed to enhance the natural soft texture of her skin rather than diminish it. Although Doc was the only one slightly winded from the quick trip up the stairs, they all stood with their mouths opened.

She quickly tried to take in what she was seeing. To her far right stood David. Standing behind him and peering over his right shoulder stood an elderly man with blond hair and a full beard, about two inches shorter that David. He was almost as thin as David. His eyes seemed to twinkle a bit.

A second man stood in front of him to David's right. He appeared to be middle aged, but she was so surprised to see a grown man wearing such baggy long shorts and odd shoes with anklets that she did not notice much more about him in the initial instant allowed. A less secure woman might have felt jealous that his shirt was a more feminine blue than hers. Alongside him stood the final relative David had told her was coming. He was an older man, heavier than the others, with a silver goatee, wearing worn jeans with a red knit short sleeve shirt.

That was about as much as she could absorb about her guests in the brief time it took her to open the door and say, "Happy Birthday, Birthday Boy!"

He was a little disappointed she just stood there standing in the doorway, holding the doorknob now with her right hand to keep the door open. *"A big birthday hug would be nice,"* he thought, but he appreciated her prudence in not wanting to embarrass him with any public display of affection in front of the three guests. He decided to follow her lead.

"Kay, this is Dr. Tew, I-I mean my Uncle Dave, um, Tew. Call him Uncle Dave. It's a long story," he said with nervous laughter that indicated more about how nervous he was than how funny he was.

Dr. Tew held out his right hand and shook hers gently as he said, "Please, call me Dave."

"Very nice to meet you, Uncle Dave," she replied, noticing the similarity in his voice and David's. She wanted to be kind, so she tried to ignore his silly shorts which were long enough to reach to his knees, which were still a long way from the top of his anklet socks. She was too polite to notice for long, as she was fascinated to study the obvious similarities between uncle and nephew. He had the same blue eyes — although they somehow didn't seem as trustworthy, — the same George Washington nose, the same height and similar body build, but the moustache was definitely not an asset. Something about him made her feel a bit uneasy, a bit self-conscious. He certainly was not timid about looking at her, and his eyes studied a lot more than just her face. She was almost relieved when David continued the introductions.

"And this is...well, we all just call him 'Doc', and you should, too," he said, bowing slightly toward Doc and extending his right arm.

"Well, um, 'Doc', it's a pleasure to meet you. I'm so glad you came," she said warmly as Doc came toward center and also shook her hand while Dr. Tew stepped back toward the rail. Doc's smile warmed her heart as he looked into her eyes. He reminded her of her own grandfather a bit, except for the jeans. His blue eyes seemed younger than the rest of his aging body and danced behind his glasses with an unspoken but obvious interest. His face was fuller than Uncle Dave's, but he too had the trademark Tew nose, although his looked a little broader, a little fleshier.

"I can't tell you how nice it is to meet you... We've all heard such nice things about you," he replied, as if his thoughts were distracting him from speaking smoothly, his eyes locked with hers.

David continued with the introductions. "And last, but certainly not least, this is Pops, the grand patriarch of the clan," said David as he backed away and to his left, opening a gap for Pops to step forward. As Pops stepped forward he opened his arms and she politely indulged his harmless invitation, giving him a hug. Kay had learned that in the South when meeting close friends of friends for the first time, hugs were not unusual. Pops fully embraced her, burying the left side of his face into her left shoulder saying nothing. As they hugged David studied the responses of Dr. Tew and Pops. Both men observed the situation closely, their attentions seemingly trained on Kay. David observed that neither did anything to betray a previous acquaintance with Kay, so maybe she was not in on their birthday appearance. She certainly had indicated nothing in that regards by her initial reactions.

Before his embrace became embarrassing to either, Pops disengaged and stepped back. He seemed visibly taken by her presence and he spoke now with a voice that was softer but earnest, somber and sincere.

"David has told us what a beautiful young lady you are, but his descriptions fall short of telling the full story. It is *so* nice to see you, Kay."

David's mind studied the situation further. *"I don't remember telling him how beautiful she is. But there's no way he's just acting. Kay is not in on their trick, whatever it is. She's looking at them like she's never seen them before. What was I thinking inviting them here? What do they want?"*

Kay was momentarily taken aback by the effusive praise, then collected herself, her face flushed, as she said, "Oh, my, forgive me for letting you stand out here. Come in, come on in! It is so nice to meet you all."

They filed into her apartment and stood, looking around. On the far wall in the kitchen taped to the cabinets over the counter were sheets of notebook paper, each with a separate large hand-colored block letter that spelled out 'Happy Birthday'. On the counter David spied a cake dish he had not seen before, but it was covered, so he could not tell what it contained. In the center of the small square dining table in the kitchen was a fairly large box wrapped in dark blue paper with a white ribbon and bow. No candles or silverware, however, and no flowers. The record player on the shelves along the left side of the living room was playing a Barry Manilow album — David knew it was her recently purchased *This One's For You*.

To the right of the door there were three chairs near the wall, facing toward the sofa — two unmatched folding beach chairs and a third metal folding chair that matched the four folding chairs around the table in the kitchen.

"Make yourselves comfortable," she said in a warm and cheerful voice. "My interior decorator tells me that backyard chic will be big next year," she added, smiling at the beach chairs.

Doc and Dr. Tew positioned themselves at either end of the sofa, neither speaking, each man's mind seemingly whirring to process the information they had gleaned from their intense study of Kay. Pops seemed a little more composed, offering a bit of humor by asking, "Can you first point me to the little girl's room?"

Kay, momentarily caught off guard, wrinkled her brow, then, getting the joke, said, "Oh, by all means. Go down the hall to the right, through my bedroom and you'll recognize it on the left."

She quickly turned to David, startling him, as she blurted out, "Ooo. Before I forget, your parents just called here looking for you —"

"— Is everything OK?" interrupted David.

"Yes, they just wanted to let you know there had been a change of plans, so instead of you calling them collect between five and seven this evening, they will call you here at around four o'clock. Is that OK?"

"Well, of course. They called at daytime rates to say that…and they are going to call back at daytime rates just to say 'Happy Birthday'? Did they say why? And how did they get your number?"

"Your father said you'd be impressed that they 'lost it' and were willing to pay the rates for his 'only oldest boy'. Apparently they've got some evening plans that just came up yesterday and they wouldn't be able to be close to a phone that you could easily call in to, so they decided to call and let you know that they'll call you when they are through seeing patients this afternoon. They called your dorm this morning, but when there was no answer then and again later in the morning and again a few minutes ago he used the itemized phone bill he had from when you called me here from his house during spring break — you remember the call that Thursday night? He remembered you still owed him for the 13-minute call, and was glad he remembered the number was listed on the bill. He took the bill to work with him this morning just in case he needed it, and so he did. So the condensed version is, since they knew I might know where you were or where you would be at four o'clock, we agreed you would stay here until they call then."

"Sounds like a plan," said David.

She sat in a chair facing the sofa, and redirected her comments to her guests and thoughts of 'backyard chic'.

"Jennifer and I sort of borrowed things from our parents to furnish the apartment," she explained, and then set off on a fairly detailed description of the visible items in the apartment — whose they were, how they came to be needed, etc. Dr. Tew and Doc relaxed and became a willing and attentive audience, peppering her with questions that led to yet another round of discussion about the accumulated "yard-sale-in-waiting" as she self-deprecatingly referred to her creatively appointed abode. By the end of their discussion about the only thing not mentioned was the big blue box on the table.

David felt a bit guilty for not already knowing the history of each piece — she had obviously put a good bit of effort into creating the setting. She concluded her descriptive tour and realizing her hostess responsibilities, asked, "Can I get you something to drink?"

David and Doc both answered her by a shake of their heads 'no' as Dr. Tew asked, "Do you have any Diet Coke?"

She and David looked at each other briefly, puzzled. Dr. Tew read their faces and immediately corrected himself. "I mean do you have any Tab?"

"Yes," she interjected, and headed to the refrigerator while he continued his thought.

"Some people call Tab 'Diet Coke' because it was really supposed to be a diet version of Coke. In 1963 the powers that be at Coke were afraid to call it anything having to do with the Coke name, so they called it 'Tab'. Something to do with being able to 'keep a tab' on your calorie count. Didn't seem to hurt the Pepsi brand image when they created 'Diet Pepsi' in 1964, although I still prefer Tab."

"Oh, I can't imagine life without Tab! It is my new-found addiction since coming to UGA," she called from across the kitchen as David listened interestedly and Doc rolled his eyes at Dr. Tew's predictable thinly veiled attempt to impress the good-looking girl.

"I forgot how boring he was," mumbled Doc to David, who was standing at the end of the couch where Doc sat.

Kay returned with the Tab for Dr. Tew and he thanked her as he took the cold pink can, rejecting her offer of a glass with ice. He studied the pull top briefly, then opened the can carefully as she spoke.

"Excuse me while I work on a few things for lunch."

"Need any help?" asked Doc.

"Oh, no, I'm fine. You guys just relax and keep the Birthday Boy entertained," she said as she walked back to the kitchen. She took a head of lettuce from the refrigerator and turned on the water in the sink.

David positioned himself on the couch between Doc and Dr. Tew as the first sip of Tab was about to be enjoyed.

"Ooo, cyclamates!" Dr. Tew said with a disappointed look on his face. "I remember now why I never learned to drink Tab," he said in a comment directed to Doc, inaudible to Kay over the running water and Barry Manilow.

"I never could stand the taste of diet drinks," said David.

"You will," said Doc and Dr. Tew, together.

David folded his hands together, shaking his head in disbelief as he leaned forward and looked at the floor. Speaking softly enough not to be heard by Kay, he said, "You guys just won't quit. I don't know what you're up to, but *please* don't do anything to mess up this afternoon with Kay. She'll have us all committed to the asylum if she hears all this futuristic mumbo-jumbo stuff. Besides, Dr. Tew on the way over here you said the birthday present would be white. There's a lot you've said today I could never confirm, but that fact is indisputable — it's blue. There seems to be a hole in your trick. So tell me, what's the deal?"

"No tricks at all," replied Dr. Tew in a hushed tone. He took another sip of Tab, frowned, and continued, "I said the *box* was white — I didn't say anything about the wrapping paper."

David's retort, "That's lame," came from his heart, but that was not the way he would normally address an adult. He was starting to feel apprehensive about the potential predicament he had allowed himself to be part of.

He looked back over at the blue box as Kay glanced over from the sink where she had been busily washing salad ingredients. She winked and gave him a full and enthusiastic smile while swaying with the music as "Weekend in New England" finished and the turntable went silent. She was in her element and enjoying the moment.

"I couldn't help but notice what a beautiful *blue* centerpiece you have there," David said, directing his comment to her, his barb to Dr. Tew.

"Oh, I hope you'll like it!" she said excitedly. "Do you want to open it now?"

"Sure!" came the obvious answer.

She turned off the water, drying her hands on a towel as she asked, "Do you men want to come sit her at the table and watch David open his presents?" As they started to stir from the couch, she said, "I'll let Pops know you're starting presents," as she headed down the hall. Standing now, David saw her stop at her bedroom door and look inside. "Poor sweet baby," she said quietly, and she went in to her room, closing the door quietly behind her.

Dr. Tew looked at Doc and shrugged. "Do you guess we should finish making the salad?" asked Doc. Dr. Tew nodded, answering, "Might as well. Might keep her from putting olives in it." They busied themselves at the sink, with no mention of concern for whatever it was that was making Pops a 'poor sweet baby'."

"Do you think we should check on Pops?" asked the concerned David.

"You can if you want, but I'll bet he's OK," answered the unconcerned Dr. Tew as he poured his full can of Tab down the sink.

"Well I think I'll check then," said David, walking down the hall. He stopped at the door and knocked softly. "Is everything OK?" he asked through the closed door.

"Yes," replied Kay, "We'll be out in a minute."

This seemed strange to David. Did this have something to do with the blue present awaiting him on the table, or something to do with the bigger picture of whatever had been going on all day? He walked back to the kitchen where Dr. Tew and Doc were working on the salad and talking. Not wanting to be rude, he listened as they continued.

"Man, I was shocked to see how young she is — you forget those things," said Doc.

"And you got to admit, she looks great with a tan," added Dr. Tew.

"Ironic, wouldn't you say?" responded Doc.

"Yeah," laughed Dr. Tew, good-naturedly.

Realizing they were probably talking about Kay, David was ready to change the subject. "Kay says Pops is doing OK and they'll be out in a minute."

"Just as I thought," said Dr. Tew.

Doc chopped carrots. Dr. Tew chopped lettuce. David sat at the kitchen table. As he sat he noted now that in addition to the large blue box, there were what appeared to be a wrapped record album, and two smaller blue packages leaning against the back side of the large blue present. Kay had gone all out. He didn't know whether to feel proud or scared. They had only been dating eleven weeks and four days. What would he do for her birthday in November?

No one spoke, but they could hear nothing from the bedroom. Doc started working on the tomato and Dr. Tew the mushrooms. *"Hope this is what she had in mind for the salad,"* thought David. *"If, in fact, these men knew Kay, they had not seen her recently. Maybe they knew her as a child... they were friends with her dad and he had something to do with today...or her mother..."* but that didn't seem plausible, either. *"What are she and Pops talking about?"* This lull in the action was giving him plenty of time for questions, but no answers.

David was growing uncomfortable with the quiet, with nothing to do, with Kay's absence, with Doc and Dr. Tew, so he said to both of them, or to himself, "Guess I'll put on some music." He walked over and flipped the album to its 'B' side, then for lack of anything else to do, went back and sat at the table.

"Not a bad album," said Doc. "I was always surprised that "Jump, Shout, Boogie" didn't get more airtime," he said.

"Or "Weekend in New England"," added Dr. Tew.

"How do these old guys know so much about Barry Manilow? But what's not to like?" David thought. "It's OK, but some of the songs are a little weak," said David, not wanting to appear too big a fan of such sentimental music. "Mushy music gets a little old after a while. Better to stay with Chicago," he countered, not fully expressing his true love for all things Barry.

With that, the discussion turned to the brassy rock band Chicago and their music, but Doc and Dr. Tew seemed to know more about Chicago than David did, so David listened while they discussed Chicago and songs he had never even heard of before. What he knew of Chicago he had learned from Will Rice, who loved Chicago, and had all their albums. David would have to buy one of their albums someday.

Pops had walked into Kay's room and then bathroom, thankful for the opportunity to compose himself. He was not really surprised with the impact seeing Kay had on him, just unprepared. It stirred his heart to see her looking so good, so young, so healthy. He was chagrinned with himself at having to claim to need to use her bathroom — he had just used the one at Reed Hall 15 minutes ago. The advantage of having an 80-year-old prostate was that nobody else seemed to think this was unusual.

He turned on the sink and splashed cold water on his face and burning eyes. Rising from the sink he looked at the mirror in front of him and saw a picture Kay had stuck in the lower right corner of the frame of the mirror. It was a picture Kay's mother had taken on the night of Kay and David's pizza date. David had arrived, been welcomed into the house, and chatted with Kay's mother and father. As he and Kay headed out the front door, Kay's mother had them pose on the front stoop, the front yard as the background, while she snapped a quick picture of the two of them. Pops studied the picture — what a great smile Kay had, how she tilted her head just a little toward his shoulder as they stood beside each other. Tears welled in his eyes and he splashed more water on his face. He turned off the water and grabbed the hand towel beside the sink. He held the towel in both open palms and pressed it against his face to dry off. He smelled the faint scent of Kay on the towel, and was racked with sudden uncontrollable sobbing. He muffled his sobs with the towel while he walked back to Kay's room to sit down. He sat on the side of her bed, then stretched out prone, burying his face in her pillow to further muffle his agony, but her scent was only stronger on the pillow. He silently rocked and pulsed in grief on the bed for several minutes, feeling this wave of woe sweep over, then beyond him. He was beginning to gain control when he heard Kay say, "Poor sweet baby," and enter the room, closing the door behind her.

Pops was embarrassed to be seen this way, but comforted by her words, by her presence. He dared not speak lest he break down again. He was grateful that if anyone had to enter, it had been Kay. He did not want to disrupt the happy party planned in the next room, nor to cause her distress, but her sensitivity and discernment were appreciated at this moment. He felt his secret safe with her. She did not try to coax him into conversation, choosing instead to sit tacitly on the bed beside him gently scratching and stroking his back while the last sobs exited as deep breaths.

There was a knock at the door, and they heard David from the other side ask, "Is everything OK?"

"Yes," replied Kay, "We'll be out in a minute." She continued to patiently, quietly wait for Pops to say something.

"I'm sorry," he eventually said. "This is supposed to be a happy day, and I've intruded. I didn't mean to."

As he spoke he sat up and swung his legs over the side of the bed, so he was now sitting alongside of Kay. He wiped his face with her towel and continued, staring at the towel in his lap.

"It's strange how I'm doing OK then it just hits me," he said softly, not being completely honest with himself. She nodded as if to understand. His voice began to strengthen as he continued.

"Kay, did you ever see the movie *Romeo and Juliet*?"

"Yes," she replied.

"There is a beautiful love song, the theme song for the movie — I'm sure you know it-"

"Yes, definitely," she said.

"The lyrics say

A rose will bloom,
it then will fade
So does a youth.
So does the fairest maid

The words have bothered me for a long time. I guess that's true for Romeo and Juliet, but for most of us, the rest of us, that misses the bigger point. I've grown a lot of roses in my life, and you know what I've learned?"

"What?" she replied.

"Only after the rose has begun to fade does its true beauty, its true value, which is its fragrance, begin to reach its fullest potential. If you smell a perfectly formed rosebud, you only get a hint of what the ultimate fragrance of that bud will be. But if you leave that bud in a vase of water for a few days that bud will fill an entire room with its true fragrance as it opens into full bloom. People may value the appearance of the rose bud, but in reality the ultimate value comes later in its life, only after its physical beauty has peaked. Do you see what I'm talking about?" he asked.

"Yes, I guess," she tried not to lie.

"Too many people think that once the bloom starts to fade that life is over. I can tell you, our society places too much value on youth, not that youth isn't a great thing, but there is no substitute for life's experiences. There are too many people that would be bored to find out that if Romeo and Juliet hadn't died, they could have had an even greater life together, every day falling more in love, with a life full of shared experiences. It is those shared experiences that help make a marriage uniquely rich; that's when the fragrance really becomes beautiful. As exciting as it is to be a rose bud, I'd far rather have the pleasure of being in full bloom, and beyond. I have a feeling you are going to make your husband a very lucky man. The good fortune he finds in you will only begin with the fact you make a lovely rose bud, not end there."

Kay blushed at such a complement from the relative of the man upon whom she could project her futuristic thoughts and dreams. "That's a really beautiful thought," she said. "I hope you're right."

"I am," he replied. "And I hope even more so that you will know beyond a shadow of a doubt, each and every day of your marriage, how much his love grows for you, that he never passes up the opportunity to tell you what a lucky man he is." His voice shook slightly as he slowed now, his speech more deliberate with emphasis, "and that you know in a *powerful* way what *complete* joy and meaning you give his life. Most men probably aren't very good at telling their wives that, but I hope you will know it, that you will feel it in whatever inadequate ways he demonstrates his love to you. You deserve all that and more."

Kay felt herself trembling — she wanted to cry. This was so raw, so intense, so heartfelt, she did not feel worthy to be the recipient of such a blessing of hope. This description of love, of marriage was a description of all she wanted and more someday. She just never expected it to be verbalized by a little old man. She and David had certainly never had such a conversation.

"You have a *very* lucky wife," she said, softly, when she thought she could speak. "You do have a wife, don't you?" she asked, not certain how to phrase the question to which she did not know the answer.

"My wife...My Kitty... let me tell you about her..." he said, as he began his story.

Kay knew she had stumbled upon the right question by the way he seemed to brighten up as he now spoke freely.

Kay came up the hall from out of her bedroom followed by Pops. If there had been a problem, none was evident, although *"They certainly were in there a long time,"* thought David as he stood up from the table. But so much about this day seemed weird that having his girlfriend in her bedroom with a strange old man, a room where he knew her parents had made it clear that no male was ever to go, seemed like just another piece in the puzzle, a puzzle that was still in a million pieces and made no sense at all.

Kay took control of the conversation and asked cheerfully, "Well now, who's ready to open presents?" She noticed the finished product of the salad-makers in a bowl on the counter and said, "Oh, wow! That's a beautiful salad. Thanks, salad fairies, whoever you are, for doing such nice work!" Doc and Dr. Tew beamed like six-year-old boys with her praise.

She plugged in her frying pan and turned it on, saying, "I better get this started," as she put the large prepared salad into the refrigerator. She briefly looked into the oven, then walked to the table and picked up one of the two smaller packages. "This one first," she said, placing it in David's hand. He opened the present, a big bag of Raisinets, impressed that she remembered how much he liked them. When had he told her about that?

"Wow! A half pound bag of Raisinets — a single serving size!"

Kay giggled.

"And it's yellow," observed Dr. Tew, with a cocky nod toward David.

"Next open this one," said Kay, ignoring Dr. Tew's remark which made no sense to her. She handed David the smallest remaining package. He hoped it was what it felt like. Opening the present, he said, "Vanilla Creams!" and tore the rest of the paper off. "Hmmm... six Vanilla Creams and only five of us. If my math is correct, that means...Kay gets five and I get one, and you guys go hungry!"

They all laughed at his self-perceived wit while Kay gave him a friendly slap on his arm with the back of her hand. "You should be writing these down," he told her, with a wink to Doc, who had moved behind where Pops was standing and had briefly massaged Pop's shoulders as if to convey a message of support.

"Is it OK if we eat these now? I don't think I need to worry about ruining my appetite. I could eat steak on a full stomach!"

"You're the Birthday Boy — you decide," replied Kay, glad to see her gifts being so well received.

David opened the pack of Vanilla Creams, careful not to spill any crumbs on the floor, and held the pack out to each one present, starting will Kay. Everyone took a cookie, but waited for David, as if observing Communion. As Pops was being served last, he held his cookie up with his right hand and said, "I propose a 'toast'. To David, may you always know where to seek happiness, and having found it, enjoy it!"

"Here, here!" barked Doc and Dr. Tew as they all lifted the cookies high, then ate in unison with sighs and moans of ecstasy. "I forgot how good these were," Doc exclaimed, as David offered the sixth and final Vanilla Cream to Kay. She shook her head and said, "Oh, no, it's your birthday, birthday boy. You should have the last one."

"I could never win an argument with you," he smiled, and bit into the last cookie, as Doc was starting to say, "Hey, what about me?!"

He stuck the cellophane wrapper in his pocket as Kay picked up the next package and said, "Now, for your next surprise."

He skillfully peeled away the blue paper and revealed the Lettermen's album, *All-Time Greatest Hits*. "I love this album! Thanks Kay!" he exclaimed.

"Rex said you were going to wear out his cassette, so I thought you might need a copy for over the summer," she replied.

Dr. Tew took the album from David and started reading the song titles out loud. "'Going Out of My Head'... 'When I Fall in Love'... 'Put Your Head on My Shoulder'...I like your taste in music David. I'm glad you're not afraid to listen to a little 'Mushy Music', as some might call it."

David took the album back and headed for the turntable as he removed the cellophane. "I think these guys are amazing vocalists. You don't mind if I play it now, do you Kay?"

"Not a bit — you're the boss!" she decreed.

As The Lettermen filled the room, he returned to Kay and the group in the kitchen. "Well," said Pops, "Looks like it's time for you to eat!" seemingly ignoring the large blue box that was now the solo item on the table.

"It's such a pretty centerpiece, it would be a shame to open it up," teased Doc.

"It wouldn't be polite for me not to open all my gifts before lunch now, would it Kay?" David replied eagerly.

"You're the boss," Kay repeated. And with that, David excitedly began to peel away the paper, revealing a large white box with green letters on the side that read 'Rich's'. "I had to borrow a department store box for reasons that will become apparent in just a second," advised Kay.

David separated the taped top from the bottom and lifted off the top to reveal the contents, which were buried in a large volume of white tissue paper. When he dug to the bottom of the paper, he felt a firm object and lifted it out. He immediately realized that this was a replacement arm rest for the Marvelous Maverick.

"How did you get this?" he exclaimed with obvious delight.

Kay smiled proudly as she explained that she had made her purchase at a large junkyard on Highway 78 halfway to Atlanta. David slowly rotated the armrest in his hands. It was like new — he couldn't believe it had ever been in a junkyard. "It's perfect!" he said.

Dr. Tew and the others had been an appreciative audience to this point, but now he spoke up, observing, "It is such a perfect match to the *beige* interior of the car."

David froze with this reminder as Kay replied, "Yes, I got lucky. I left them my phone number the first time I went and they didn't have it. Then called them every week, and on the third try they told me I could come out and look at a recent drop-off. It was a perfect match. Sad thing to see what happened to somebody else's Maverick, though. I'll always wear my seatbelt."

"Beige," David repeated, holding his gift with both hands.

With the present opening completed, Kay set about to cook the steaks in the frying pan that was now at cooking temperature. The men congregated around the table, which made things a little tight for the cook in the small kitchen, but she voiced no complaints. She enjoyed the banter as the guests asked David various questions about his family, friends, and childhood memories of earlier birthdays. Occasionally they crossed over the conversation to include Kay, who was glad not to be too distracted from her cooking, but still shared fun stories about growing up with James, John and Martha. She appeared to be quite busy between the frying pan, the oven, the refrigerator, the sink, and the toaster oven. Gradually, a table cloth then two settings of china appeared at the table. She confirmed with the others they were certain they didn't want to eat, so she set out three extra water glasses and napkins, assigning Dr. Tew the responsibility of getting the extra folding chair from the living room and placing it at one corner of the table so he could sit between Doc and Pops, while she and David each had a side of the table to enjoy their soon to be prepared lunch. Silverware and candlesticks appeared, which she asked Doc to light, perhaps intentionally interrupting a somewhat lively discussion that bordered on an argument between Doc and Dr. Tew about the relative merits of margarine vs. butter. Then she pulled an arrangement of flowers in a glass bowl from the refrigerator and placed the lovely azaleas and pansies on the table. With each addition to the table a complement was paid the hostess who was having a fun time not being a pre-med student.

David went over to the record player and flipped the album to its reverse side when it completed, then returned to the table. The room was filled with the sound of fun and the Lettermen, while the aromas of steak, rolls, and baked potatoes intensified. The salad was set out with two choices of dressing (she knew he wanted Thousand Island and she wanted Bleu Cheese) and dinner and salad plates for two appeared. Then, in what seemed be perfect timing, Kay magically added a plate with a foil-wrapped baked potato and still sizzling steak to her place and to David's place at the table to complement the just poured Tab for her and milk for him. She surveyed the table as Dr. Tew announced, "There's something burning in the toaster oven!"

Flustered, Kay turned back to the toaster oven and opened it with a cloth pot holder, rescuing the tray of four now black-top rolls from their incinerator. She placed them on the stove top, found a knife from the drawer beside her and picked up a roll to try to scrape off its blackened layer, but quickly dropped it back to the tray as she yelped, "Hot!" Not deterred, she picked up the tray with the pot holder and sheepishly presented the tray to David.

"My goal in life is to learn how to cook bread," she said. For some reason Pops, Doc and Dr. Tew all found this to be very funny now, and laughed. She seemed to be a good sport about it all as David quickly lifted two rolls off the tray. If she had been hurt by the laughter she had unwittingly spawned, it did not show. He tried to sooth her spirit by noting, "This is how I like my marshmallows and my rolls." He then got up from the table to pull her chair out for her.

When they were both seated he blessed the food and they ate. David enthusiastically dug in to his special birthday dinner while the three guests provided plenty of lively conversation on a wide variety of topics, always returning to find yet another thing about which to complement Kay — her appearance, her apartment, her grace, her appearance.

Kay took no offense at Dr. Tew's ribbing of David's food favorites — "You're killing me with all these saturated fats," — since a special day deserved a special menu. She could not be expected to understand the double entendre intended by his humor.

History will remember that the rolls were burned on top, yet not done in the middle. The steak was not cooked into medium doneness as David would have preferred, but rather past well done, with no pink color and little juice remaining. The baked potato was crunchy — who knows how much longer it should have baked. But he did not even try to scrape the burned tops off of his rolls. He ate everything exactly as it was presented, thankful that butter (or was it margarine?) covers a multitude of sins, and that the olives remained forgotten in the refrigerator. When he had finished, he pronounced it to be the best meal he had ever eaten. Kay knew he was lying — she elected not to finish her steak, potato or single roll. Had it only been the two of them she might have spoken up. Yet again, he was such an appreciative eater, she didn't want to interrupt. On that day she found one more thing she really liked about this David Patson guy.

When David's plates were empty, Kay rose and quickly cleared their dishes, then just as quickly set out five dessert plates and forks. The men did as they were told and stayed seated, their offers to help having been rejected. She refilled David's milk glass and offered milk to the other guests. Dr. Tew turned down the offer for milk when informed she had no skim milk, just 2% low fat milk, and he similarly refused another Tab. "Ice water will be fine," he stated. Pops and Doc both selected milk for the next course. She was glad she had purchased a full gallon.

From his place at the table David couldn't see what she was doing behind him at the counter, so he played dumb as she took the top off the cake dish and placed the candles while the men discussed Phil Niekro and the physics of the knuckleball. David then started to explain why he thought Hank Aaron's record of 755 home runs would stand forever when he heard her striking a match and smelled the sweet acrid scent of the fresh strike. She started singing as the others quickly joined in for yet another verse of "Happy Birthday", and he was yet again impressed how nicely his three surprise guests harmonized and blended, now even sweeter with Kay's cheery soprano melody as the cake blazing with candles was placed in front of him. "You guys sound great — the Lettermen don't have anything on you!" he exclaimed as all clapped at the end of the verse.

"Make a wish!" reminded Dr. Tew as David drew in a deep breath and extinguished all twenty candles with a single gust.

"Let me guess," said Doc, "you wished that one day you'll be as good looking as I", "or me," added Pops. The festive atmosphere even whetted Dr. Tew's dry humor. When all eyes turned to him expecting a similar comment, he flatly added, "You wish — let's eat some cake, but just a small slice for me, please."

"Kay, I can honestly say you bake the best carrot cake I've ever eaten," said Doc as the others chimed in their agreement, five empty plates now on the table, plates spattered with crumbs and streaked with icing.

"You're too generous," she replied. "But I can't take all the credit. My mother mailed me that recipe — it was her mother's. Then last night Mother talked me through some of it on the phone. I'll have to make it again someday."

"I'm sure you will," predicted Doc.

"Soon!" urged David.

"Well there's still a half cake there, does anyone else want any more to eat or drink?" asked Kay. There being no takers on this generous offer, Pops spoke up.

"We've still got some time before you have to go to work Kay. Why don't we go over to Reed and install this arm rest in the Maverick. I can't wait to see how it looks."

"Great idea!" agreed David.

"Sounds fine with me," said Kay. "I even happen to have just the right tool to make the job easier. I had to remove the armrest at the junkyard myself. Fortunately my brother, James — he drives a Mercury Comet similar to the Maverick — knew just what I'd need and advised me on what to look for in the Craftsman section. So I'm now an expert remover and installer of passenger-side arm rests for 1973 Maverick Grabbers."

"And here I thought you were just another pretty face," teased Doc. "You can bake the world's best carrot cake and remodel cars!"

The installation of the armrest went off without a hitch, capped by a brief ceremony in which David spoke a word of thanks to the old armrest for its faithful miles of service, then unceremoniously threw the old armrest into the dumpster outside the west end of Reed Hall. They all returned to Kay's apartment, now well after three o'clock.

"You men feel free to make yourselves at home," instructed Kay. "I need to change and get ready for work," she added as she disappeared down the hall and into her room.

David walked over to the turntable and flipped the Lettermen album and commenced the playing of side 'A'.

"She's really a beautiful girl," complemented Doc with a remark aimed at none but heard by all.

"I can't believe she was ever that young," added Dr. Tew, as if he had been looking at an old photograph. "Just to think, she was starting to drive two years ago."

"That is a long time," observed David, wanting to be part of the conversation, if only to represent Kay's interests since she wasn't here to defend herself. He could tell the conversation was headed back toward the on-going joke of the day that somehow he was entertaining three time travellers from the future, each claiming to be him from a future point in time, whose lives had all conveniently converged with his on this his twentieth birthday.

"But you should see her now," said Dr. Tew with a tone that did not sound complementary.

"There you go again!" shot back Doc. "You're a pig. You should see her *now*! She's beautiful, inside and out!...Which is more than I can say for *you* when you're sixty. Look at me! All that crazy jogging you're so into has left *me* with a bum knee that's going to have to be replaced sooner or later," he said, massaging his right knee. "I've gained fifty pounds because I can't run and now I spend every day listening to diet advice from my patients who show no mercy after all *your* years of being such a sticker for diet and exercise. So where did it get *you*? It got you here!" he said, patting either side of his belly.

Dr. Tew cocked his head to the right and then straightened it back up. With a bat of his eyes he advised, "You should take better care of yourself."

"Gentlemen," Pops interrupted, "We didn't come here today for this."

Hoping to find them now off-script, David responded, "Why did you come here today?"

Pops leaned back in the lawn chair he occupied and said, "Well, David, I'm not totally sure. I know now that I can't convince you that I'm just as real as you. But I don't want to, or need to, for the purpose of today's visit. I do wish I could convey to you what I've learned in life to save you a lot of pain and hassle." He spoke so sincerely that the other three listened intently.

"I have observed there are Four Seasons of Life for men. These seasons typically define and predict priorities, interests, or drives seen in the lives of most men as they proceed through life — with a lot of overlap and residual effect. But I've seen a pattern occur over and over in so many different men that it is worth noting and perhaps gleaning something from. I call the Four Seasons the Four S's. Are you following me so far?" he asked.

"Yes," David assured him.

"OK. The Fours Seasons, the Four S's are:
First: Sex. From adolescence until about age thirty, men are directed by their sexual drives in their courting and how they spend their money to draw attention to themselves. Sex helps determine with whom they want to associate. Many of the poor choices they make during this stage of life can be blamed on testosterone, but they are mistakes nonetheless, and sometimes have lifelong consequences. Not surprisingly, some men never seem to leave this season. But by about the time they hit their late twenties, they've married and settled down, at least a little, and the second 'S' comes into play. Can you guess what it is?"

"Tell me," said David.

"I see you're not there yet," Pops joked. "But the second 'S' is Success. From 30-45 years of age men switch from basing their decisions on sex to being controlled by a desire to win the game, to be successful. This can be good if it means providing for their families, but bad when it competes with their families and becomes an end unto itself. All too often men think they are climbing the corporate ladder for their families, moving all around, leaving friends and family behind, submerging themselves in their work, but the only person actually enjoying the climb to the top is the man, while his wife and kids suffer from neglect. Sadly, in the future this second 'S' will characterize more and more women also, much more so than the first 'S' does for the average woman."

"Fortunately, my Kitty is no average woman," muttered Doc to Dr. Tew with a nudge of the elbow and a raised left eyebrow.

"Pig!" retorted Dr. Tew in mock disgust.

"Gentlemen...listen now, you may learn something, too," Pops said, pausing.

He then resumed, "The third 'S' season is Security. Sometime around 45 years old and carrying to 60 and beyond men will really ramp up their efforts to create more financial security. They save more money, sacrifice today for tomorrow, become more conservative in how they manage their finances, only to realize as they begin to achieve some semblance of financial security that their friends are starting to die off and the real security they seek is fleeting. A cruel transition occurs during this season as men begin this period thinking security comes through financial assets, and emerge from this season realizing how little security exists in their wealth as they watch people they know in their late fifties and early sixties begin to get bad diseases, suffering from disability and death. They realize that the best security is actually good health, and even that will be fleeting."

Doc's face seemed to be reflecting on this last comment more than Dr. Tew or David, but all three listened in solemn silence.

"And so we men enter into the final phase, probably much later in life than the average woman does, but we enter into a search for the final 'S', Significance. How will the future remember me? What can I do to impact the people around me who are for the most part younger and have so much more life ahead of them? What can I do to make life better for them, to prepare them to make the experience better for themselves?"

"So, if you ask me why I came here today, maybe that's the birthday sermon I wanted you to hear. Sometimes vision for the future is a matter of perspective, and my hope for you is that your perspective will always give you 20/20 vision. Try to remember that."

David replied, "I don't think I'll ever forget anything about today. You've been a great birthday addition. I really appreciate all the effort you went to, all three of you, to be here today. I don't understand who set this up, or why, but please thank them for me. This has been fun, and unforgettable," said David sincerely.

"Glad to be invited," said Doc, who then added, "My unsolicited advice would be to never lie to your woman."

"Well I nev-" started David.

"If you lie to her," Doc continued, "about the way you like your steak cooked, you're going to have to eat it overcooked the rest of your life!"

"Got it!" agreed David.

Speaking to Pops, Dr. Tew narrowed his eyes and said, "I think there's a final 'S' season you left out — Sanctimonious. You seem to be getting close.

Lighten up. The kid's just twenty. He'll do OK. Look how I've turned out. We seem to handle the first forty years pretty well. The next forty are up to you two guys," he said, looking at Doc and Pops, while stroking his chin with his left hand.

David was a little surprised with Dr. Tew's blunt statement. His thoughts were distracted as he looked at Dr. Tew's raised left arm and the watch on his wrist. He said, "Excuse me just a second." Without first asking permission he held Dr. Tew's arm at the wrist to get a better look. It was a gold Seiko watch, with the day/date which read, "SUN 25". He looked at Doc's identical, though more worn watch, which indicated, "THU 25", and Pop's even more worn watch which was as much silver as it was gold, much of the gold plating having worn off. It read, "MON 25".

"You guys went to a lot of trouble to get all the details right, so I'm surprised you forgot to set your watches right. Today is Wednesday," said David smugly, as if he had cracked the case wide open.

"David, you're a hard sell," said Dr. Tew, looking down at the ground, smoothing both eye brows horizontally with his left thumb and index finger, a little perturbed at having been interrupted while setting Pops straight. "My watch is right, because today I'm turning 40, on Sunday, May 25, 1997."

Doc added, "He's right. I remember turning 40 on a Sunday, eating at Aunt Catfish's in Daytona Beach and getting my name up in lights on the hotel marquee. And my watch is right, because today I'm turning 60, on Thursday, May 25, 2017."

"And it's Memorial Day, another Monday birthday for me," added Pops.

David remained silent, unwilling to participate in their fantasy, unable to break away from it.

"You notice all our jewelry is the same. Look here, we only wear three things — a wedding ring, an MCG class ring, and a watch," he said, now removing the watch. "The watch is inscribed *DLP 4/21/91*. It was a seventh anniversary wedding gift, all three pieces are gifts from...can I tell him now?" Doc asked, looking at Pops.

Pops shrugged and nodded his head, "Why not? We've behaved. What harm can come from it?"

Doc continued, "The real gift for me today was seeing Kitty — Kay I used to call her, but she is now and will forever be Kitty for me. What a woman," he said almost reverently.

"David, you don't deserve her, and forty years later I don't deserve her, and never did any of those years in between. And to think, twenty years from now — Pops, do you deserve her?"

Pops shook his head slowly.

"See David, you'll never deserve her, but never stop trying to treat her like you might one day do enough to earn that right. Every day with her will only get better. I can't believe how good life is now. Pops, you must be going crazy with her if you've had another twenty years to be her husband. How great is that Pops?"

"AHEM," Dr. Tew said loudly as Kay now started up the hall toward the waiting men. The conversation slammed to a halt, as it may well have regardless the topic. Kay entered the room in her short sleeved white smock and slacks, which only served to make her tanned arms and face glow all the richer. Her beauty trumped any conversation they could have hoped to continue.

"Well, gentlemen, I hate that I have to go to work. I should have turned down the chance to work today, but they are so understaffed there, and I don't want them to think I'm not interested. I need the money," she admitted.

"And the letter of recommendation for medical school," David added proudly, glad to be back into reality with Kay in the room. He could never call her Kitty. These guys were spooky.

She turned to Dr. Tew. "Uncle Dave, do come again," she said, shaking his hand. "And next time I'll have skim milk, I promise."

"It was a beautiful day, Kay. Thanks, and I'll take you up on that offer."

She next turned to Doc and said, "Doc, help David finish up that carrot cake so he doesn't have to haul it back to Atlanta. I certainly can't have it tempting me here."

"Kay, you can trust me. I'll do my best," he said, and gave her a quick hug.

"And Pops," she said, turning now toward him, "thanks so much for coming, for all of you guys coming, and not being shy about being included in today's improvised party. You are all good sports to watch David and me eat. Next time I'll cook five steaks!"

"Sounds good to me!" said Pops as the others agreed. "Kay you are such an excellent hostess — thanks so much for letting us be a part of this."

"Thank *you*, Pops for coming. I've learned so much about you all, I feel like I've known you all my life," she giggled. Her voice softened as she added, "And thank you for sharing with me about your dear wife. Kitty sounds like she was such a wonderful lady. I'm *so* sorry for your loss and that I'll never have the chance to meet her, but she lives on in the many ways you remember her and honor her memory with others. I'm so thankful you could share such wonderful things about her with me. I hope one day I can be half the woman she was. She was a lucky lady to have a man like you."

Having said that she gave Pops a hug as his eyes again started to well up. He replied, "You will be, I'm sure." A stunned silence gripped Doc and Dr. Tew as David watched them all. Pops pulled her back away from him just far enough to look into her face, and said, "You're a special girl." Then he cupped her face in his hands and recreated the kiss on her head first given eleven weeks and four days ago, give or take sixty years.

Chapter 18
Wrap-up

David spoke first. "Well Kay, I'd better get you on down to your car."

"Oh, yes, look at the time!" he was grateful to hear her reply.

"I'll be right back," said David to the quiet guests as he headed out with Kay, closing the door behind him.

Kay started talking as they walked along the upper walkway. "Oh, David, you've got such a great family. I hope I get to meet more soon. Those guys are so friendly and engaging. They seemed so interested in everything about you and me — not at all like my uncles who would probably just sit off in a corner and talk about 'the good old days'. I can definitely tell you're related — you seem to have a bit of each of them in you, not just the way you look, but your humor, your brains, your heart."

"Well, you were very generous to let them crash your party. I'm sorry to do that to you on such short notice," he apologized.

"Never!" she exclaimed. "That would never be an imposition. I loved everything about today."

"Me too," he agreed. "The best birthday I've ever had! I was a little jealous to have to share it with them...and to share you with them," he admitted, then could not resist adding, "but at least I didn't have to share my steak."

"Sorry the steak was a little overdone," she said meekly.

"It was perfect, the whole meal was great!" he lied.

"You, Mr. Patson, are a creative thinker," she said in a most proper tone, employing a phrase they had both heard Dr. Harris use as a complement. "But they did all seem to enjoy the cake," she said proudly.

She reached out and grabbed his hand as they started down the stairs, saying, "Well they didn't get the entire afternoon. I intentionally left a little early so I could have you all to myself for at least a couple of minutes before I go to work."

"Good thing," he replied. "I'm almost surprised they didn't all come down to help me tell you good-bye," he laughed, wishing not to spend more of the little time he had left with her talking about these guys who had already monopolized the entire afternoon he was supposed to have had alone with her.

"That Pops is an amazing man," she marveled, unaware of David's birthday wish. "I work with patients at the nursing home who are his age or even younger that seem so much older than he is. You almost forget that he is eighty. He certainly doesn't seem to be slowed by it." Her voice softened a bit, "You've never said anything before about your Great-Grandmother Kitty. "Were you very close to her?"

Struggling to ad-lib now, he replied, "Well...you know...um...What did Pops have to say about her?" wondering himself what Pops wanted to tell Kay, and how she fit into this strange day.

"When I saw him in there lying on my bed I could tell something was bothering him — he looked like...well, he was... crying. I asked him what was bothering him and at first it seemed as though he didn't want to go into it. He was OK talking about Kitty and remembering her as she was — she was certainly an incredible lady — but he didn't go into why he was sad. Initially he was only talking about her as if she were still alive. He later explained that he didn't want to ruin your party. He asked me not to bring her up during lunch."

"Anyway, then he asked me if I knew what 'phantom pain' is. You know, how if you have your leg cut off, you can still feel a pain that feels like your foot is there, even though it is gone?"

"Oh, yeah," said David as they arrived at her car and he leaned against the door while she stood, not wanting to risk getting her uniform dirty.

"He told me about the first time he ever had a patient with phantom pain. The man knew exactly where his leg was supposed to be, and it hurt all over the leg, but the leg just wasn't there. He could reach down for his leg at night to try to move it to make it hurt less, but there was no leg where it was supposed to be, only pain. Pops said that his Kitty is supposed to be there when he reaches out for her at night, but she's not there, just pain. It's very sad to hear, David."

"He's never really talked much about it," David said.

"He misses her so much, David, I hope you can help him get through it. He does brighten up around you."

"He certainly does brighten around *you*," countered David. "I was afraid that Pops was being a copycat with that good-bye kiss," he said, hoping he was joking. "I should have trademarked that first kiss."

"Oh David, don't be silly. His was a peck. Your first kiss that night was *the* most romantic kiss *any* man has ever given *any* woman in the history of the world."

"*Now you're talking*," he thought.

She resumed her thoughts on Pops. "He loved her so much, and yet he says he worries that he didn't do enough for her to let her know that during all their years together. You know, to show his appreciation for the way she raised their children, to be thankful for what a great wife she was for him. It's so sad, so sweet," she said, her eyes now tearing.

Seeing her cry made the drama of the raw tragedy of her story too real, too sad for David to deny. Regardless of the facts, he needed to hold her, to comfort her. He stood and hugged her as she quietly buried her head in his shoulder. This was impossible — was he to believe that the same day he was told he would marry this woman he would also learn she would die, that he would hear it first from her own lips, and see her mourn her own passing?

"*I've got to get a grip on my thoughts,*" he told himself. "*Now I'm starting to believe this stuff myself!*" True or not, however, he did realize that today had confirmed for him what he had already determined.

"I love you, Kay."

He held her tightly, silently, and the world did not end, the sun did not fall, and she did not leave. She hugged him snugly. "*That sounded nice,*" he thought, enjoying the physical closeness and the emotional closeness. He slowly stroked her back up and down along either side of her spine and he felt her shiver.

"Rrrrrrrrrrr," she purred playfully. "You can do that all day. You make me feel warm and safe like a little kitten."

"You can be my sweet Kitten," he responded gently, realizing that the time was rapidly melting away before she would have to leave for work.

He cupped her face in his hands and recreated what he humbly agreed was the world's most romantic kiss first given eleven weeks and four days ago.

Fortunately, he reminded himself realizing a couple of minutes still remained, today he had not eaten onions.

A dark silent pall had filled the room as Kay and David closed the door and left the apartment. Doc and Dr. Tew stood motionless, processing the news Kay had just unwittingly announced.

Pops, turning to face them, said, "I'm sorry for you to hear about Kitty that way. I had hoped to go through today without her death coming up. If it's any consolation, she didn't suffer any."

Doc spoke first. "This is so bad. She's not supposed to go first. Even now at 60, I think of her as being younger and more vibrant, like when she was 20, rather than being...dead."

"Are the kids OK?" asked Dr. Tew, who himself could not imagine an aging Kay, much less his own children. He did not stop to realize his children would thus be close to his current age of 40.

"They were all devastated, of course, but they've all five been a great source of strength to me the last few months, including the younger two you don't even know yet. Rachel wrote and played a beautiful flute tribute at the funeral. Lincoln has managed to keep us smiling recalling lots of funny memories of his Mom, embellished and told as only he can do."

"What happened?" asked Doc.

"A freak accident," said Pops, shaking his head, still unable to make sense of an incomprehensible loss. "We were in Daytona last year for her 78th birthday week — we go after the Georgia-Florida game every year now. I was taking an afternoon nap and she went out for a walk on the beach after the sun started to weaken. It became overcast, then cloudy, and then she got caught up in a freakish storm down the beach about a half-mile from our hotel. She never much worried about rain, 'I'm waterproof', she always said," to which Doc and Dr. Tew nodded in agreement, smiling with the memory of her saying just that so many times over the years.

"But then a bolt of lightning struck her. Some people saw it from their hotel balconies, and said she was the only thing on the beach, and the lightning went right to her. She would have never known what hit her. It was like old pastor Ike Reinhart said at her funeral — he's eighty-six now, but wanted to speak from his wheelchair since he had performed our wedding — 'God took her straight up to heaven on an express chartered jet that looked like a bolt of lightning to those of us on Earth. That was the way He saw fit to get her where He wanted her in the quickest way possible, like he did with Elijah — in a chariot of fire.'" They both smiled thinking back on the funerals they had heard Ike preach. He always knew the right and personalized things to say to make the family smile and be able to look past their immediate grief.

"It is comforting," Pops continued, "as Ike pointed out, that she will never have to go through the slow painful process of disability and dying we've seen so many others go through, but selfishly, I'm not ready to give her up. And now I have to finish the race without her."

The silence which followed seemed more fitting than any words they could say, as each measured his loss. Then the conversation gradually returned. First with Dr. Tew, who was so far removed from the incident that he waxed philosophically about the brevity of life, and spent some time recounting her strengths, which might have taken him all day. Later Doc joined in, emphasizing what a loss for so many people — Pops, the children, her siblings and extended family, her patients, her community, her fans. Finally, Pops spoke.

"We didn't come here today to ruin David's birthday, so enough of that," he said, hoping he believed it. "Let's have some music." He went over to the turntable and started flipping through the fifteen or so albums that comprised Kay's musical library. He found her Evie album and was reading the cover when the phone rang. He looked at the others and held up his hands silently while shrugging his shoulders as if he were afraid that the phone would transmit his mime of 'what should I do?'.

"Go ahead, answer the phone," urged Dr. Tew. An eavesdropper would have heard this conversation:

"Hello, Kay Powell's apartment, this is David Patson speaking."

"Hello, David, this is Daddy. Happy Birthday!"

"Hey, Daddy! It is really great to hear your voice!"

"Well I wanted to talk with my only oldest boy now that he's no longer a teenager. Your voice sounds a little funny, son. You're not sick are you?"

"I was about to ask you the same thing. Must be the long distance wires."

"Well you sound older already. Have you had a good birthday?"

"Oh man! This is one I'll never forget! Kay pulled out all the stops and cooked me a steak with baked potato and a salad. She treated me like a king!" said the eighty-year-old son to his fifty-year-old father.

"Well son, I better let your mother say 'hello' before we hang up. We're paying day rates you know."

"Yep. I can hardly believe it."

"I told your mother you were going to think your dear old dad had lost it."

"Uh, yeah," chuckled Pops as David reentered the apartment. "Daddy, uh.. before you go…"

David quickly sized up the situation and realized the prank that Pops was pulling on his father. He slapped and held his own forehead in mock dismay, wondering if there was no limit to which these guys would not go. *"How could Daddy fall for such a poor impersonation of my voice?"* he thought.

"Yes, son," said Daddy.

"I just, uh, wanted to say thanks for going to the trouble and expense of calling me—"

"Well, you're welcome —"

"And thanks for getting me through my teens. I know I wasn't always the easiest son to raise."

"Well, you're welcome —"

"And thanks for sacrificing and saving so I could go to college. Daddy, I love you," said Pops, voice quivering in the moment. The three pairs of eyes that had been fixed on Pops shifted their gaze to the tan shag carpet.

"Well thank you Dave. You know your mom and I are proud of all six of our children. Now let me put her on so she can say goodbye, then we'll see you tomorrow."

With that, Pops waved David quickly over to the phone and placed it against his ear. While David shared some of the same things about his day and more with his mother, Pops stepped back over to Doc and Dr. Tew.

"Nice touch," said Doc softly, with Dr. Tew nodding slowly in thoughtful agreement.

"I should have said it while he was alive — he died the summer after my 55th birthday," said Pops, not telling Doc anything he did not already know, but causing Dr. Tew to slowly nod again as he processed this new information.

"Don't you want to speak to Mom?" Doc whispered to Pops as they watched David continue his phone conversation.

"Nah, I talked to her last night before I left. She's 104 now, you know, but still going strong. She lives in a basement apartment looking out over the lake at my house. She stays busy with her digital communications, photography, and writes a sponsored weekly column for the local blog called 'The Second Hundred Years' — she's good." A bemused Doc nodded his head to acknowledge his amazing mother.

"OK, I promise, 9:00 tomorrow morning, dental appointment in East Point. I won't be late — I'll leave here with plenty of time to spare. Thanks Mom. Bye!" With that David hung up.

"I have to drive back to Atlanta first thing in the morning for a dental appointment. What a way to start the summer!"

"Is that a problem?" asked Dr. Tew.

"Well, I thought maybe I'd come back here when Kay gets off work at midnight to finish off my birthday celebrating."

"Not a good plan," said Dr. Tew.

He enumerated his reasons why this was not a good plan.

"First, you've been up since five this morning."

"I'll sleep when I'm old," said David.

"Second, you've got to get up almost as early tomorrow to drive to Atlanta. You should be well rested for that drive — more than the four hours or less you'll get with your plan."

"Third," added Doc, "she is not a night person. She's been working an eight hour shift after a long day getting ready for your party then working a full shift. She'll be ready to sleep."

"Finally," added Pops, "your birthday ends at midnight. Don't push your luck."

"OK," yielded David. "It's just that she's so... great to be around."

"And don't you," said Doc, starting with a wagging of his finger at David, then turning to complete his finger wagging and sentence with Dr. Tew, "don't you *ever* forget it."

"Lighten up, Francis," said Dr. Tew, ignoring Doc's admonishment as he walked toward the record player and started to look for an album to play since Pops had been distracted from his duty by the phone call.

"Gentlemen," Pops said firmly, drawing Dr. Tew's attention away from the records as Doc dropped his arm back to his side. "We did not come here to argue."

"Well then, just why *did* you come here?" asked David impatiently, ready to have the mystery of his birthday revealed.

"I'm sort of curious to know myself," said Doc.

"Huh?" said a surprised David. "You don't know why you're here either?"

"Let me explain," said Pops, as he directed David to sit in one of the lawn chairs. Doc and Dr. Tew settled down at opposite ends of the couch. David did as he was told, resigning himself to admit defeat and surrender, or at least suspend further disbelief while a logical explanation was finally offered. Or so he hoped.

"David, you've never lost someone really close to you, yet. But when you do, you can't help but have regrets. And perhaps the more important the relationship, the greater the regrets. Experts will tell you that in the situation of a terminally ill patient, it's important to say goodbye. That provides comfort to the patient, and to those left behind. When Kitty died, I didn't get to say goodbye. Today, thanks to you, I did."

David remained composed despite the sense of frustration and even anger he felt from this fantasy that Pops refused to quit acting out. Pops continued, "But the experts will tell you that it's important to be able to say more than 'goodbye'. You need to say 'I'm sorry', 'I love you', 'forgive me' — all the things that remove items from the slate that otherwise turns into a list of regrets. Unfortunately, life happens fast, then death happens faster. I didn't get to do all of these things as well as I wish I had before Kitty died. Today I think she heard me."

"You didn't tell her that you think you are me, did you?" asked a very concerned David, defensively.

"No, but I communicated how I felt about Kitty and somehow that seemed to help me. I explained that at times in my life I was unkind, I was selfish, I was hurtful. I disappointed Kitty, and for that I'm sorry."

Doc couldn't help editorializing with the cynical humor that was his trademark, ill-timed though it was. "You could generalize those remarks to pretty much every female with whom you've had a relationship since you were four years old." His use of the second person pronoun did nothing to absolve him of guilt, however.

"Thanks, Doc, but I think I can handle this mea culpa on my own." Pops resumed his explanation. "Kay and I had a nice discussion. I told Kay that while I was raising my sons and now seeing my grandsons, I was reminded of the man I aspired to be at their age, and how I failed that standard more than once in my choices, my thoughts, my actions — in my decisions and behavior. Raising daughters, I thought about the type of men I wanted them to date, the way I wanted them to be treated, the type of men I wanted them to marry, and realized I would have fallen short of that mark more than once."

Pops paused to think, and then continued. "I told Kay that over these many years I've come to understand better the man God would want me to be. I ask myself, 'What do I need to do to become the man God envisioned while He was designing me?' I hope that I have grown closer to that ideal, and that the growth continues daily. I told her, 'It's awkward for me to be saying this, and probably awkward for you to be hearing it, but for me to be the man I want to be I should have said this to Kitty' — and yes, Doc, you're right, several other women —, 'but you'll have to do, so thanks for listening.' She seemed to understand. She's a good listener."

"You make it sound as if I'm a terrible person who has done terrible things," said David.

"Oh, no, not at all," replied Pops, "and maybe that's part of the problem. In all too many marriages, in all too many relationships, it's not the big things, but the little things that wear away at the bonds that should be holding the two together. If we think we've done something terribly wrong, we will usually apologize immediately if we are still interested in the relationship. But if we think it was just a little something, a minor offence, a misdemeanor, we'll cut ourselves some slack — we'll grade ourselves on the curve — and figure that we don't need to apologize for such a minor infraction. But a little speck of dirt between a couple gets very gritty over time, like a small speck of dirt in your eye that becomes more irritating until the entire eye is red, and can become very significant. The Grand Canyon wasn't formed by a huge bulldozer, but rather by the constant wear and tear of little grits of sand in the water — all it took was time. Over time, both sides see more of how they were wronged than what they did wrong. Soon pride and 'winning the points' seem to become more important than settling the issue and going forward as a couple. Way too many marriages end in divorce, or are terminally flawed, because one or both parties become less interested in being a partner than in being right in a silly argument."

"Did you and Kitty have a good marriage?" asked David.

"Oh, yes!" responded Pops immediately. "I guess that's why I'm so thankful to her, she made it so. I hoped to somehow convey my thanks today, and simply by talking to Kay today she reminded me of the ways that I did express gratitude over the years. But no, we didn't have a bad marriage. We were a great team. About the worst fight we ever had was how to load the dishwasher."

With the mention of a dishwasher, Dr. Tew broke in loudly and commandeered the discussion. "I just don't understand what is so hard about seeing that you rinse the dishes and immediately put them in the dishwasher! No matter what the Bosch salesman says, you *have* to rinse the dishes, or they'll come out spackled with baked-on particulate matter. Don't stack the dishes all up in the sink when you clear the table. That just makes them dirty on both sides. Rinse them and put them in the dishwasher immediately! That way you only have to handle them once. It's so much more time efficient. What is so hard about that?!"

"Exhibit A," Doc said calmly to David while nodding toward Dr. Tew.

"Well I'm right," fumed the prideful Dr. Tew.

"And I was willing to die on that hill and a hundred others, and almost did, but fortunately we were smart — well, Kay was smart, and I was lucky — and we made it all work out. So I sometimes thanked her for the little stuff along the way, but never really thanked her often enough for the big picture. She is what made my life great..."

"OK, so I promise to be a good husband, and let her do all the dishes, any way she wants to. But that doesn't tell me how you are doing this trick. How do you know all this stuff about me and Kay and why do you pretend to know about the future and why do you even care?" David said all in one breath.

"David, have you ever heard of Mackinac Island? "

"No," said David, wondering where this was going. *"Why do old people take so long to say anything?"* David thought.

"Well you'll have a great vacation there one day. It's an island between the two Michigan peninsulas. There was a strategic U.S. military fort there in the early 1800's and an Army doctor there, William Beaumont, had to care for a trapper who showed up with a gunshot wound to the abdomen. This trapper survived but never completely healed, so for the rest of his life he had a fistula — an open tract — from his abdominal wall right into his stomach. Dr. Beaumont thought that was pretty neat — he used to look down into it or tie food onto a string and drop it into the stomach then pull it back out after a while to observe the effects of digestion by acid in the stomach. So Dr. Beaumont made medical history with significant advances in the world of gastroenterology by studying an abnormality and reporting his observations. This is often how advances in medicine are made. By studying an abnormality, you learn a lot about normal function."

Dr. Tew and Doc had both been listening to Pops' medical history lesson with interest, nodding at times in agreement. Dr. Tew, apparently having put the dishwasher irritations behind him, then added, "That's how most of the understanding within the science of neuroanatomy first came about. A patient would suffer a head injury or stroke, and have a corresponding loss of function. After the patient died, an autopsy would reveal the specific area of the brain that had suffered the insult, and so the brain's areas of function were eventually mapped out. A person who had a stroke and lost the ability to speak was found more often than not to have had an injury in his left temporal lobe. A person who lost the ability to move his left hand was predictably found to have an infarct in the right frontal lobe, and so on."

"Exactly," said Pops. "By studying the abnormal, we learn a lot about the normal."

"Well I have to admit," said David with an uneasy laugh, "there's been a lot more abnormal about today than normal, but I still don't understand what you're trying to say—"

"Because I haven't said it yet," interrupted Pops. "Was I ever this impatient?" Pops impatiently asked Doc and Dr. Tew, who shrugged.

"OK, now, where was I?" he asked, immediately regaining his composure. "Oh, yes, abnormal. Well, anyway, for a long time the government has been interested in sleep — normal and abnormal — trying to discover a way to make sleep less necessary for people. You can understand how this would be in the military's interest — it really bogs them down when troops are on the move across a country and have to stop to sleep after sixteen hours on the move. That potentially leaves a lot of troops very vulnerable and exposed. As is so often the case, original research opens a door that lead down paths which were originally unanticipated, and dream research is one of those paths resulting from the military's interest in sleep."

"Stop right there," said David. "You're telling me I've been dreaming this whole thing? No way...no way!"

"Well you're an intelligent guy. Do you have a better explanation?" asked Pops more calmly this time.

"I've been trying to come up with one all day," said David in an anxious, pressured response. "I've gone through an entire list of options — a weird experiment by the Department of Psychology here, an elaborate scheme involving my parents, or Kay, or Will Rice, or...who knows? I've even gotten crazy enough to consider time travel or space aliens. But you're going to have to come up with a better explanation than a dream. You and I are as real as this chair!" he said, grabbing both arms of the chair he was sitting in and aggressively rattling it side to side.

"Dreams can be deceiving," Pops replied.

"But you can't know that you are dreaming while you are dreaming!" David countered.

"Well, actually, you can," interjected Dr. Tew with a professorial tone. "There are dreams — lucid dreams, they're called — that occur where the dreamer knows he is dreaming. They've been known about for decades, just poorly understood. They start out as a dream, then the dreamer reaches the conclusion that he is dreaming while he is still asleep. That's a fairly uncommon event, however, but scientifically proven to exist in some people."

"Well then, I can't be dreaming about the future," countered David.

"Wrong again, but thank you for playing," said a sarcastic Dr. Tew, sounding like a game show host. "There are those who study the ability to see the future in dreams. 'Oneiromancy' it's called. Joseph accomplished it in the Bible. Shakespeare referred to it in *Julius Caesar*. Abraham Lincoln reportedly had a very graphic dream predicting his assassination. So I wouldn't write it off entirely."

"*I wish this was just a dream,*" thought David, rolling his eyes as he took a deep cleansing breath.

"Interesting topic," added Doc. "I've been fascinated by dreams all my life. They do seem to be necessary and provide some sort of benefit to the dreamer — we just haven't figured out what that benefit is. Some have hypothesized that dreaming allows us to put order and structure into the things we don't understand, or to have 'fire drills' to practice our response to threats and emergencies, or to simply entertain ourselves. Dreaming might also allow us to repackage our short-term memory into long-term memories. Who knows? I used to like to study at night right until bedtime. That seemed to give my brain something to process while I slept. I usually felt like I knew the material better, more deeply, in the morning than I had when I went to bed."

"I know what you mean. I do that, too," said David, drawn into the conversation. He then instantly felt as if he had just been suckered back into this trick — or was it a dream? — that these guys were all three versions of himself.

"Well you're not alone," continued Doc. "There have supposedly been famous discoveries and inventions — the sewing machine, the structure of the benzene ring, as I recall — that occurred as a result of dreams. Paul McCartney said he first dreamed the song *Yesterday*, then awoke and wrote it down. Similar stories for the writers of *Frankenstein* and *Dr. Jekyll and Mr. Hyde*."

"So you can see one of the spin-off reasons that researchers would want to know more about dreams. Imagine the power of dreaming if we could better understand the process of dreaming and use dreams to access the facts we have already stored in our heads, or to manipulate the information we have acquired to create better solutions to the problems that confront our world," added Pops.

"Sounds pretty far-fetched," said David.

"At least two Nobel Prize winners attribute a part of their discoveries to insight they gained from dreaming," said Doc.

"I wonder if all that German I learned in college is still deep down in my brain somewhere," said Dr. Tew.

"I'll never forget the German I learned this year," thought David, proudly.

"It probably is," said Pops. "It was there once, and research indicates it is your *access* to the data, not the data itself, that causes you to 'un-learn' things you once knew." Dreams may reveal a way to re-establish that access."

"In the process of trying to research the mechanism to best enter into dreams, scientists studied patients with various forms of dementia — senility, as you call it," he said nodding to David, "or Alzheimer's Dementia, as you call it," he said nodding to Dr. Tew. "But a better term is to describe the group of dementing illnesses as the CDD's — Cognito-Degenerative Disorders. That's fairly irrelevant for the discussion at hand, however."

"My thoughts exactly," thought David to himself.

"Anyway," continued Pops, "while the specific types of CDD's aren't important for our discussion, studies of the CDD's have revealed some interesting findings. Here again — another fine example of studying something abnormal to better understand that which is normal. One interesting observation was that some individuals with various CDD's have what is known as Dream-Enactment Behavior."

"Great!" thought David. *"Now, not only are you going to tell me this is a dream, but that I have brain damage."*

"Dream-Enactment Behavior is a disorder of REM sleep where the person's body acts out portions of a dream. Usually we are very still during dreams, but these people may move their arms and legs, kicking, striking out, and so forth. In more severe cases, seen in some people with CDD's, the patient seems to awaken from sleep, but may spend several minutes or more acting out their dream while appearing to be awake. It's a very strange thing to observe, as the person is essentially sleep walking, sometimes with a glazed-eye look. But these unfortunate people will make phone calls, try to leave their homes, argue with their spouses, all while having this Dream-Enactment Behavior, which then gradually wears off as their day begins."

"Very odd," said Dr. Tew. "I can't say that I've ever heard of that before."

"It is odd indeed, and a tragic diagnosis when combined with a progressive CDD. But again, as a result of the areas of the brain involved in these patients, and research into the specific neurotransmitter chemicals known to be necessary for normal function in these areas of the brain — predominantly in the parietal lobe — researchers have made leaps and bounds in understanding sleep and so are beginning to be able to manipulate it."

"Are you telling me that some mad scientist is trying to manipulate my dreams — without my permission?" asked David.

"Oh no," Pops assured him. "That would be unethical. But the process is very interesting. In order to induce a dream, the researchers first have you increase your level of neurotransmitters with a modified form of dopamine, a very important chemical in the brain. Then, while still awake, you do a 'walk through' of what it is you want to dream about or remember. The closer to true and pleasant reality the 'pre-dream' is, the more likely it is that a similar dream will follow when you go to sleep. The theory is that a dream is like a bubble, and the more stress you put into it — unpleasant memories, or things that never happened that thus require more thought to process them — the greater the surface tension, the more untenable the contents, the more likely the bubble will burst, as if to preserve the psyche."

"So you're trying to tell me that someone slipped me some modified brain chemicals to make me have a dream that doesn't seem like a dream? This is just too crazy to believe. Come on, Pops, get serious. Do I seem that gullible?" asked David.

"No. Medicating you without your permission would be unethical, too."

"None of this makes any sense!" shouted David, now becoming angry and impatient. "What gives you the right to come and invade my birthday... my dream then? Just what?"

Pops continued calmly. "Well, David...I'm afraid you've got it backwards. You see, you are not dreaming about me...I am dreaming about you." David's mouth dropped and he remained still and silent as Pops proceeded.

"I'm participating in a study of Reality Enhanced Dream Manipulation.

It's real pioneer research, but it could affect the way we all sleep, learn, study, and are entertained. I'm the first subject. The researchers at Emory Sleep Institute thought I'd be an ideal candidate. For now, they are studying only patients 80 years and older, but they and I were both so excited to get started that we did the study as soon as I was eligible, today, my 80th birthday. They all think people who are 80 and older will be more easily induced into Reality Enhanced Dreams with standard doses of the study drug. They never really said so, but I think they believe that patients over 80 are more likely to have early but not yet detectable CDD, and thus, they hypothesize, be more likely to be susceptible to the process of dream manipulation. I was glad to see that in the pre-treatment screening exams I had no evidence of CDD — that would have excluded me from the study since they don't want to appear to be taking advantage of someone who might not be able to reason perfectly — but that can't last forever. I'm definitely noticing some things just don't bother me like they used to, so maybe I'm having some early frontal lobe decline. And my memory certainly isn't what it was when I was twenty, but, as you know, the diagnosis of CDD requires more than simply a little memory loss."

"True," replied Doc, who appeared to be quite interested in this entire explanation, as did Dr. Tew.

"Nonetheless, I do have a positive family history for CDD, and I carry the ApoE4 gene, so that increases my risk also. Dr. Allen and the team at the sleep center also liked me because I'm a widower, so nobody is depending on me, in case their concerns are validated and something goes wrong with side effects causing permanent changes. Another reason they selected me, for the same concerns, was because I have good long-term care insurance. But the clincher for choosing me was that I am a doctor. They figured that only a doctor had any hope of actually understanding all of the complicated explanations and possibilities spelled out in the 127 page informed consent form that the Institutional Review Board and the research panel's lawyers finally hammered out."

Doc rose from the couch with a little effort as he groaned a sincere, "Fascinating," and headed back to the kitchen for a second piece of cake. David could not comprehend how the others seemed to be taking all of this in stride.

David spoke. "Pops, this is crazy! You must be crazy if you think I'm going to believe this is a dream — your dream! I feel so alive, so right, at twenty."

"David," Pops interrupted, "did you ever have a dream where you were back in kindergarten or back in grade school?"

"Sure, but —"

"And while you were dreaming you were in kindergarten, you weren't dreaming you were an adult attending kindergarten, you were actually once again, in your mind, five years old and in kindergarten. Well, today in my mind, thanks to this Reality Enhanced Dream Manipulation, I'm twenty again, and I love it.

This is the coolest thing I've ever done. The research team tried to prepare me for what I could expect, but this is better than anything they described. They said that hallucinogenic drugs created an experience that was 95% hallucination and 5% reality, but their hope was that Dream Manipulation would create about 5% hallucination and 95% reality, establishing access to information long ago stored in my brain."

"Well I'm not buying it," argued David. "That's just crazy. Maybe I am just having my own crazy dream. I've been under a lot of stress with final exams."

"Too far-fetched, not plausible" said Dr. Tew to David. "I'm voting for Pops' explanation."

Doc returned holding a plate with an oversized piece of carrot cake which he had already diminished significantly. He joked, "Maybe it's my dream. The only way I'll look that good when I'm 80 is in my dreams!" At this Dr. Tew and Pops both joined Doc in another good laugh.

"I've still got it," said Doc, congratulating himself as he sat back down on the couch.

"This carrot cake is *so* good!" continued Doc. "David, the girl can cook. She makes the best cake, the best bread, the best bean soups, the best cinnamon rolls — oh man, can she cook!"

"*She didn't seem so great at it today,*" thought David, who instead replied, "I didn't know she could cook all of those things."

"Oh, she can't yet. But get ready. It's going to happen," predicted Doc.

Doc looked back at Pops. "How did you get to looking so good, Pops?" he asked between bites of the world's best carrot cake.

"Genomics," Pops explained. "Research has really taken off, unlocking and understanding genes. I guess that's one of the advantages of the Baby Boomer generation's pursuit of the fountain of youth. Lots of worry about aging, and it all seems to boil down to genes and how they are activated and inactivated. As is so often the case in science, once the ball got rolling, more has happened in gene science in the last twenty years than had happened in the previous hundred. After researchers overcame the problem with oncogenes and fears of activating cancer, much more could be done. Advances continue to come in bits and pieces, but the gene for hair color can now be turned back on, although it also stimulates skin pigmentation. Interestingly, that gene seems to be activated back to the age of mid-childhood, but I don't mind being blond again. They aren't sure why yet, but when you activate the hair color gene, you also seem to turn on the hair growth stimulant gene or genes. I've never been able to grow such a full beard until now."

"*Nice sideburns,*" David admitted to himself.

"Unbelievable! What did you do about this bum knee?" asked Doc, rubbing his right knee.

"Tissue transplant," said Pops. "Wish I could have done it years ago."

"So now you're running again?" asked Dr. Tew, interviewing the patient. "You look like you do a great job maintaining your weight."

"Wish I could take credit for that, but that gets back to genomics. Reactivated some of those metabolic genes that shut off soon after adolescence. Makes a reasonable diet so much more rewarding," revealed Pops.

"Unbelievable future you live in," said Dr. Tew. "So why did you choose this particular dream sequence? You could have selected any topic, any day to go back to. Why today?"

"I wanted to relive a time that I spent with Kitty. I thought about our wedding day, but that day was shared with so many other people, I didn't actually see Kitty until that night when she was walking down the aisle. Any one of the five births of our children would be fun, but again, the focus would, in a large part, not be just on Kitty and me. I even thought about going back to the last day Kitty and I spent at Daytona, but I was advised the trauma of that day might disrupt the dream manipulation and burst the bubble. On the other hand, my twentieth birthday was a wonderful day — one of the best days in my entire life. The memory of it has been engraved in my brain for all these years, so it wasn't hard to do the pre-dream walk through. It was a carefree day, no responsibilities or tests or deadlines. It was the first day I told Kitty I loved her. What a great day!"

"It was one of the best days of my life," said Dr. Tew wistfully.

"Agreed," chimed in Doc.

"And I was able to work in our first date and blend in fun memories of Rex and Will and Mad-man."

"So you've been happy with the results of this dream experiment?" Dr. Tew asked Pops.

"Oh, yes! It's worked beyond my wildest imagination. I can't wait to file my report and have my post-dream debriefing interview with Dr. Allen. I just hope I remember the dream. I hadn't thought of that until now, but what if I forget this dream?"

"It happens," replied Doc.

"Well I hope not. This has been such fun. It's as if I'm actually here."

"We *are* actually here," said David, unable to accept the latest explanation as anything more than another man's psychosis.

"The details have been so sharp and so precise with so much I had forgotten, down to such little details. I was surprised, too, with how good the food tasted. I haven't had Vanilla Creams or a Blimpie's in years, but they were great!" said Pops.

"I could have done without the Tab," droned Dr. Tew.

"I'll be sure to include that in my report," said Pops sarcastically. "There were some surprises along the way, minor though they were. For instance, I expected I would show up as the twenty-year-old me, not the eighty-year-old me. So in that regard this dream has been sort of like a split screen. And for that matter, I didn't request that my other two versions, Dr. Tew and Doc, as it were, be here. But somehow you two showed up, and that's been sort of fun, actually."

"Our pleasure," said Dr. Tew, bowing, as Doc added, "Wouldn't have missed it for the world."

"Well is there anything else then, before you have to go?" asked David, hoping that if these guys would just leave his life would return to normal. He still had packing to do before his early start tomorrow. "You do have to go, don't you?" he asked, almost politely.

Dr. Tew ignored David's attempt to steer the conversation as he continued with Pops. "Next time, I think I would try to make the dream a little more...Freudian," he said, choosing his words delicately.

"Well, I'll be sure to include that in my report, too," replied Pops with a roll of the eyes. "But since, for now at least, the pre-dream sequence has to be written out, reviewed and approved by the research committee, I didn't feel inspired to be very creative along those lines. With the way they have me all hooked up for sleep with EEGs and polysomnographic equipment, I might set off an alarm with your plan. Besides, my hormone levels are lower than yours. Next time, get your own dream. I'm sure your testosterone-saturated brain would love to get its hands on this technology. But from what I see of the statistics, most people seem to do fairly well on their own in that department without dopamine enhancement."

David furrowed his brow and tilted his head as if to imply this conversation was beyond his comprehension.

"Can you just imagine the surprise if the dream had a minor malfunction while twenty-year-old David is snuggling with college student Kay and she suddenly morphs into my almost eighty-year-old Kitten?" asked Pops, laughing as David silently shuddered, Dr. Tew frowned and Doc smiled.

"The shock to the brain might be too great and burst the dream bubble. But come to think of it," said Pops, "the part about Vicki Post wasn't in my pre-dream. She just appeared, yet she seemed true-to-life, from what I can remember of her."

"Yes, that part of the dream was nicely developed," noted Dr. Tew with an intentional double entendre wasted on no one.

"Pig!" exclaimed Doc as if disgusted, although David noticed his eyes seemed to brighten a little at Dr. Tew's recollection.

"Boob!" shot back Dr. Tew with an insult and a smile.

"Your clever humor suddenly seems to be *bust*ing forth," responded Doc with a remark he could well have pulled out of a drawer in his memory labeled "Sixth Grade Jokes".

"I'll keep you a*breast* of any changes," promised Dr. Tew with a similarly crafted response.

"Ahem, 'Gentlemen', and I use that term loosely," scolded Pops in disgust, "Please! It is fairly evident that the testosterone levels in this group get toxic quickly in the absence of the moderating influence of a female. Enough of this tit-for-tat."

"*These guys are all weak,*" thought David, who could not help himself but was not sure he was invited to join in this adult humor. (Or was it grammar school? His comedic palate was not yet that discerning.) "*What the heck!*" he thought, "*It's my birthday!*" He added to the conversation with a nervous titter, "I think you guys have about *milked* that joke for all it's worth."

"Just *skim*ming the surface," said Doc with a smile.

"Well," said Dr. Tew to Doc, "I could probably come up with a clever milk joke, but it would likely just go over your head, or at least *past-your-eyes'd*."

With that all four had to laugh. David had always been his own best audience.

"Well, Pops," said David good-naturedly, deciding to play along, as if he had a choice, "since you are here for my birthday, why don't you give me that cool jacket you were wearing? Is that what clothes will look like in the future?"

Realizing that David was still not believing his explanation, an exasperated Pops said, "Sure. I left it under your bed. But that's not the current style. I just made that part up in the dream. I've always thought that with time the materials we wear would get more interesting, but for the most part they haven't — just the way the materials are cut and sewn seems to change."

Sensing the frustration in Pops' voice, not wanting to appear too unappreciative for the effort expended for his birthday, David tried again to play along with today's game, sort of. "There are less than eight hours left in the day, and then you guys might turn into pumpkins, or some such. So what else did you mean to tell me?"

"Oh, not much. What would it matter? But I do thank you for being a gracious host. You've been kind to let us invade your birthday. And it's nice to see you," replied Pops, as he continued more seriously, ignoring David's flippant attitude. "Before I look in the mirror every morning, I am you, and then I have a harsh reminder of the inevitable march of time as I see not you but me. You are very much alive in my memory and always will be. I will be you a lot longer than you'll be you."

Still more than a little confused, David replied, "So why are we having this discussion if it doesn't matter?"

"Out of habit, I guess," admitted Pops. "We've been having a discussion all my life. I'm the person you hope to become, and there is always that dialogue, that conscience about how to get there with the least amount of damage to yourself, if not others. And now that I'm 80, I find myself having more conversations with the guy that I was at 20. Did I do everything right? What did I leave out? What do I regret? What will be my legacy?"

"The loss of Kitty was infinite, or at least more than I can recover from in the years that I have left. That serves to increase my search for that fourth 'S', significance. So I volunteered for this dream study. It really could revolutionize the way we look at sleep. Perhaps when future generations sleep, they'll accomplish just as much while asleep as when they are awake. They won't see sleep as being such a waste of time. They won't want to wait until they're old to sleep. This study on dreaming might be the best thing I can do with the time that's left. What's the worst thing that can happen to me? I lose my memory? Do I have that much to lose?"

"Being eighty gives me a more complete view of life and what happens. Want to know a secret? Here's the big picture. We all die. The rest is just the minor details of what happens in between being born and dying. Given that big picture, you'd better have a darn good plan of how to make the most of every day, as every day leads to the next, and the next. I don't view today as simply today, but rather I see it as the most immediate link with the future, a reminder of constant change, change which makes children grow up, parents get old, and spouses die."

Dr. Tew entered back into the conversation. Even he realized this was a lot to be dumping on a fellow on his 20th birthday. "So what he's trying to say David is 'Happy Birthday!'. Now I think maybe I'll try some of that milk with a little slice of cake."

"Have some for me," joked Pops, who then continued again more seriously. "I realize now I probably made a mistake by coming here today. Not that I didn't enjoy being here and reliving old memories and creating a few more. I have always treasured my 20th birthday as one of the best days in my life. Many of the details of that day remain fresh in my memory sixty years later. I had no responsibilities that day — school was over, I hadn't yet started working for the summer, nothing that had to be done except celebrating with Kitty. That day was the first time I ever said to her, or any other girl, 'I love you'. But now, listen to me. I'm starting to sound like an old guy, repeating myself," said Pops.

"I may be eighty now, but I learned something today. I don't think saying 'I love you' was such a big deal after all. That's a powerful phrase — 'I love you' — but it can cause a lot of different emotions and results. In the past tense it can be hurtful. If we're mad at someone we might say 'I loved you', but now I hate you. We think that we hurt someone when we stop loving them, but we can damage ourselves or deprive ourselves just as much. Just look how destructive a force divorce is. What a terrible thing that is. Yet all too often it happens because one or both have decided to hurt the other. So they stop trying, thinking the next time things will be better, that marriage with a different person would be so much better. Oftentimes that's just not the case. I remember a patient who was in her second marriage telling me, 'It wasn't until my second marriage that I realized my first marriage wasn't all that bad, it just wasn't perfect. So I lowered my expectations when we had a few problems in my second marriage, and we've made it work for fifteen years.' That's the key to making marriage work — realizing we're all just humans. It does take work, it does take commitment. So instead of just saying 'I love you', I think we should more often repeat a portion of our marriage vows, and say, 'I will love you', with a promise about the future together, rather than just an occasional potentially self-serving attempt at sweet talking."

David sat silently listening. Pops was not certain if David was absorbing anything he was saying or just being a patient audience. That no longer mattered. Pops would have been just as happy talking to himself. So he continued, "I just hope I didn't blow a once in a lifetime chance by targeting this day for my dream creation sequence. I thought that to see Kitty again on such a special and memorable day would somehow relieve some of the unbelievably oppressive grief that I've felt since she's been gone. I thought it would be rejuvenating to see her all young and tan and fresh and smooth. Then, while I was talking with her, I realized that what made her so treasured to me was not the woman that she was when I was 20. The Kitty I miss is far more interesting, far more beautiful, far more vested in me than the girl I knew when I was 20. That college girl is forever gone, and has been for many, many years. I feel sorry now for men who waste away their lives wishing for something they can never have, the young girl they married, not embracing the woman she has become. The Kitty I miss is the one who grew old with me, whose youth was spent and forever changed carrying and raising our five children, whose psyche had weathered the storms the children and I had thrown her way. Through it all she just got better every day. Ultimately she grew emotionally and spiritually with me in all our years together. She comforted me through major losses and disappointments."

Pops paused, then added, "David, your Kay has only known you a brief time. Knowing none of your faults, she thinks you are perfect. My Kitty has experienced and suffered from so many of my faults, tolerated my imperfections, yet she thought I was perfect for her despite my failings...I can't believe she's gone...I will always love her."

All inside the apartment was very quiet. After a moment they all heard a woman's voice they did not recognize, "David...David Patson," she called from the outside.

Pops walked over to the door and opened it. He looked outside, not locating the source of the voice. He looked back inside over his shoulder as he told the others, "Guys, it's been fun but I think I'm going to have to go soon."

Epilogue

Our life is twofold; Sleep hath its own world,
A boundary between the things misnamed death and existence:
Sleep hath its own world, and a wide realm of wild reality,
And dreams in their development have breath, and tears, and tortures, and the touch of joy;
They leave a weight upon our waking thoughts,
They take a weight from off waking toils,
They do divide our being;
They become a portion of ourselves as of our time,
And look like heralds of eternity;
They pass like spirits of the past—they speak like sibyls of the future;
They have power— the tyranny of pleasure and of pain;
They make us what we were not—what they will,
And shake us with the vision that's gone by,
The dread of vanished shadows—Are they so?
Is not the past all shadow?—What are they? Creations of the mind?
The mind can make substances, and people planets of its own
With beings brighter than have been,
And give a breath to forms which can outlive all flesh.
I would recall a vision which I dreamed perchance in sleep
For in itself a thought, a slumbering thought, is capable of years,
And curdles a long life into one hour.

      From "The Dream" — Lord Byron

Chapter 19
Postlude
May 26

"David…David Patson" he heard a voice say and as David Patson became aware of his surroundings, he felt twenty years old. With his eyes closed, his body at perfect rest, he didn't know how old he was.

About the Author

David Anders (UGA Class of '79) lives in Peachtree City, GA where he practices Internal Medicine and Geriatrics. In his free time he enjoys playing trombone. He met his wife, Kenya (UGA Class of '80), at the University of Georgia in an Honors English class. Kenya and David both received their M.D. degrees from the Medical College of Georgia. Kenya is a full-time mom and a part-time dermatologist, harpist, and clarinetist. She is known across the region for baking the best sourdough bread ever tasted. They have five children: Rebekah, Lloyd, Luke, Rachel, and Lincoln.

David welcomes your comments to him by
e-mail c/o his Executive Assistant at:

Attn: Fred Carey, Executive Assistant
2080@AndersUSA.com

Or write via U.S. mail at:
David Anders Publishing House
PO Box 2422
Peachtree City, GA 30269

Drop by our website at
www.AndersUSA.com

Find us on Facebook at
David Anders Publishing House

David Anders Publishing House — a Writer's Studio® was established to provide new authors assistance with access to the world of professional publication. As a publisher of quality writings we hope to be adding continuously to our studio of writers and the list of their fine works.

If you have a friend who is trying to get a book published, tell him or her about us — or maybe you are ready to take that step yourself. Visit our website and bookstore at www.AndersUSA.com.

Books we are proud to be featuring currently include:

Octogenarians Say the Darndest Things
by David L. Anders with Rebekah Yates Anders

Life doesn't begin at 80, but it doesn't have to end there either. This mother-son team of physicians with over 75 years of patient care experience recalls the humor, wisdom, pathos and surprises revealed while caring for this remarkable group of people.

The Silver Bell
by Rebekah Yates Anders
with illustrations by Rachel Elizabeth Anders

In this short story for children and adults, a young boy demonstrates caring and another view of the love of Christmas is revealed.

Signs of The Times
by Kenya Houghton Anders

By combining familiar traffic signs with valuable scripture verses, students of any age will find learning Bible verses easier and more enjoyable.

You Might Be a Problem Drinker If...
by David L. Anders

Hilarious and yet insightful, more than 100 ways to know if maybe it's time to cut down on the drinking (or increase your life insurance coverage!).

You Might Be a Problem Drinker If... Let's Have Another Round!
by David L. Anders

Picking up where he left off with the first volume in this series, the author provides more than 100 subtle or not so subtle signs that alcohol is causing problems for you or those who nag you.

www.ingramcontent.com/pod-product-compliance
Lightning Source LLC
LaVergne TN
LVHW061344060426
835512LV00012B/2562